A STUDY ON WOMEN INDUSTRIAL WORKERS IN LEATHER FOOTWEAR INDUSTRIES

By

L.ANITHA M.H.R.M

D1728240

DECLARATION

I Mrs.L. Anitha here by declare that the thesis entitled **"A study on women industrial workers in Leather Footwear Industries in Chennai City"** Submitted by me for the Degree of Doctor of philosophy (Ph.D) in Economics is record of research work done by me as a full time research scholar under the guidance of **Dr.S.SURESH,** Associate Proffessor, Department of Economics, Presidency college, Chennai- 600 005 and that the thesis has not previously formed the basis for the award to me of any degree, diploma and associateship, fellow ship or other similar title.

ACKNOWLEDGEMENTS

I deeply owe my profound gratitude and sincere thanks to my revered Ph.D., and Supervisor **Dr.S.SURESH,M.A.,M.Phil.,Ph.D.,** Associate Professor, Post Graduate and Research Department of Economics, Presidency College, Chennai -600 005 for his invaluable guidance, inspiring discussions and heartfelt motivation, timely help and encouragement which enable me to complete this thesis successfully.I will be failing in my duty, if I do not place on record my heartfelt respecet to him for his excellent teaching skills in the fields of methodology and application of statistical tools which helped me immensely in my research analysis.I will forever be in his debt I feel proud to be his ever green protégé.

I thank the principal **Dr.R.SABANAYAGAM, M.sc.,M.Phil., Ph.D.,** Presidency college Chennai- 600 005 for the opportunity given to me to pursue my Ph.D.,Programme in this prestigious institute.

I take this opportunity to express my sincere thanks to **Dr.S.KARTHIKEYAN,** Head of the Department, all Faculty Members of the Department of Economics, Presidency college, Chennai -600 005 for their constant encouragement in my research work.

A very special Thanks to Doctoral committee Members (DCM) **Dr.A.MUNIYAN,M.A,B.Ed.,M.Phil.,Ph.D.,** Associate Professor, Departmentof Economics, Presidency college, Chennai -600 005 and **Dr.R.BALASUBRAMANIAN,M.A.,M.PHIL.,Ph.D.,** AssociateProfessor, Department of Economics, **D.G.Vaishnav** college, Chennai -600 106 for all the support and encouragement in my research endeavours.

I Express my most sincere thanks to **Dr.JAYARAMAN, Dr .ARIVAZAKAN, DR.YOGANATHAM, Dr.VARATHAN, Dr.ANABALAGAN,** Associate Professor, Departmentof Economics, Presidency college,Chennai -600 005for their constant support an helpful comments on the substance and style of my research work.

Particular thanks go to **Sr.Principal Scientist S.MATHIVANAN (Shoe Design & Development Center) CLRI Adyar, Chennai-20** whose enthusiasm has inspired me in this project. I am grateful thanks to the institutes such as CLRI, IIT Madras etc., for help in literature survey.

I thanks the **N.ARAVAZHI** Sr.Technical officer -Librarian of the central Leather Research Institiute Adyar, Connemara public Library, British Council Library Madras institute of Development studies (MIDS)Adyar,Anna university ,University of Madras

I would like thank **Dr.GIRIYAPPA KOLLANNAVAR** Technical officer E-II (sociologist) Economics Research Division in Central Leather Research Institute

I place on record my sincere thanks love and affection to My Father **M.LAKSHMANAN** My Mother **L.KABILA** for their everlasting love, support, inspiration and blessings which have made me what I am now. They have been a real source of strength and encouragement.

I would like to thanks **DR.G.SUNDARVADIVEL** Asst.professor Dept of adult & continuing Education university of madras, **DR.J.KHAJA SHERIEF** faculty of Dept of Management studies university of Madras Chennai -5

Published papers relevant to this work

Publications/Journal

Sl No	Title of the Article	Name of the Journal	ISSN/ISBN
1	Inclusive Growth of Import & Export in Leather Footwear Industry during the 11th Five year plan Period	Southern Economics January 15,2013 Volume 51,Number 18 Page 15-18	ISSN0038-4046
2	Information of Communication Technology (ICT) & Women Empowerment	International Journal of advanced Research in Management and Social Sciences Page 143-152	ISSN 2278-6236

CONTENTS

ACKNOWLEDGEMENT

DETAILED CONTENTS

LIST OF ABBREVIATIONS

LIST OF IMAGES

LIST OF TABLES

LIST OF CHARTS

5.27	Job stress diminish the health status	170
5.28	Poor didn't night sleep affect the health	170
5.29	Measures are taken to reduce the intense of occupational hazards	171
5.30	Indusrial wastage are disposal in healthy way	172
5.31	Dye chemical didn't affect health of theworkers	173
5.32	Dust levels emitted within the presciribed intensity	173
5.33	Management provided all the protective equipments for the workers	174
5.34	Workers get back from the work with aches regularly	175
5.35	Hazardous to wris t and hand in working in themachinery without proper protection	175
5.36	Immediate attention given during emergency	176
5.37	Unhygienic water in the industries didn't affect the health of the workers	177
5.38	Management provide adequate protection measures to the workers	177
5.39	Job is the first priority rather than the family members	178
5.40	Not enthusiastic to take up the responsibility in the company	179
5.41	Dedication provide promotion and incentive in the job	180
5.42	Presently holding interesting job	180
5.43	Hard work acknowledged with incentives in the company	181
5.44	Comfortable environment persuade to work effectively	182

CHAPTER I

CHAPTER II

CHAPTER III

CHAPTER IV

CHAPTER V

CHAPTER VI

ABBREVATIONS

IMAGES

APPENDIX

BIBLIOGRAPHY

CHENNAI CITY MAP

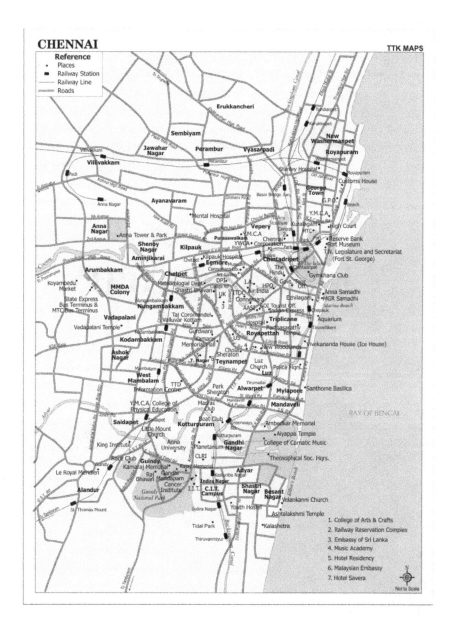

List of Abbreviations

CDI -Caste Development Index (CDI)

CEDAW - Convention on Elimination of all forms of discrimination against women

CLE – Counsel Leather Export

CLRI – Central Leather Research institute

DFID -Department for International Development

DC - Developed countries

DAW-Division for Advancement of Women

ERP - Early-reform period

EPZ -Export Processing Zones

GDI-Gender Development Index

GOI - Government of India

HDI - Human Development Index

ILO- International Labour organization

IFAD - International Fund for Agricultural Development

ILDP - Indian Leather Development Programme

KINFRA - Kerala Industrial Infrastructure Development Corporation

LFPR – Labour force participation rate

LRP - late-reform period

LDCs - less developed countries

MDGS – Millennium Development Goals

NCAER -National Council for Agro-Economic Research

SC - scheduled castes

SNA – Standard National Activities

ST - scheduled tribes

UPS - Usual Principal Status

UPSS - Usual Principal and Subsidiary status

UN -United Nations

UNIFEM - United Nation Development Fund for Women

UNDF - United Nation Development Fund

WPR -work participation rate

WHO - World Health Organization

WB - World Bank

WFO - World Food Organization

WIEGO -Women in the Informal Economy Globalizing and Organizing

CHAPTER I

A study on Women industrial workers in Leather Footwear industries in Chennai City

1.1 Introduction

Leather footwear industry occupies a place of prominence in the Indian economy in spite of its massive potentiality for employment, growth and exports. In fact, backed with strong raw-material base and a large reservoir of traditionally skilled and competitive labour force, the Indian leather industry has made significant strides during the past two decades. Not only that, this industry has undergone a dramatic transformation from a mere exporter of raw materials (like tanned hides and skins) in the 1960s to that of value added finished products from the 1970s. Policy initiatives taken by the Government of India (GOI) since 1973 have been quite instrumental to such a transformation. The structure of the Indian leather industry is quite interesting. It is spread in different segments namely tanning and finishing, footwear and components, leather garments, leather goods including saddlery and harness etc. The industry uses primarily indigenous natural resources with little dependence on imported resources. Hides and skins are basic raw materials for the leather industry, which originates from the source of livestock, India has a very large share of the world bovine animal population. Further, an overwhelming proportion of the total production of this industry comes from an unorganized sector, i.e., small scale, cottage and artisan sector. The major production centres are spread over selected areas in a few states, such as selected places in Tamil Nadu, Kolkata in West Bengal, Kanpur and Agra in Uttar Pradesh, Jalandhar in Punjab and Delhi. The major export market for Indian leather goods is Germany, with an of take of about 25 percent of India's domestic production followed by the USA, the UK, France and Italy. The important export items are leather handbags, footwear and leather garments. Official policies/programmes are undertaken to facilitate the growth of the leather footwear industry including de-reservations of 11 items (particularly

1

semi-finished hides and skins, leather shoes and leather accessories for leather industry) in 2010 , abolition of the license system in case of manufacture of most of the leather items. Some items are still reserved for exclusive manufacture by the small-scale sector, but non-small scale units can also obtain approval for the manufacture of these items provided they meet an export obligation of 50 per cent of their annual production. In the same line it also generates the huge employment opportunities to the people ofIndia in which women constitute the major portion. The present study would try to understand the conditions of women workers in the leather footwear industry in a holistic perspective in Tamil Nadu[1].

1.2 Labour in India -An overview

The industrial development in the post independence era culminated definite improvement of the conditions of labour in the organized sector. The corresponding benefits however, did not filter down to the workers in the un-organized sector which accounts for more than 90 per cent of total work force in the country. The National Commission of Labour, which looked into this matter, inter-alia, recommended, "A better understanding of the problem of different categories of un- organized Labour is essential to the formulation of suitable ameliorative measures and detailed surveys about the conditions of work in these employments should be undertaken."In India, a vast majority of the labour force is employed in an unorganized sector employments. The organized/informal employment is characterized by its casual and self employed nature. Self employed persons and those employed in unorganized sector enterprises are not eligible for many benefits including social security benefits to which the organized sector workers are entitled. According to the results of the last quinquenial Employment & Unemployment

---

[1] Indian Leather Industry – Perspective Planning and Intervention Strategies to Reach US $ 7 billion exports by 2010-2011, CLE New Delhi

survey conducted by National Sample Survey Organization in the year 2009-10, the total work force in the country is about 469 million and only 7 per cent of them are employed in the formal or organized sector (and all public sector establishments and all non-agricultural establishments in private sector with 10 or more workers). While remaining 93 per cent of the total work force is employed in the informal or unorganized sector[2]. This vast majority of an unorganized labour force has not been able to organize itself due to various constraints. They have remained a neglected lot as most of the labor acts enacted are concerned about the welfare of the organized sector workers. The workers in an unorganized sector were left to fend for themselves and were rendered vulnerable to exploitation by the employers as they could not organize themselves into a force to reckon with. High rate of illiteracy among unorganized labor has also added to their problems. The various government agencies charged with the responsibility of suggesting effective ways and means to ameliorate their conditions could also do little due to the absence of basic data on this labour segment. The appalling conditions of labour in an unorganized sector attracted the attention of policy makers. But they however, found themselves ill equipped to do anything significant to ameliorate the conditions of workers as no reliable data relating to their working and living conditions was available.

1.3 Economic Significance of Women's Role

Women play a key role in the family. The biological division of roles in the family assumes that generally men engage themselves in productive and economic activities outside the household, and women are to be engaged in caring the hearth and home. Usually, any economic value is not attached to the multifarious jobs women perform in the family. In some of the families, women are the breadwinners

---

[2] NSS 66th Round: Report No. 515(61/10/1), Part II, (July2009-June2010):"Employment and Unemployment Situation in India".

who sustain the family by toiling whole day inside and outside the household[3]. The history of rural women's relationship to nature's resources has been marked by a struggle to provide for family subsistence. Women are noted to have been the first farmers, potters and weavers. In hunting gathering societies, childe notes: "to accomplish the Neolithic revolution... womankind has not only to discover suitable plants and appropriate methods for their cultivation but must also device special implements for tilling the soil, reaping and storing the crop and converting it into foods. Technologies such as the digging stick (used to dig out tubers and wild plants, and precursor to the plough), hoe, the saucer shaped stone for grinding grain, baskets and vessels for grain storage, jars, jugs, strainers and beakers for holding water and fermented liquor, the over for baking bread and the loom, are all attributed to women, as are techniques such as hoeing, winnowing, making bread, spinning and weaving, and the chemistry of pot making. "Food gathering itself demanded and elaborated knowledge of food and medicinal properties of plants, fruits and trees-including wild 'reserve' knowledge of edible plants not normally used but critical to tide over prolonged shortage of other foods during climatic disasters." Women collected edible seeds of wild grass ancestral to our wheat and barley, and to them are attributed the decisive step of deliberately sowing seeds on suitable soil and cultivating the sown land by weeding and other measures. "Indeed it is women's daily activities that are assessed to have sustained the family on the other hand male hunting typically being supplementary, less dependable and more risky source of food supply."(Bina Agarwal 2001)[4]

---

[3] Agrawal, Sarita (1993): "Gender Discrimination in the Labour Market: A Review of Literature"; The Indian Journal of Labour Economics; Vol. 36, No. 2.

[4] Agarwal, Bina. (1985): "Work Participation of Rural Women in Third World -- Some Data and Conceptual Biases"; Economic and Political Weekly; December 21-28, Pp. A-155 to A-164.

1.4 Gender Disparity and Institutional Economics

Institutions as generally accepted (spatially and temporally positioned) regulate social norms for behaviour in a specific social situation, which are subject to self-regulation or external authority. Approaching institutions in this way permits theorization to extend without dismissing, a concern with the real constraints that institutions impose on individual behaviour to consider how they contribute to perceptions of interests and, correspondingly, the legitimacy of existing social relations as well as attempts to alter established patterns. In the context of this research it is important to recognize that institutions central to the labour relation are gendered in essential ways. As "gender bearing" institutions labour markets and relations are instantiations of the gender roles and patterns of the society in which they are embedded. Stereotypes associating authority in the workplace with masculinity, and suggesting that there is 'man's work' and 'woman's work' are inscribed in social institutions and it effect the types of work endorsed for, and acceptable to men and women. Cook et al have claimed that the gendered division of labour both within and outside the household has profound repercussions for women's market labour involvement: "women do enter the public sphere but are often constrained by their roles in the private sphere and frequently undertake activities in the labour market which are an extension of their activities in the private sphere" (In the South Indian case, gender, mediated by caste and class, is a powerful constraint on rural women's mobility, public visibility, and autonoy. Women lack (enforceable) ownership rights over land and other productive assets their works are valued far less than men's and is accordingly remunerated, their mobility is limited, and so their power to bargain over contracts, prices, and wages is severely constrained. However, as noted by Morgan and Olsen (2009) institutions may alter somewhat over time through a series of interrelated cultural changes. Transformations in areas of the political economy and available technologies, as well as collective or cumulative processes of bargaining and negotiation can lead to adaptation and change in accepted social norms, processes which are evident and ongoing in South India's rural labour markets, roles and relations[5]. Throughout India the composition of rural labour has altered over the past three decades. Casual daily wages agricultural labour has increasingly become the domain of women accompanied by subjection to many of the labour relations that men have sought historically to exit, including tied labour disciplined by debt relations. The rural non-farm labour force has remained disproportionately male, with women most prominent in the most casual or intermittent activities offering the lowest levels of remuneration (bidi and match production; outsourced, home-based handicrafts and food processing; construction; mining), where work sited are commonly located within, or near to, their homes The production relations of this type of work are typically characterized by "excessively long hours, especially [for] young women...low piece-rates (with delays in payment in many cases)... unhygenic working conditions...[and] lack of pension benefits" (Mehrotra and Biggeri 2005)[6].

1.5 Work Environment and the Discrimination

People spend more than a third of their working life time at the workplace. Work place characteristics, likewise material or non-material exposures (e.g. psychological distress), hence are major determinants of health. As people continuously enter and leave the labour force, the world of employment and the world of unemployment are strongly interwoven[7]. Rates of unemployment, or economic trends like boom and recession might have an impact on perceived as well as on de-facto job insecurity of both employed and unemployed individuals. This

[5] Morgan and Olsen (2009) "The Strategic Silence: Gender and Economic Policy"; London: Zed Book with the North South Institute.

[6] Mehrotra and Biggeri 2005. "Status of Indian Women"; Kanishka Publisher, New Delhi.

[7] Busse, M. & Spielmann, C. (2003) *Gender discrimination and the international division of labour.* HWWA Discussion Paper 245 ISSN 1616-4814 Retrieved on April 20, 2009 from http://www.hwwa.de/Publikationen/Discussion_Paper/2003/245.pdf

research work would try to explore   more about the relation of macro-level variables like income, income inequality, access to employment, social dialogue, workers' rights and equality , education and discrimination, to health outcomes. Furthermore, the study would like to know how the macro-level variables are connected to, or partly can be explained through micro-level variables such as social support, work-related stress and job satisfaction with in the realm of gender dimension, Hence this overview is mainly structured by the big fields of income, education, unemployment, control, stress, and social support, and by those diseases that have the biggest influence on mortality or on the economic burden of disease, respectively.

1.6 Women work situation

Time immemorial, women are described as the better half of men. But in reality, the women in developing countries do not tally with this description. It is well known fact that women have played and continue to play a key role in conservation of basic life support systems such as land, water, flora and fauna. Women have to play a dual role, as a housewife and as income earners. Women have the burden of preparing food for the family, besides fulfilling their fundamental role of nurturing and caring for the children and tending to elderly members of the household. Even then they suffer from being economically and socially invisible. There is continuous inequality and vulnerability of women in all fields like socio-economic, political, education, health care, nutrition etc. Women constitute nearly one half of the world's population having enormous potential but the being underutilized or unutilized for the economic development of the nation. Indian situation is not an exception for this. In India, women have remained as a neglected section of work force. They were not considered on par with men. Women are lagging behind men mainly   because   of the relative   absence   of economic opportunities   and minimal participation in decision making process. Women's access to land ownership is extremely limited. Educational

7

backwardness is another major reason why women are lagging behind men. The latest census reports revealed that female literacy rate in India was 54 per cent, as compared to the male literacy rate of 76 per cent. However, the life expectancy of female was 65 years in contrast to 64 years of male. The work participation rate of women was 54 per cent as compared to that of 21 per cent in respect of men. However, the time spent on non-market activity by women was only 65 per cent. The participation of women in professional and technical work force is as low as 21 per cent. Therefore, the organizations concerned with the development of women are considered as an empowerment to women and as a solution to these problems.

1.7 Women's work and Wages

Women workers have been undergoing serious discrimination in the labour market, Labour legislation, and as far as the workers are concerned are inadequate for the women. It does not fully safeguard their interests wherever they are employed. The essential principle of labour legislation should be not only to prevent employers from taking advantage of workers' helplessness and weaker position but also to compel them to adopt measures which ensure the rights of the workers especially women to overcome handicaps peculiar to them. But too many demands and restrictions on the employers are bound to affect the employment of women adversely making it difficult from the point of view of the management. Women are usually employed in lighter occupations compared to men who are employed in heavier occupations. Even when they work in similar occupations, distinctions are made sometimes. There is no reason why women are not paid equal wages for equal work[8].

---

[8] Mathur, A. (1994): "Work Participation, Gender and Economic Development: A Quantitative Anatomy of the Indian Scenario"; The Journal of Development Studies; 30(2): Pp. 466-504

1.8 Constraints of Women Workers

Certain problems are common to women workers. A study of the problems of women workers will indicate the need for the welfare measures to be adopted along with proper lines of approach. Woman is physically weaker than man. In addition, she has to bear the child which requires her to take rest before and after delivery. Where there is no coverage of maternity benefits, it may sometimes become takes occasional disability. Then she has the burden of the growing child; its care taking much of her time. She has also to function as a housewife with all household responsibilities. The family is a grave for the women in our country than her western sister. Her social and economic status is very low[9].There are several additional gender-specific dimensions which affect women's work situation. The gender based inequalities in the family in the provision of basic necessities also create health problems for women. Further they are exposed to health hazards arising from the nature of their work. There exist several types of exploitation by employers and money lenders also.

1.9 Empowerment of Women and work situation

Empowerment is a process of creating awareness and the capacity for building, and leading to a participation and greater decision making power. The process of empowerment strengthens their innate ability through acquiring knowledge, power and experience (Murugan and Dharmalingam, 2000). To raise the status of women, they must be empowered socially, economically and politically. Empowerment can serve as a powerful instrument for women to achieve upward social and economic mobility and to achieve power and status in the society The tenth five year plan (2002-07) has made a major commitment towards empowering women as the agent of socio-economic

---

[9] Mehta,Arati and Menon,Latika (1998): "Status of Indian Women"; Kanishka Publisher,New Delhi.

change and development. Based on the recommendations of the committee on National Policy for Empowerment of women, the tenth plan has suggested a three-fold strategy for uplifting the status of women through social, economic and political empowerment. Social empowerment is to create an enabling environment through various developed policies and programmers for the development of women, besides providing them easy and equal access to all the basic minimum services such as education, nutrition so as to enable them to realize their full potentials. Economic empowerment is to ensure adequate provision for training, employment and income generating activities, with both forward and backward linkages. Gender justice is to eliminate all forms of gender discrimination and thus, allow women to enjoy their rights and fundamental freedom in all spheres of life. The provision of 33 per cent reservation in the 73rd amendment of the constitution endowed rural women with platform to enter into the perview of decision making and planning. This provides for the development of leadership quality among women which results in political empowerment.The specialists in economic development have considered entrepreneurship development as a postive approach to empowerment of women. A women as an entrepreneur is economically more powerful than as a mere worker, because ownership not only confers control over assets but also gives her the freedom to take decision. This will also uplift her social status in the society.At present women perform exceedingly well in different spheres of activities like academics, politics, administration and social work. It is now widely accepted that if national development and women's development have to be purposeful and relevant, women have to be fully fledged participants in economic activities. Participation of women in economic activities is now emerging as an universal phenomenon. Alternatively stated, women are increasingly joining the world labour market and also assuming the role of entrepreneurs all over the world. In India too, significant changes in women's rate of participation in the economy are taking place with the pace of liberalization and privatization sweeping across the country[10]. The role of women as entrepreneurs and economic workers are already visible, the enterprising females are relatively a new breed of women in India. Wealth is created only by doers in the arena who are marred with din, dust, blood and sweat. These are producers who strike out on their own who know high high's and low low's, great devotions and who over extend themselves for worthwhile causes.

1.10 Global commitment for uplifting women's status

Improvement on the status of women status has been remaining on the agenda of United Nations (UN), right from the beginning. For this purpose in 1946 it setup Division for Advancement of Women (DAW). For propagating awareness about women issues 1975 to 1985 was declared as a decade of women equality, development and peace. The UN and related agencies also organized various conferences periodically on women's issues. The main agenda of these conferences was to eliminate the gender discrimination and to involve women in development process by promoting education and providing better health facilities etc. At present different commissions and agencies are working and funding the projects related to women issues i.e. Division for Advancement of Women (DAW).United Nation Development Fund for Women (UNIFEM), International Fund for Agricultural Development (IFAD), World Food Organization (WFO), United Nation Development Fund (UNDF), Department for International Development (DFID), World Health Organization (WHO) and World Bank (WB)

---

[10] Mahapatra, Suhasini. (2002): "Women Participation in Labour Force", New Delhi: Rajat Publications, Pp. 46-54.

11

1.11 Women workforce in informal economy

Women workers in the informal economy is associated with low levels of organization, small-scale production, and casual employment, little or no social protection and lack of job security or health insurance. The most vulnerable sections of the society comprising of women, children, minorities, and illegal immigrants are prime targets of this exploitation. The informal sector organizations do not seek to overturn the class system, but represent a challenge to hierarchical class relations. The informal sector often supplies vital services and goods to the formal economy at cheap rates due to low labor and infrastructural costs. It is where the growing number of workers in the developing countries is concentrated.The estimates by Women in the Informal Economy Globalizing and Organizing [WIEGO] suggest that informal economy accounts for over half the urban employment in Africa and Asia and a quarter in Latin America and Caribbean. In Asia and the Pacific, women in the informal sector are concentrated in small enterprises. These are often family based using simple labor-intensive techniques of production, which involves repetitious monotonous work. These jobs are unregulated, vulnerable and dependent on sub contracting.

1.12 Labour Market discrimination and Gender

Labor market discrimination consists of treating equally productive people differently in the labor market based on characteristics unrelated to an individual's productivity. Most studies on discrimination in developed countries have focused on explaining wage gaps between men and women and between races. The primary approaches in the literature include the neoclassical approach [primary among them Becker (1957), Arrow (1972), Blinder (1973) and Oaxaca (1973)], statistical discrimination approach [Aigner and Cain (1977)] and segmented labor market approach or the dual labor market hypothesis [(Doeringer (1986); Reich et al.

(1973)][11].Bhattacherjee (1985) estimated the extent of wage discrimination against low caste workers in a Bombay automobile firm. Based on the Oaxaca decomposition of the wage gap, he found evidence indicating that wage discrimination was reflected in the under-valuation of lower caste human capital and other characteristics, and this discrimination mostly stemmed from differential access to resources important to developing skills for the labor market.

1.13 Women Labour in Leather Footwear Industries

It is a contention of the literature that harsh conditions in export factories are an outcome of the decision to locate production in areas where labour is 'cheapest and most exploitable'. Accordingly, labour's subordination is claimed to arise primarily from the greater mobility of capital in a world of uneven development. However, labour's containment is not settled by the selective recruitment of particular kind of workers from 'spatially- differentiated labour markets' This can make a difference but at some point production must still proceed and then there is the problem of getting work from workers. In the Indian leather industry, It was found that production for an overseas market stimulated changes in the responses of local owners and production managers to the 'problem of labour' which entailed a furthering of the real subsumption of labour to capital. These changes to the social form of the labour process had a generally positive impact on workers' capacities to unionize at the enterprise level as they increased 'the spatial boundaries' of labour's 'organizational coherence'. Whereas the labour perspective pays great attention to the effect of the mobility of capital on labour's bargaining status. It is the common supposition of the existing literature which pertains to garment industries that women workers predominate in export factories because they have – or are at least perceived to have – characteristics that their employers prefer: namely, greater manual dexterity, a lower supply

---

[11] Ibid

13

price, and 'less disruptive' attitudes than men. As a corollary, the employment of women workers is thought to be a factor which explains low levels of unionization in export factories,the results of many related work shows that the employment of women as sewers was not a strategy which owners and managers in the Indian garment industries pursued to ensure a more disciplined workforce and that their actions in hiring women instead were an immediate consequence of certain taken-for-granted assumptions about the nature of women and the tasks which they perform. This is not a particularly surprising finding, yet it challenges the standard feminist view that the employment of women in export factories is principally the result of the rational economic calculations of their employers. In the modern leather industry in the India, as internationally, machine and hand sewing are predominantly done by women, while men are exclusively engaged in the tasks of laying out and cutting,. bleaching, cleaning. Although the owners, production managers and some trade union officials attributed this occupational segmentation to perceived natural differences between men and women. It is important that this should not be considered as an adequate explanation   rather, to avoid the assumption that 'a transhistorical structure is built into gender by the sexual dichotomy of bodies. It is essential to look that the existing division of labour along with the gender lines must also be seen to have a history, in which it was first laid down in the nineteenth century in the transition from artisan to capitalist forms of production and the concomitant shift to mass-produced, ready-to-wear items of clothing[12]. In this regard   employers' rational economic calculations plays a greater role in the past in establishing industrial sewing as 'women's work' than they do currently, when the gender division of labour is fully institutionalized. Most of the detailed discussion of the reasons for women workers' employment in export factories was located within the literature on 'women and development' which debated changes in the gender division of labour with capitalist

---

[12] Labour practices in the Footwear, leather, textiles and clothing industries, International Labour Office, Geneva, 2000

development and the impact of these changes on women's socio- economic status in society which is replicated in the labour division as well, women work has not adequately recognized with the appropriate incentives in the leather footwear industries, in Tamil Nadu plethora of the studies illustrated the vulnerability of the women force in leather footwear industries especially in leather garments industries.

1.14 Selection and justification of the study

Women workers in 'export' (or 'world market') factories have been a popular target of academic and journalistic research since the late 1970s.Export factories are work sites in developing countries that are linked to the emergence of a 'new international division of labour' in which, it is argued,that low-wage countries become manufacturing sites for consumer markets in the advanced industrialized world through transnational production arrangements involving direct investment or international subcontracting. In that the term 'export factories' refers specifically to the sites of production in transnational production arrangements, it is not limited to 'factories' per se, but also includes more 'informal' establishments and home-working. Despite this diversity in possible employment forms, the argument is that working conditions in export factories are universally poor on account of their vulnerable position in the society which inhibits the scope for collective bargaining, and their establishment in places where labour is especially 'cheap to buy, abundant and well-disciplined' Accordingly, the literature is characterised by the assertion that low wages, inadequate health and safety standards, and an absence of union representation are all defining features of export factories.This thesis challenges the perspective on labour in export factories, most specifically the assertion that transnational production arrangements geared to exporting are a particular cause of low levels of unionization. The structural and cultural subordination of women in India strongly defame the quality of the women and underestimate their labourious contribution either at home and the working place. Women predominately constitute themselves

15

as agricultural labour that has also been largely engaging in garment industries. Their proportion is high in the leather footwear industries; unleash lot of negative consequences on the workers in terms of health and other occupational hazardous. In this context the study would propelled to asses the conditions of women in leather footwear industries in terms of contribution in the production, incentives received, job stress, job involvement, engagement in the production process, with in the realm of gender dimension in Tamil Nadu. In the Tamil Nadu garments industry in the early 1990s, It was found that women workers were not in fact generally able to establish and sustain independent unions in the industries. Thus, the study would propel to understand the contributions and conditions of Women in the leather footwear industries in Tamil Nadu.

1.15 Statement of the problem

Women constitute larger proportion of the workforce in the leather industries and plethora of the studies have advocated the research in leather footwear industries within the framework of challenges and contribution of small scale industries on economic development, environmental related issues, health related issues, very few studies concentrated the workers issues in general and few studies have concentrated on women issues in particular but not in holistic dimension by considering the lacuna in the existing literature. The study would propel to concentrate on the challenges and contribution made by the women workers in the leather footwear industries in Tamil Nadu, women constitutes larger segment of the work force in the leather footwear industries but none of the studies were focused on this core issue with more comprehensive manner. The present study an attempt to fill that gap and would like to ascertain, the women workers conditions in leather footwear industries in terms of their contribution, remuneration, incentives, challenges in working place, oppression in the industry, health hazardous, equity and various similar kind of unnoticed dimensions would be interrogated in more comprehensive ways, Since Tamil Nadu economyis known for its urbanized and industrialized face it is worthwhile to introspect how did it addresses the issues of women and whether women workers get adequate recognition for the service they rendered to the leather footwear industries.

1.16 Need of the study

The study would be an important tool to exemplify the issues confronted by the women workers in the leather footwear industries. As the modern development encapsulated the concept of women empowerment but it is imperative to examine whether the cultural constraints would enable the women to obtain their required share in the domain. At this juncture the study would give the clarity to the policy makers and the leather garment industries to conceive the polices to protect the rights of the women workers and facilitate them to participate in more effective way in the production process thereby ensuring the optimum productivity in one hand and the workers job satisfaction on the other hand.

1.17 Objectives of the study

Within the broad scope outlined, specific objectives of the study are as follows.

- ❖ To examine the socio-economic conditions of women in leather footwear industries workers in the study area
- ❖ To examine the job satisfaction and job involvement level of women worker in leather footwear industrial worker in the study area
- ❖ To examine the health hazardous encountered by the women workers in the study area
- ❖ To ascertain the perceptions of the women workers on the protective measures provided in the work place
- ❖ To examine leather footwear industries practice gender discrimination in the provision of remuneration and incentive to workers
- ❖ To formulate the suitable policy measures on the selected domain.

1.18 Hypotheses

To give a specific focus to the objectives, a few hypotheses have been drawn up to be tested using appropriate statistical tools in the analysis chapter

❖ *Ho: There is no significant influence of socio-cultural factors on the wage and incentive determination for Women workers in leather footwear industries.*

❖ *Ho: There is no persuasion of working environment on the worker health deterioration*

❖ *Ho: There is no relation exists between protective measures and labour security in the Industries*

❖ *Ho: There is no significant influence of work environment variables on job satisfaction and constraints in the job profile*

❖ *Ho: Job, education and self confidence are not the determinant of women empowerment*

1.19 Methodology

Sources of Data

Both secondary and primary data have utilized for the study purpose

1.20 Secondary Data

The sources of data, sampling frame, method of data collection and the non-sampling error of the study are presented in this section. The present study is based on primary as well as secondary data. The relevant and available information were collected at various levels. Secondary Data were collected from:(I) Census of India (ii) National sample Survey reports (iii) Report of Annual survey of Industries (iv) Annual Reports of the Industries and commerce of India,(v)ILO reports, Besides the

18

above books, Journals, Reports, News paper, Seminar, conference papers, Economic magazines of the banks on this subject matter have also been referred to.

1.21 Primary Data

Primary Data were collected from the women leather workers across Chennai through interviews and discussions with the officials involved in manufacturing at various levels. The Method of Data collection was personal interview with the respondents by administering the questionnaires. The structured questionnaire conceived to obtain the relevant information from the respondents,

1.22 Selection of sample

Stratified random sampling method was adopted to select the sample for the study. The leather footwear industries location were classified into three segments like North, Central and South Chennai, out of 56 leather industries in Chennai 23 industries located in South Chennai, 14 industries located in Central Madras and 19 industries located in North Madras, 100 samples from each region were selected for the study as number of workers in the each companies differs. Thus the researcher adopted the region wise representation for the sample selection rather than company wise selection. For example each industries consists of 250 to 700 workers in accordance with the size of the company. Thus region wise selection is close to the proximity of the study.

1.23 Questionnaire design

The questionnaire formulated in various sections in which first part of the schedule is designed to collect the demographic information of the women leather footwear workers. This is used to study the income, employment, asset, savings, indebtedness .The next section deals with the working time and the structure of the industries which would be helpful to understand the amenities made available for the workers in the study area. The Next section of the schedule derives the information on the health conditions of the worker next section collect the information on the work environment and the job engaging practice of the industry which would enable to assess the job satisfaction and job involvement of the workers. Next section would receive the opinions of the workers on various issues which pertains to the work through which women workers perceptions at comprehensive manner in gender dimension.

1.24 Sample size

In Tamil Nadu 8,07,732 women are employed in both public and private sector in 2011, out of which 1,54,391 are engaged in Manufacturing industries, especially in Garment industries 78 percent of the female are employed and nearly 40 thousand women employers represent leather footwear industries in Tamil Nadu, With respect to sample selection three industries were taken for the study. The first industry consists of 900 women workers, second Industry comprises of 870 women workers and the third industry consists of 926 women workers. Stratified random sampling method was deployed to select the sample for the study and 100 sample from each industry were selected and the systematic interviews were conducted with the respondents and registered the information for the study purpose.

1.25 Analysis of Data

Statistical tools like percentage analysis, cross tabulation chart analysis, frequency distribution, and correlation ANOVA, Logit Regression, are applied to find out the major factors determining the socio economic status of agricultural women labourers.

1.26 Limitations of the study

The study introspects the perception of the employes on health status but it didn't carried clinical test to find the health status

20

Women employed in the industries as the recognized workers were interviewed it didn't include the information of the un-organized workers who are working from the home.

1.27 Chapterization

The first chapter contains the basic contextual background of the importance of the women leather footwear workers and various elements of women workers like significance and the features of the workers in India, changing role of women and significance of the study, selection and justification of the study, methodology, objectives have been structured and illustrated in the introductory chapter.

The second chapter consists of literature review pertaing to the women workers on both Indian and international studies, job involvement, job satisfaction, health hazardous and the gender discrimination in the industrial set up.

The third chapter examines the various theoretical insights of the women and work. It begin with the feminist perspective and women labour position in the production function theory, Marxism and women, first wave feminist analysis, second wave feminist analyses, psychological theories of women and work, international statuary protection for Women agricultural workers and status of women in the family system have been critically analyzed with the perspective and women empowerment.

Fourth chapter describes the profile of the study area, it deals with the historic significance of Chennai, climatic conditions of the study area, tropical, demographic situation of the Chennai have been illustrated, details of the administrative set-up, Medical and educational infrastructure, rain fall, irrigation sources, land use patern, size of land holding, crop production, information on industries and marketing facilities have been illustrated in the chapter.

Fifth Chapter describes the analyses of the primary data and the inferences derived from the analysis have been displayed.

Chapter six exemplifies the summary and conclusion which includes the major findings and general observation made by the researcher apart from the empirical insights, suggestions, policy recommendations and scope for future research.

2.1 Introduction

In this chapter, an attempt has been made to present the literature pertaining to the past research work related to the present study. Systematic perusal of the literature of the chosen domain categorized in various segments viz., Studies pertaining to Women Labour force in the Economy, Studies pertaining to constraints faced by the Women workers, Studies pertaining to the Gender based labour market discrimination, Studies pertaining to the dual role of working women, Studies pertaining to Globalization and its impact on Women workers.

2.2 Studies pertains to Women Labour force in the Economy

Vinamazumdar (1975)[1] In her article 'Women Workers in Changing Economy' state that in the traditional economy women have played integral and protected roles in agriculture, industry and services development with increasing complexity of markets, production techniques and technological changes have been the relevant force which has displaced large masses of working women with their traditional occupation, made their productive and professional skills absolute, and reduced them to the status of unskilled unwanted workers. The alternative opportunities that have opened up as a result of development in services or new industry are for a different class of women educated and with new type of skills. They cannot absorb the displaced women who are mostly illiterate, rural and with restricted mobility.

Delia Dawn (1978)[2] In her study tells that working women are a great revolutionary force. We convey our high respects to the revolutionary women of all countries and warm greeting to the working women of all nationalities in our country. It is important as Lenin taught as to get women to take part in socially productive lab our, to liberate them from 'domestic slavery' to free them from their stupefying and humiliating subjugation to the external drudgery of the kitchen and the misery Mao Tse Tung has said: "Time have changed and today men and women are equal what ever men comrades can accomplish women comrades can too. The women of our country must live up to our great leader's earnest expectation. They should aim high, study hard, and strive to make new and still greater contributions to socialist revolution and

---

1 Vina Mazumdar 'Women workers in changing Economy' (Yojana vol. 19: p.7, 1975)

2 Delia Davin , 'Women – work' women and the party in Revolutionary China (Oxford university press, 1978), March 8th international working women's Day, p: 212

socialist revolution and socialist contusion" Mao has always given great encouragement to women.

Ghosh (1993)[3] writes that in developed countries (DCs), urban work participation rates are higher than rural rates, whereas in Less Developed Countries (LDCs) rural participation rates are higher than urban rates. In DCs females are more inclined to work in the urban areas than to rural; whereas in LDCs, female are participating at higher rate in rural areas. It appears that the proportionate distribution of population between rural and urban sectors, and the economic structure is responsible for these differentials. It should be noted that female education is less valued in rural areas. But after the age group 15-19 years, a larger proportion of females remains permanently absent from work-force, mainly because of high fertility performance: child bearing and child rearing.

Kundu, Amitabh (1997) [4]examined the work participation rate (WPR) in India both in rural as well as in urban areas, the data taken decennial censuses as well as by the N.S.S support this proposition. The urban 19 rates of work participation are lower than the rural ones, for both males and females. The reason mentioned by Kundu for this trend is the agrarian nature of Indian economy because agriculture sector has the 'capacity' to carry a large number of disguised unemployed persons to absorb them at low levels of productivity. This is particularly true for women. The 1991 census recorded a significant growth in the number of total female workers during 1981-91 viz 40.4 per cent. The corresponding figure for males was 20.8 per cent only. As a result, the percentage share of total female workers moved up from 19.7 per cent to 22.3 per cent while for male workers, it declined from 52.6 per cent to 51.6 per cent Importantly the WPR of females has gone up both in rural as well as in urban areas. The opposite is true for males. Furthermore, the increase in the WPR for women in rural area works out as higher than thatin urban areas during 1981-91.

Papola .T.S and Sharma.N.Alakh (1997)[5]examined that in 1980's the female employment in urban India increased at 4.33 per cent per annum , faster than male employment which grew at 3.12 per cent per annum. Between 1983 and 1993-94, WPR of women increased faster by 1.97 per cent while that of males it increased by 1.55 per cent. The sex-ratio of the workforce

3 Ghosh, S. K., Women in a Changing Society, Asia Publishing House, New Delhi, 1976.

4 Kundu, Amitabh (1997): "Trends and Structure of Employment in the 1990'sImplications for Urban Growth"; Economic and Political Weekl;, June 14,Pp.1399-1405.

5 Papola .T.S and Sharma.N.Alakh (1997): "Employment of Women in India: Some Reseach and Policy Issues"; The Indian Journal of Labour Economic; Vol. 40,No.2, April-June, Pp.348-355

improved from 139 women per 1000 men in 1981 to 178 in 1991 according to census and from 260 women per 1000 men in 1983 to 268 in 1993-94, according to N.S.S.O.

Nirmala, V and Bhat, Sham. K. (1999)[6]in their paper attempted to analyze the female labour participation and examine the impact of technological changes on female labour employment in rain fed agriculture in Tuticorin district of Tamil Nadu. It was observed that technology adoption had positive impact on female labour employment. Cotton crop created better employment opportunities accounting for 77.12 man days/ha as compared to Cumbu (37.93 man-days/ha) and Cholam (44 man-days/ha). But the percentage of family female labour to total labour decreased with the increase in the level of adoption of technology.

Tripathy, S. N. and Das, Soudamini (1999)[7] conducted study on the role of informal groups in increasing women's participation and employment generation among rural poor. The groups were selected from two different project areas viz. Chitradurga district in Karnataka and Periyar district in Tamil Nadu. The study revealed that in terms of occupational pattern of members, agricultural labourers constituted 70 per cent of the membership of the group. The additional employment generated through the informal group lending worked out to 172 person-days per member undertaking supplementary activities such as animal husbandry, poultry etc. and non-farm activities like petty shop, kirana shop, flower selling business etc. provided employment to a greater extent. The annual employment available for the group members increased to 85 per cent during post-group formation period when compared to pregroup formation period. The informal groups of rural poor with active intervention of NGOs, adequately supported by training and financial assistance ensured and also significantly improved women's' participation both from economic and social aspects.

Agarwal, Bina (1999)[8] has attempted to examine the changes in educational and employment status of female labour in rural areas of Amritsar district of Punjab at two points of time *i.e.*, 1990-91 and 1997-98. The data was collected from 200 female workers based on three stage random sampling procedure. The employment of female labour in the

6 Nirmala, V and Bhat, Sham. K. (1999): "Female Work Participation in the Emerging Labour Market In India"; The Indian Journal of Labour Economics, Vol. 42,No. 4, Pp. 613-624

7 Tripathy, S. N. and Das, Soudamini, Informal Women Labour in India. New Delhi: Discovery Publishing House, 1999

8 Agarwal, Bina (1999) "Work Participation of Rural Women in Third World; Some Data and conceptual Biases " Economic and Political Weekly, Vol. 20,No. 51, 1999

primary sector declined from 60 per cent to 53.5 per cent, but it showed upward shifts in secondary and tertiary sectors. The number of illiterate female workers declined from 44 per cent to 39 per cent between 1990-91 and 1997-98 with a proportionate increase in the number of literate female workers. Their share in the family income from primary, secondary and tertiary activities showed increase from 12, 15 and 18 per cent in 1990-91 to 15, 17 and 20 per cent in 1997- 98.

Mishra (1999)[9] in their paper have examined the extent and proportion of women labour participation in paddy cultivation and gap in wages between men and women labour in Kymore Plateau and Satpura hill region of Madhya Pradesh. The participation of women labour was higher in transplanting of paddy, inter-culture and harvesting while, operations like preparatory tillage, sowing, manuring and fertilizer application, irrigation and threshing operations were performed jointly with men. The use of women labour (both family and hired) in paddy cultivation constituted 53 per cent of the total human labour employment. The hiring of women labour was highly associated with the increase in the size of farm. The result of the study also showed that the wage gap was more than 71 per cent between men and women for all operations. The study suggested that diversified farming such as dairy, poultry etc. can help to increase the employment opportunities of women.

Gumber, Anil (2000)[10] locates the importance of women as workers and as managers of human welfare who are central to the ability of households, communities, and nations in tackling the current crisis of survival. The process of development taking place in almost all the Third World countries is linked up with the global economy, where the key issues are growth versus people-centered development, export-led growth versus inward oriented production, problems of impact of capital and technological and its appropriation. These contradictions reflect the conflicting interests of different groups where the interests of lowest rung in the caste, class and gender hierarchy are deteriorating. If rural women as a group are taken they are the providers of entire range of so – called basic needs. Therefore, if the impacts of development strategies are to be understood properly, then the starting point has to be that of viewing women as principal producers and workers. However, the approach is a blend of gender and class. Referring to the

---

[9] Mishra, Bimlesh Kumar, "Women Workers Deserve a Better Deal." Yojana,Vol. 34, No. 12, 1999, p.19

[10] Gumber, Anil (2000): "Correlates of Unemployment Among Rural Youth in India: An Inter-State Analysis"; The Indian Journal of Labour Economics, Vol. 43(4),October-December, Pp. 657-671.

26

effects of land reforms, the study says that they have often reduced women's control over land by recognizing male heads of household, resulting in more seasonal, casual, temporary nature of work of the landless women. And, where agricultural mechanization has occurred, it worsens or at least does not improve women's absolute and relative economic position

V.Nirmala and K.Sham Bhat (1999)[11] observed that since 1971 there has been a stabilization of women's employment. The ILO database shows no rise in women's economic activity rates for India during 1972-2002. These data show 31 per cent of women working in 1970, 31 per cent in 1980, 27 per cent in 1990, and 30 per cent in 2000. In other words there is no substantial change, according to this source. The measures of work participation obtained by the National Council for Agro-Economic Research (NCAER) in their survey in 1997 showed labour force participation rates of 52 per cent among men and 26 per cent among women. Their calculations used both usual and subsidiary status. At the all-India level it raised women's labour force participation from 18 to 26 per cent. The NCAER figures closely mimic the Indian Census figures for 1991. The Census showed 27 per cent of women and 53 per cent of men were in the labour force using the combination of usual and subsidiary status. Furthermore state differences in work participation rates are given using NCAER data. The change in female work participation rates due to including subsidiary status has different effects for different states. For those with low participation rates under the heading of 'usual' status (for women), there is a huge difference. Adding subsidiary workers in some cases doubles the work participation rate, e.g. from 9 to 29 per cent in the Punjab, and a similarly large jump occurs in Uttar Pradesh.

Greed (2000)[12] addresses the question of whether an increased number of women entering the construction professions is resulting in the build-up of critical mass, with associated changes in the culture of the construction industry, and thus in its organization and conditions of employment. The study identifies the change agents such as governmental regulatory bodies, and bottom-up agents such as minority groups and community organizations which are responsible for the changes in the construction industry. One important professional body is the women-led Equal Opportunities in Construction Taskforce, which has produced and is promoting guidelines for equal opportunities in the industry. The study reveals the trends which work against the build-

[11] V.Nirmala and K.Sham Bhat: " Female Work Participation in The Emerging Labour Market in India"; The Indian Journal od Labour Economics; Vol. 42.4,1999

[12] Greed, C. (2000, July) Women in the construction professions: Achieving critical mass. *Gender, Work and Organization, 7(3)*, pp. 181-196(16)

up of critical mass and culture change. They are high job turnover among women in construction, occupational isolation, and limited promotion prospects.

Study of Mitra, P.P. (2001)[13] presents that urban employment has grown at a faster rate than that of rural - largely due to growth of informal sector. The annual growth of employment in urban areas during 1972 to 1987 had been as high as 4 per cent as against the corresponding growth in rural areas of only 1.7 per cent. The era of eighties has been characterized with jobless growth as employment in the organized sector grew at less than 1 per cent per annum while the labour force in the country grew at 2.5 per cent per annum. He also mentions that in all industries, the proportion of contract workers in total workforce has increased from 8.3 per cent in 1984-85 and 9.1 per cent in 1991-92. There has been perceptible decline in the self employed status of workers both on the basis of Usual Principal Status (UPS) and Usual Principal and Subsidiary status (UPSS) except in the case of urban males. Although there has been an increase in the proportion of female workforce in the category of regular employees, but the decline in the case of male workforce has been so fast that there has been an overall decline in the proportion of regular workers.

N. RAJESESWARI (2002)[14] The socio-economic conditions of Handloom weaves in Taminadu in India reference to their occupation, income consumption, debt , education , job statisfication, investment, sources of finance expenditure savings health environment conditions, welfare schemes etc., are useful for determining their economic independence majority of the handloom weavers earn very low monthly income and they live below poverty line. The handloom sector has to be saved from global competition failing which the sector and weavers will lose their economic positions

According to Jha (2002)[15] the construction sector in Nepal plays a vital role in providing employment for a large proportion of the poorest sections of the population in Nepal. The study reveals that the main priority of the construction workers is to find work on a regular basis and improve their income. Male workers can raise their income considerably by acquiring skills and it is rare to find an unskilled male worker having more than five to seven years of experience in this

13 Mitra and Muopadhyay, (2001), Spatial dimensions of Labour Absorption, Economic and Political Weekly, Bombay.

14 N.Rajeshwari, "Socio- economic conditions of workers in estate: A survey" southern economist, February 1, 2002, Vol.40.'p.19.

15 Jha, K. K. (2002) Informal labour in the construction industry in Nepal. Sectoral activities Programme, Geneva: ILO.

sector. Thus men in Nepal are trained through on the job training. But this opportunity to acquire skills is denied to female labourers. The contribution of women to the construction industry of Nepal is significant. It was found that the women constituted 25 to 40 per cent in roof casting groups and roughly 75 per cent in production of construction materials. The female construction workers are exploited also in terms of lesser wage rates than their male counterparts. In Nepal, females are employed only as helpers and continue working as helpers throughout their working lives.

Elumalai and Sharma (2003)[16] in their study on non-farm employment for rural households in India have found that the employment of wage labour has been declining in agriculture, while it is increasing in non agricultural activities. The non-farm activities provide opportunities to earn income during the slack season in agriculture. The study also revealed the multi activity nature of the workers. About 62.13 per cent of the person-days spent in agriculture as principal activity by the rural male, also spent 3.35 per cent and 4.34 per cent of the person-days as self-employed and wage labour in non-agriculture respectively. The per cent distribution of male workers in non-farm employment in 1999-00 was the highest in Kerala followed by Himachal Pradesh and the per cent distribution of rural female workers in non-farm activities was the highest in West Bengal followed by Kerala. The study concludes that augmenting rural investment in the development of non-farm sector will increase the income of rural households and thus reduce poverty.

Mohanty, S.K.(2004)[17] examined that overall levels of WPR is likely to be lower. The WPR is derived from the occupation of the labour force. It is found that the WPR in urban India has remained constant at 55 percent at both early reform and late reform period for the population aged 20-59.The WPR by broad age group showed that there is sharp decline in the WPR for the age group 45 and above where as there is no/marginal change for other age group. For the age group 20-24 the WPR has increased from 19.2 to 20.6 percent while it has increased from 37.6 to 38.8 for the age group 25-29 in urban India. But the WPR has remained stagnant at 64 percent for the age group 40-45, declined from 62 to 59, 51 to 49, 44 to 31 and 35 to 21 for the age group 50-54, 55-59, 60-64 and 65+ respectively. The NSSO findings revealed that there is decline in overall work participation rate during 1993- 94 and 1999-2000 in all the age group where as this

16 Elumalai and Sharma (2003) "Measuring women's work in agriculture"; Food and Agricultural Organization Report; Pp. 1-15.

17 Mohanty, S.K.(2004): "Employment and Unemployment in a Society of Transition"; The Indian Journal of Labour Economics; Vol. 43, No. 2 Pp. 8-17.

finding shows such a decline in elder ages. The NSSO finding reveals that the WPRs had declined from 420 to 395, for both sexes, from 545 to 527 for males, and from 286 to 254 for females per 1000 work force. The sex differential in work participation is quite distinct in urban India in both early-reform periods

(ERP) and late-reform period (LRP). While the female work participation rate has increased the male work participation had remained constant the ERP and LRP for the age group 20-59 years. But the decline in work participation is observed for higher ages irrespective of sex. The female work participation in urban India still remains low. Further it may be noted that the male work participation rate reaches its peak at the age of 30-34 years and the female work participation reaches its peak at the age group 35-39. This is true both in ERP and LRP. The NSSO finding reveals that the age specific WPRs per 1000 work force on the usual status had declined for all age group in urban India and for both sexes.

Meer Muhammad Parhiar (2005)[18] has investigated in his research article entitled "Understanding Poverty in Rural Sindh" that rural women do all On Farm/Off Farm works. Her day begins from pre-dawn with crushing. If the family is fortunate enough to have cattle and end up by taking leftover bites of bread and bowl of porridge. Their traditional role of housekeeping has been extended to collect firewood, fodder, and working on farms. Owing to social taboos, ignorance, financial constraints, inadequate education facilities, and non-availability of lady teachers in rural girls', schools have not opened the doors of literacy for them. Agriculture-dependent rural people have struggled to improve their economic conditions. On the contrary, shortage of water, dry spell cycles, decrease in cultivable area due to soil deterioration, extension of towns and villages, contraction of infrastructure, rising cost of inputs, non-availability of high yield quality varieties seeds to small farmers, un-checked population growth, etc, have together adversely affected the lives of rural people

Korinek (2005)[19] in the OEDC Working Paper "Trade and Gender: Issues and Interactions" examines ways in which greater integration through trade impacts women

---

[18] Meer Muhammad Parhiar (2005): "Globalization Vs Skill based Technological Change: Implications for Unemployment and Wage Inequality";The Economic Journal; Vol. 115, No. 503. April, Pp. 391-393.

[19] Korinek (2005) The Economic Status of Women: An Analytical Framework,-in The Role of Women in Contributing to Family Income (Proceedings of the regional workshop in Bangkok, July, 2005) Friedrich- Ebert Stifling, pp 45-67.

and men differently, and ensuing implications for growth. The paper finds that trade creates jobs for women in export-oriented sectors. Although women are more than ever formally employed, differences in wages earned by men and women persist in all countries. Women also have less access to productive resources, time and, particularly in many developing countries, education. Professional women continue to encounter discrimination in hiring and promotion, including in OECD countries. The study suggests that women comprise between 53% and 90% of the employed in many export sectors in middle-income developing countries. These jobs bring more household resources under women's control, which in turn has a positive effect on investments in the health and education of future generations. However, there is some evidence that women are constrained from moving into more skilled, higher-paying jobs created by trade liberalization because they have less access to resources, education and time.

According to Ahsan, Ahmad (2006)[20] there has been growing concern with Indian employment trends in recent years. Although the Indian economy witnessed robust and sustained growth rate of about 6 per cent per annum in 1990's but employment trends presented a worrying picture. By official estimates employment growth rates almost halved in 1990's, compared to 1980's. Further, there has been a marked fall in participation rates and unemployment rate and casualisation rates both have increased. When the first result of the 55th Round of the National Sample Survey (conducted in 1999-2000) was released, it was already apparent that there had been some major shifts in patterns of employment, especially in the rural areas. The 55th Round indicated a substantial decline in the share of agriculture and a rise in the share of non-agriculture in employment. In itself this could be a positive sign of progress and diversification, but it was associated with a fairly large drop in work participation rates of both men and women, which indicated a deceleration in aggregate employment growth. Such a deceleration has now been confirmed by data emerging from 2001 Census. When the estimated population is used to estimate the total number of those in some form of employment in 1999-2000, it yields results which show an even sharper drop in the rate of growth of rural employment generation than was previously supposed, although the fall in urban employment growth is less severe. Thus, the combined estimates suggest an average annual rate of growth of aggregate rural employment growth of only 0.58 per cent over the period between 1993-94 and 1999-2000. This makes it not

[20] Ahsan, Ahmad (2006))Studies of educated working Women in India Trends and Issues, Economics and political weekly,vol.14 (13)

only as low as around one-fourth of the previous period's rate, but also the lowest such rate of increase observed since the NSS first began recording employment data in the 1950s.

2.3 Studies pertaining to the constraints faced by the Women workers

Kaveri (1995)[21] notes that in Tamil Nadu women and children on worksites are called *chithals*, literally small people. Male workers on the other hand are *periyal* or big people. On large construction sites, *periyals* act as watchmen. They often have the responsibility for curing operations at night that require watering freshly laid cement at intervals so that it sets without cracking. The *periyal's* wife is expected to help him with this job but it is he who gets paid for it. Women construction workers in Tamil Nadu are employed only on a temporary and casual daily basis as unskilled workers (lifting earth loads, cutting soil, mixing cement, breaking stones) and not as masons. There is also considerable hostility from the contractors and male workers to women masons.

Deshpande, Sudha (1996)[22] conducted a study by pointing out that the country points to the awful conditions of women workers in the informal sector. Ignorance, traditional bound attitudes, illiteracy, lack of skills, seasonal nature of employment, heavy physical work of different types, long hours of work with limited payment, sex discrimination in wage structures, lack of guarantee of minimum wages/ comprehensive legislation/ minimum facilities; migration and disintegration of families, bondage and alienation etc are some characteristics of employment of women in this sector. But these unattractive sectors still involve many women because they search these jobs for their livelihood

Deshpande (2000)[23] examined the role of caste affiliation as an indicator of inter-group disparity. She formulated the Caste Development Index (CDI), based on the Theil index, to measure caste inequality and defined caste disparity as the distance between the CDI for low caste groups and for others (non- low castes). She analyzed between-group and within-group disparity focusing on the southern Indian State of Kerala which has experienced greater

---

[21] Kaveri, (1995) Excerpts from *women, work and inequity - the reality of gender*. Edited by Cherian Joseph and K.V. Eswara Prasad, National Labour Institute.

[22] Deshpande, Sudha, (1996), Changing Structure of Employment in India, The Indian Journal of Labour Economics, Vol.39, No.4.

[23] Deshpande, A. (2000, May) Does caste still define disparity? A look at inequality in Kerala, India. *The American Economic Review*, 90(2). Papers and Proceedings of the One Hundred Twelfth Annual Meeting of the American Economic Association, pp. 322-325.

social and labor reforms thanks to a communist regime and where caste is expected to be less important in the society. She used the Consumption and Expenditure Data from the National Sample Survey Organization for 1993-94, and considered three groups - the scheduled castes (SC), scheduled tribes (ST) and others. She found that overall inequality was not on the higher side, as was expected given the State's social and political history. Contrary to expectations, she found evidence of inter-caste disparity in both rural and urban areas. But she found that the problem of within-group

According to Nirmala, V and Bhat, Sham. K. (1999)[24] the degree of casualisation is found to be more in the case of rural females as compared to the rural males. The ratio of female casual labour to male casual labour shows a continuous decline over time since 1972-73 and shows a slight rise in the period in internationalization of agriculture. The ratio of casual labour to regular employees is much more in the case of rural females as compared to rural males. Urban India is characterized by more regular employment and casual labour forms only a fraction of it. Though over a period, the ratio of casual labour to regular ones tends to increase for males but the corresponding ratio is much higher for females. They also concludes that the marginalization of women manifests itself in declining work participation rates and a shift of low paid occupations rather than in increased unemployment rate and increased casualisation.

Ravindar (2003)[25] analyzed the time use pattern of the poor so that employment and welfare programmes could be planned for them. A survey was conducted covering 2000 households (1000 rural and 1000 urban) spread over 11 divisions categorized by the Slum Clearance Board of the Coimbatore Municipal Corporation. It was found that the average household size was 3.97 in rural areas and 4.12 in urban areas. 71% of the rural households were nuclear and in urban areas 59% of the households were joint families. Overall, only 6% households in rural areas and 8% in urban areas were headed by women. In rural areas 49% of the women were working while in urban areas 31% women worked. About 58% of the working women in rural areas were in the active working age group of 15-35 years, 38% were in 36-59 years age group, and 4% were 60+ years. More than 90% of the working women were married, widowed or separated. About 91.82% of the working women in rural areas were in full time jobs, and this percentage was 65.60% in urban areas. On an average in rural areas,

[24] Nirmala, V and Bhat, Sham. K. (1999): "Female Work Participation in the Emerging Labour Market In India"; The Indian Journal of Labour Economics, Vol. 42,No. 4, Pp. 613-624.

[25] Ravindar (2003) Avinashilingam Institute for Home Science, Dept. of Economics, Coimbatore.. Labour force participation and time management of women in slums in Coimbatore district. Coimbatore : AIHS-DE. 8 p.

males spent about 6.223 hours in a day on SNA activities (Standards of National Activities) and 0.7155 hours on extended SNA activities. In rural areas, females spent about 2.8252 hours on SNA activities and 3.4466 hours on extended SNA activities in a day. In urban areas, the time spent by females on SNA activities was only 1.6374 hours, while males spent 5.3108 hours on SNA activities per day. Females spent about 5.8457 hours in a day on extended SNA activities, while males spent about 1.6487 hours in a day on extended SNA activities in urban areas. In rural areas working males spent about 11.81 hours on personal care, while females spent about 10.96 hours per week. Females spent 1.86 hours per day on cooking, 0.97 hours on washing clothes, cleaning utensils and cleaning the house. The economic cost of activities such as cooking, washing utensils, washing clothes and cleaning the house were estimated in monetary terms. It was found that the per capita monthly expenses incurred would be Rs.40 for each of these activities. It was recommended that a macro level policy is needed that could integrated women's paid and unpaid work, reduce their drudgery, and lessen the burden of extended SNA activities.

Bhatt, Aparna and Sen, Aatreyee (2005)[26] defines a domestic worker as "Someone who carries out household work in private households in return for wages". The report focused on the findings of two public hearings in Mumbai and Delhi. The hearings investigated cases of gross human rights violations against domestic labourers/ workers by both state and private parties and aimed to report, campaign and litigate for the same. A gathering was organized with 140 domestic workers in Mumbai and 200 domestic workers in Delhi. These hearings had a multi-disciplinary panel consisting of professionals ranging from lawyers, journalists, activists to academicians, etc. Domestic workers were categorized into 3 groups namely child domestic workers (CDWs), live in workers (full timers), and part time domestic workers. The problem of each type of worker was not very different from the other but the intensity of exploitation increased with lower age groups (children). The report showed that poverty was the main factor responsible for the plight of domestic workers. Several other problems faced by domestic workers were strenuous working hours, low wages, no job security, physical assault if the work was not done, frequent scolding for minor things like breaking a cup, and most of the times salary was deducted for any breakage or minor

---

[26] Bhatt, Aparna and Sen, Aatreyee. (2005).Report on domestic workers. New Delhi: National Commission for Women. 98 p.

accidental damage while at work. One major problem faced by live in workers/ full timers was trafficking. They were trafficked from villages and brought to Bombay or Delhi by giving them high expectations of better lives and most of the time false hopes. All the full timers and part time domestic workers complained that no yearly increment, holidays, bonus, medical allowances and maternity leave benefits were given to them. Suggestions given/ made by panelists were that CDWs should be treated like children not as slaves or bonded labour by their employers; compulsory registration of domestic workers should be done to avoid the problem of very young children working in homes; awareness and sensitization programmes should be launched for both politicians and government servants on the plight of domestic workers; all domestic workers throughout the country should be guaranteed minimum wages, paid work off, adequate and free medical treatment; and the Labour Commissioner of the states should register all CDWs under the provisions of Child Labour Act.

Singh, D.P. (2005)[27] conducted the study to know the socio economic status of women workers in the brick industry of Haryana. It investigated the different economic activities adopted for survival; and explored various aspects relating to the family, migration, and women's working conditions. A sample of 410 women workers were drawn using multi stage random sampling technique. Structured interview schedules were used, and employers and significant persons were interviewed to gather information. More than 87% women workers of brick kilns were found to be less than 45 years of age. The largest number of workers was from the neighboring states namely Uttar Pradesh (32%), Bihar (29%), Haryana (22.68%) and Rajasthan (13.41%). For most of the women, it was the husband's decision to work in the kiln. The chief attraction was that money could be obtained in advance. Women workers in brick kilns were at the bottom of the hierarchy. Only a few of the respondents (6.34%) mentioned that women were either looked down upon or physically harassed. Almost 98.04% workers came to the brick kiln only for the season, that is, from October and November to May or June. Family size of workers varied from two to five members (67.56%), six to ten (24.15%), and eleven to fifteen (8.29%). In all the brick kilns of this area employers gave some money to workers for their day-to-day expenses on the 15th day of the month. This money was actually paid to the male workers, and women did not receive money for expenses separately. Most of the women said that their families were unable to save. Control and decision making usually rested with males. The lives of women working in brick kilns was exhausting and

[27] Singh, D.P. (2005) Women workers in the brick kiln industry of Haryana. Indian Journal of Gender Studies, 12(1) : 83-97.

tough because of the double burden of working at home as well as at the work site. They hardly got any time for recreation or leisure activities. Although all of them contributed to the family's survival, it was disheartening to note that they did not receive any independent income and had to depend upon their men folk entirely.

Vanker, Purushottam. (2005)[28] was undertaken a study to assess the challenges faced by construction workers, due to mechanization, wage structure, etc. The sample consisted of 250 workers (150 females and 100 males) in the construction sector. For every 3 females 2 male respondents were picked up at random from each of the 50 kadiyanakas (labour points) of Ahmedabad. Due to rampant unemployment, many educated people and unemployed factory workers had joined construction work. Increased competition led workers to work for lower wages and sometimes they failed to find work. Also, migrant labourers worked for very low wages and further harmed prospects of the regular workforce. Respondents said that communal violence also affected their work as they were scared to move to another area in search of work. Mechanization had also led to a decreased demand for these workers. More than 30% of the total workers reported that they had met with an accident or had experienced an episode of sickness related to work. This led to declined work efficiency in addition to medical expenses. More than 3.2% of the workers met with accidents. 16.4% of the female workers faced sexual harassment, while 9.2% of the workers faced mental harassment due to abusive language and low wages. It is necessary to provide workers with skill training to enable them to adapt to the rapidly changing construction industry. Construction Workers Welfare Board should compensate workers for accidents. Also, it is important to identify the safety measures and equipment that is required and to ensure the implementation of safety norms and measures.

Rao, K. Hanumantha (2006)[29] identified the states where the number of female workers grew faster than that of male workers, viz Andhra Pradesh, Himachal Pradesh, Karnataka, Madhya Pradesh, Maharashtra and Tamil Nadu. These trends indicate feminization of rural labour markets. The data of NSSO for the years 1987-88 and 1993-94 point out that the phenomenon of landlessness has considerably reduced in several states, which is a welcome sign from the view-point of unemployment and poverty eradication. Male workers joined the ranks of agricultural

[28] Vanker, Purushottam. (2005) At the Kadiyanaka : challenges faced by construction workers in Ahmedabad. Ahmedabad : Self Employed Women's Association. 31 p.
[29] Rao, K. Hanumantha (2006): "Female Labour Participation in Productive Work"; Man and Development; Vol XXVI, No. 1, March. Pp. 167-173

labour and a reverse pattern i.e. rise in 'cultivator' category was observed among female workers. The most recent reports relating to employment trends were released by the NSSO in the closing weeks of 2006; these are based on the 61st Round of the NSS, covering 2004-05.On the face of it, going by these reports, it would appear that there has been a revival of employment growth, after the sharp deceleration in the late 1990s, both in rural and urban India, over the first half of the current decade. Labour force participation rates, for both males and females, have recovered the lost ground and the aggregate employment growth rates for both males and females in rural as well as urban areas were close to the rates achieved during the period of 1987-88 to 1993-94. Nonetheless, in spite of the recovery, unemployment rates, both in rural and urban India (taking the current daily status measure) have continued to rise. Moreover, possibly the most striking results from the latest survey relate to the shift in the type of employment. Essentially, self-employment among major segments of the workforce has witnessed very significant increases. For instance, annual compound growth rate of agricultural self employment, which was as low as (-) 0.53 during 1993-94 to 1999-2000, jumped to 2.89 between 1999-2000 and 2004-05. The story is no different in urban areas, as there too self-employment accounts for the dominant share of the increase in aggregate employment since 2000.

2.4 Studies pertaining to the Gender based labour market discrimination

Hakim (1976)[30] analyzed whether Women's employment has been and still is characterized by high levels of occupational and sectoral segregation by sex. The study elucidates the segregation through the distinction between vertical and horizontal occupational segregation. The usual trend in the employment of women is downward, gaining proportionately less than male employment in the upswings of business cycles. Differences in wages due to a variety of discriminatory practices are designed to perpetuate the vertical as well as horizontal division of labour markets leading to gender based segregation and stereotyping of jobs resulting in women being concentrated in a few occupations.

Usharani et al. (1993)[31] conducted a study to examine the gender differential in work participation in various operations of crop and livestock enterprises in semi-arid areas of Haryana. In the study female labour days of 8 hours were converted into man-equivalent days. One day work of woman was taken as equivalent to 0.75 man day. The major female labour absorbing operations are weeding, harvesting and threshing. Farm women spent about 85 per cent (on large

[30] Hakim.J(1976),Labour Market Discrimination in a Poor Urban Economy; Journal of Development Studies,Vol.19, No.1.
[31] Usharani et al. (1993) Extent and causes of gender and poverty in India: A Case Study of rural Hayana. Journal of International Women's Studies, 7(2): 182 -190

farms) to about 89 per cent (on marginal farms) of their time in these operations only. The overall women participation rate in dairy enterprise was as high as 94 per cent as against 6 per cent only for men. The women work participation was minimum on marginal farms (86.24%) and maximum on large farms (99.12%) indicating positive relationship with the size of the holdings. In all farm size groups, female labour use was 58 per cent of the total labour use. With the help of the primary data collected from a sample of 150 farm couples

Jayawardane & Gunawardena, (1998)[32] made an analysis of human resource development issues in the Sri Lankan construction industry shows that the work force in Sri Lanka consists of 51 per cent unskilled workers and 49 per cent skilled workers. The highest percentage of skilled workers is aged 30-39 years. Approximately 86 per cent of the skilled work force has received informal training only. Low income, lack of job security and difficulty in finding regular work are the causes for dissatisfaction of more than 20 per cent of the work force. The study compares the HRD practices in Sri Lanka with the USA and the UK and reveals that Sri Lanka needs to adopt a more formal training system and proper grading of the skilled work force.

Saxena (1999)[33] examines the working conditions for women in India, in industry and analyses possible discrimination against women with the view to shape future strategies from four perspectives: the woman worker, the male worker, the management and union leader. It looks at specific working conditions like wages and timings, promotions and benefits, facilities, occupational health and safety, collective bargaining and harassment at the work place. The study also tried to surface any best practices with respect to women workers so that worker's organizations could use these as precedents to advocate change in working conditions, of workers in general and of women in particular. The key findings in the study are women are slotted into certain jobs, based on the real differences caused by their differential access to skills and perceived constraints which takes the form of jobs predominantly staffed by women, categorized as low skilled and low paying. The second and more overt form of discrimination found is unequal pay for equal work. Inequity in pay was also dependent on the following factors: Women not deployed for overtime or night shifts where payments are higher. In general, men receive more promotions and for men, unlike women, the nature of their jobs often changed with these promotions. A higher proportion of men received benefits in all categories compared to women. The presence of unions has generally meant more benefits for the workers, including women.

[32] Jayawardane, A. K. W. & Gunawardena, N. D. (1998, September 1) Construction workers in developing countries: a case study of Sri Lanka. *Construction Management & Economics, 16 (5)*, 521 – 530
[33] Saksena, A. (1999) Gender and human rights. Status of women workers in India. Shipra Publications

Ray and Haque (2000)[34] in their paper have examined the employment per acre, operation wise labour use and wage differential between migrated contract labour and local hired labour employed. The study revealed that in Hoogly district of West Bengal contract male and child labourers migrated to the study area and were employed predominantly in sowing and harvesting seasons of boro and aman paddy. No female contract labour migrated to the study area. Poverty was the main reason for migration. Besides, lower wages and low employment opportunities also caused migration.

Solanki and Sharma (2001)[35] in their study 'Impact of Economic Reforms on Rural Employment-A case study of Jhakam Irrigation Project, Rajasthan' revealed that there is a significant impact of economic reforms on rural employment through irrigation. The 'with and without approach' of impact analysis was used. A sample of 100 farmers was selected for the study from two villages, 50 each from irrigated command area and un-irrigated command area. The study revealed that the total labour use in crop production activity in the command area was higher compared to non-command area. The use of family labour, attached labour and casual labour were also higher in the command area. The share of female workers in total labour absorption in crop production was found to be 42.45 per cent per farm in the command area compared to non-command area. The labour in the non-command area which was left out of irrigation suffered diversification from crop production and diverted to other activities in search of gainful employment.

Singh (2005)[36] have conducted a study on labour wage discrimination in agriculture. The study was conducted in six states using stratified random sampling technique. The results of the study showed that women worked less hours per day compared to men. The allocation of time by women in the six states varied from 7.3 hours per day in Ranchi (Jharkand) to 9.5 hours per day in Adilabad (A.P.). The work performed by women are weeding, spraying (assisting to men), irrigation, harvesting, threshing, drying up of pods grains *etc.* Wage disparities were found to be higher among men and women in agriculture. Labour wages of male over female in agriculture were found to be higher (47%) in Ranchi

[34] Ray and Haque (2000) "Challenges of Decent work in the Globalising World";The Indian Journal of Labour Economic; Vol. 48, No. 1, Jan- March, Pp. 6-7.
[35] Solanki and Sharma (2001) : "Impact of Female Work Participation: A Study of Agricultural Labourer Households; The Indian Journal of Labour Economic;Vol. 48, No. 1, Jan- March, Pp. 6-7

[36] Singh (2005): "Economic Reforms and Female Employment: Issues and Challenges"; Man and Development; Vol. XXVII, No. 1, March, p. 1-13

(Jharkand) and lower (31%) in Coimbatore (Tamil Nadu). The CV of labour wages of male over female in agriculture was 42.1075 while in others (non-farm) it was 32.875.

Rana, A.S, Jasbir Singh and Kulwant Singh (2002)[37] in their study on non-farm employment for rural households in India have found that the employment of wage labour has been declining in agriculture, while it is increasing in non agricultural activities. The non-farm activities provide opportunities to earn income during the slack season in agriculture. The study also revealed the multi activity nature of the workers. About 62.13 per cent of the person-days spent in agriculture as principal activity by the rural male, also spent 3.35 per cent and 4.34 per cent of the person-days as self-employed and wage labour in non-agriculture respectively. The per cent distribution of male workers in non-farm employment in 1999-00 was the highest in Kerala followed by Himachal Pradesh and the per cent distribution of rural female workers in non-farm activities was the highest in West Bengal followed by Kerala. The study concludes that augmenting rural investment in the development of non-farm sector will increase the income of rural households and thus reduce poverty.

Muniyandi et al. (2003)[38] studied the 'Changes in Rural Non-Agricultural Employment in India'. The present study examined the changes in the labour force and workforce participation rate, sector wise distribution of this workforce, employment status of this workforce in the two sectors and the relationship between the level of poverty and employment in India. The analysis of the study was mainly based on the NSSO Data gathered over different rounds. The study revealed that the labour force participation rate in rural area (male and female) and in urban areas (female) during post reform period showed a decline, while the urban male labour force participation rate showed an increase. The workforce participation rate of male and female in urban and rural areas showed a marginal increase in the post reform period. The sector wise distribution of workers in rural areas indicated that workforce participation rate in agriculture sector has been declining and that in non agricultural sector has been increasing. The study emphasizes the need for encouraging the workers to establish non-farm enterprise by providing appropriate training facilities at a reasonable rate of interest.

---

[37] Rana, A.S, Jasbir Singh and Kulwant Singh (2002) "Female Labour Participation in Productive Work"; Man and Develoment; Vol XXVI, No. 1, March. Pp. 167-173.
[38] Muniyandi et al. (2003). Changing Role of Women "A Study of Small Manufacturing Enterprises in India"; Journal of Economics and Social Development; Vol. II,No. 2, July- Dec.

Luke and Munshi (2005)[39] assess the role that women might play in reducing the disparities in income and education that persist across social groups in India. In the South Indian setting, low caste women - who have historically been disadvantaged in terms of both caste and gender - emerge as agents of change, using their income to move their families from the traditional network-based economy to the modern market economy. An exogenous increase in low caste female income, net of total household income, weakens the family's ties to the home community as the woman gains bargaining power within the household. The children are significantly less likely to marry in the traditional fashion, to be schooled in the ancestral location, and to ultimately settle there. At the same time, an exogenous increase in relative female income increases the educational attainment of the low caste children, particularly the girls. Female income effects, in contrast, are absent among the high castes, emphasizing the importance of social affiliation in shaping household decisions in a developing economy. The results in this paper suggest that historically disadvantaged groups and in particular, the disadvantaged individuals within those groups, may in fact be most responsive to new opportunities when resources are made available to them.

Madhok (2005)[40] reports that work on construction sites is invariably divided along gender lines. The types of work that men do are labeled as skilled work and fetch higher wages than the work that women are allowed to do. Women are restricted to head loading and *beldari* jobs that involve fetching and carrying of materials and this type of work is labeled as unskilled work. Naturally, unskilled work is paid less than skilled work. This division of labour seems to be prevalent everywhere in the country. Even where men are hired to do *beldari* jobs, they are, by custom, paid a higher wage than women. The Equal Remuneration Act is flouted everywhere. On some jobs, men and women are treated as a couple and wages are paid to the man, not the woman. Assisting a mason and anticipating his exact requirement so that work can progress smoothly requires a high degree of skill, as does climbing scaffoldings and balancing loads of brick. However, these are not considered skilled activities.

Suchitra and Rajasekar (2006)[41] focus on the promotional aspect of employment security in the context of unorganised workers. Regarding skill in case of construction workers, they find that skill level and continuous improvements in the same are very important for upward mobility.

[39] Luke, N. & Munshi, K. (2005, February) Women as agents of change: Female income, social affiliation and household decisions in South India. Retrieved April 20, 2008
[40] Madhok, S. (2005) Report on the status of women workers in the construction industry. New Delhi: National Commission for Women.

[41] Suchitra, J. Y. & Rajasekar, D. (2006, July - September) One size does not fit all: Employment insecurity of unorganized workers in Karnataka. The Indian Journal of Labour Economics, 49(3), 455-473

There exists a marked hierarchy among these workers based on their skill levels. The sample construction workers included skilled, semiskilled and unskilled workers. Skilled workers include masons, painters, polishers, carpenters, electricians and road layers. Semi skilled workers usually belonged to the category of apprentices. They are those learning a particular skill such as masonry or carpentry. The unskilled workers constituted helpers in all trades, and usually, they were involved in carrying mud, bricks and cement. These workers were highly marginalized and vulnerable in terms of the competition they faced and the low wages that they were paid. A gender differential was found in the case of construction workers and skill levels. Women construction workers are, in general, unskilled workers and are paid wages even lesser than those paid to the men unskilled workers. The few women workers interviewed mentioned that no matter what skills they learnt (for instance, some had learnt bricklaying and basic masonry), they were always classified as unskilled and paid the associated wage. The study finds that the key factors that determine the employment security of the construction workers are area of residence, human development, average wages and age of workers.

2.5 Studies pertaining to the dual role of working women

Sharpe (1979)[42] in his book titled 'Double Identity' stated that, there are some signs of change. Men are now recognizing and having to reconcile work and family demands. When it comes to the division of labour in the home, however, despite some optimistic fore casting women still do the large majority of tasks associated with house work and childcare. Thus while men are increasingly making career discussions with their partners and families in mind, nevertheless most men do not do their share of house hold and child care tasks. This makes it more difficult for most women to be serious contenders in the competition for promotion in their career.

Rosemary (1982)[43] in her book stated that more women are moving into managerial and professional occupations (the fastest-growing occupational category) and this trend shows no sings of slackening. It is true that women tend to be located in 'Gendered Niches' with in managerial occupations. Nevertheless, such jobs will usually generate an income, which is sufficient to live interpedently. Managerial and professional women are likely to enter into relationships with men in similar occupations at a similar level, and to remain in paid employment after the birth of their children, such households will require various services which

42 Sharpe (1979) The dual career family. Human Relations, 22 (10 3 -30.

43 Rosemary (1982), Trends and Prospects for Women"s Employment in 1990"s, European Commission

have to be purchased, either directly through the employment of paid domestic help or indirectly through ready meals, restaurant, dry cleaners and so on. More generally, two earner house holds (that is not only managerial and professional) will be more likely to buy services of all kinds. More men will be an increasing move of men into services occupations, thus further blurring the boundaries of the gender divisions of labour in the sphere of paid employment.

Jaya Arunachalam (1984)[44] in her report on "Empowering Women for a positive revolution" revealed attitude of families towards women's domestic responsibilities, the unsympathetic attitude of employers, lack of training, limiting employment opportunities and above all, women's low perception in the labour market and had provided ample impressions both to employers and the society that women work only to make subsidiary income to the families, whereas the principal breadwinner were still men. It had also given rise to belief that women were not career-minded and therefore does not mind dead and hobs without promotion options. The facts mentioned precede that even that small percentage of women who get into formal sector, face discrimination and exploitation in their factories and were pushed to accept jobs not accepted by men. A critical examination of these facts would reveal how labour intensive industries had more women workers on low schedule of payment leading to capital accumulation.

Lalitha K. Nair (1984)[45] conducted a study on "Women's two Roles" and said Women's occupational status had always been closely associated with the home and the family. There was a clear conflict between the socially approved status of women, as house wife and mother of children on the one hand, and their status as more productive worker on the other. Children of 20% respondents were looked after by their parents when the respondents were at work, 26% by the husband's 18% by servants, 20% were schools going children and 16% had no children. 30% reported that their children were too yond to judge their scholastic performance. 86% families had strong economic support due to respondent's income, which was spent to meet family needs. 50% felt it was necessary to work. 46% had satisfactory relations with their supervisors and colleagues. 52% liked both home and their job as against 25% who liked only their home and 28% liked only their office. 62% were fully satisfied with their dual role of working and housewife.

---

[44] Jaya Arunachalam (1984). Status and Role Perception of middle class women. New Delhi : Puja Publishers

[45] Lalitha K. Nair (1984) Women's Two Roles. A Study of Role Conflict. Indian Journal of Social Work. 2494), 337-380.

43

Madula Sherwani (1984)[46] in her studies on "Why more women entering work force" has observed Indian women still operate under creation limitation and hardship. One of the most common problems faced by a woman was the dual role; she had to play on the domestic front and the shop floor. Particularly the married working women with the small children found that dual responsibility a source of great mental and physical strain. For them the working hours were long 8 hours at the place of employment and at least 4 hours at home. Usually husbands and sometimes even in-laws did not extend any help in the household chores. Again after all this hard work, tragedy was that working women couldn't claim independent economic assets. Most of the salary earners had to surrender their pay pockets to their husbands in the case of married women and to their parents in the case of unmarried girls. They were allowed to hold back only a small amount for spending on transport and tea.

Kuppuswamy. B (1989)[47] discussed in the traditional joint family, social life of women was largely confined to family and relatives. Family was the only place for entertainment. There was separation of the perspective spheres of work for men and women. Men were looking after the household work. Basically the spheres of operation were separated. This separation of the sexes in the family tends to characterize social life as well. The women were forming their own social groups. They had much more restricted social life. Very few women socially free to go out of their home or house without escort. Women were not allowed to join unions' organizations or clubs. Many changes have taken place in the urban family with respect to the social life of women. The new life in the city has altered the family relations, social life because both of them are educated and are developing new relationships. Co- educated has created an opportunity for inter-mixing of boys and girls. A large number of women are working with males and making friendship with them.

Manikaramerkar (1995)[48] in his book on "Socio–economic conditions of women workers" describes that as parts of the research programmed of labour burden a field enquiry were to study working, economic and living conditions of women workers as also to assess the extent of welfare available to them vis-a vis the labour laws with a view to identifying the problem being faced by them in these various fields. These findings are recommendations were related to employment size, method of recruitment, employment status, length of service,

46 Madula Sherwani (1984): "Women Participation in Labour Force", New Delhi: Rajat Publications, Pp. 46-54.

47 Kuppuswamy. B (1989). Indian Women From Purdha to Modernity.New Delhi : Vikas Publications

48 Manikaramerkar(1995): " Female participation in farm work and non-farm work "; Sociological Bulletin;vol.25, no.2, Pp.105-110

marital status, impact of labour saving devices, wage rate absenteeism, working conditions and welfare amenities, living conditions, demographic and socio economic status of the female workers of the mines. Development efforts are to be effective. The main focus is women, as they are at disadvantageous position than men. The agreed objective of this study is growth with equity and participation, policies and initiatives to be taken for helping women among poor. The analysis is based on many case studies and throws light on a few important implications. One of the most stubborn obstacles to poor women's participation is the misconceptions held by most men and many women about appropriate roles for women. Increase in women's employment opportunities and incomes do not automatically work to their advantage, the vital question is who exercised control over their labour and income. It is clear that in some cases increased payment for women's labour lead to greater control over it by others status is considered to be one of the behavioral indicators.

Khan and Singh (1994)[49] have taken into account different spheres of decision making namely deciding family size. Even though a woman plays several roles through out her life –as daughters, sister, wife, daughter–in–law sister in law and mother, she seldom does have the power to make decisions which concern her own life vitally. Taking into account women in reproductive age in Uttar Pradesh (India) they conclude that the husband has the final in the number of children. They should have in the case of 33 percent of rural women of Uttar Pradesh, both take decision on family size and in 53% cases husbands alone take the decision. In the case of 4.3 percent of urban women, the husbands take the decision in 9.3 percent cases elder members and in 1.9 percent cases women she takes decisions.

Seta Vaidayalingam (1994)[50] discussed the problem and concerns of Indian women. According to working women are subject to more explanative problems and pressures then their non-working sisters. Finding a suitable occupation in the first problem right and proceeds it and of course fighting for the right amount of education to secure a decent job, tops it all, after having completed her education when a women steps the field of vocation are not quite correct, we find to be women's staying capacity and the usual remarks is adequate. This kind of attitude spoils a women's changes at all levels and particularly in the field of self - employment with a job come other problematic situations, kinds of people at work especially men. Number of lawyers do not encourage women simply because the later to level the office at

---

[49] Khan and Singh (1994), Modernisation and Marginalisation; Social Scientist, Vol.13 and 1994 „How real is the bogey of feminization" Indian Journal of Labour Economics, Vol.40
[50] Seta Vaidayalingam (1994): "Development Paradox in Kerala: Analysis of Industrial Stagnation;. Economic and Political Weekly; September 15,

about 6 p.m. in order to reach home early despite the fact that a busy lawyer's office is at its best after 6 p.m. Single working women have the accommodation problem, if working in a city their families do not live with them. One has heard and

Peggy Autobus, (1996)[51] in the study on "economics status and career opportunities for women in India today" has remarket that the desirability of giving important status to women society has often been expressed, thought it was denied in actual life. A women's lower status in the family was often to her exclusion from economic ability gainful employment. Recently, since the Second World War, urban women of middle and upper class, particularly, married women began to seek sinful gainful employment out of home. This phenomenon created the problems relating to women's two roles, home and work. The most popular jobs as had been seen from the number of women applicants registered in the employment exchanges were those of clerk, the highest percentage of women workers (more than 40%) was for professional technical and related jobs mostly as teachers, nurses and midwives. The next percentage (9%) that's of clerks, sales and related workers, administrative, executive and management workers from only 2%. According to the author the main reason for women's employment was economic necessity to supplement the income of her husband or of the family. Though this economic cause was most important there was also social, psychological and situational reasons for taking up employment case of high society ladies such as ambition of a career, charm of the position utilization of leisure, proper use of higher education, killing away time till marriage, escape from domestic work, freedom to mix with people and preference for outdoor life.

Parmine Sangupta (1998)[52] in her book 'women in India' states that participation of women in economic activity was very common from the time immemorial. Primitive society offered many instances of vigorous work in hunting and in cultivation by women. Women's role become more real and designed with an evaluation of an agricultural economy, Even in Moherjadaro and Harappa culture women shared a responsible position with men and helped in spinning and day modeling and other simple arts and crafts. There are more several explanations for the tendency of female participation in economic activity to deadline at the early stage of development. In addition, she states that according to Baser up Easter the most important were technical chances within the agricultural sector Unemployment policy which induces women to

[51] Peggy Antrobus, (1996), "Women and Development: An Alternative Analysis"; Journal of the Society for International Development

[52] Senguptha, P.(1998). The Story of Women in India (II edition), Delhi ;Indian Book Company

accept employment to restrict somewhat the growth of urban areas holding down the birth rate, working women poor countries can therefore reduce the burden of supporting both non–working women children and non working women by providing vocational training for employment instead of reserving employment for men.

Cherian, J. & Prasad K.V. (1999)[53] explores the causes of women's unemployment in India. The greater rush of women job seekers within a more or less inflexible employment counter, the failure of defective development process to economic transformation, the low level of educational attainment the frightening increase in female population highly prejudiced social attitude resulting in unwillingness on the part of the employers to employ women. Wide–spread sex discrimination in different productive sectors, women's preference for certain selected occupations the unwillingness of educated women to go to villages the unhelpful attitude of employers towards handicapped women and lack of provision of adequate opportunities for their self– employment ventures are the main causes of colossal problem of women's unemployment in India today.

Jhabvala, Renana and Sinha, Shalini (1999)[54] says that uses data on individual women from 1000 samples of this a picture of the labour market in each of the major metropolitan areas where these women lived is added.This helps in arriving at a picture of a relative weight that each back ground or situational factor contributes to a women's employment. A married women's score is 100 if she employed zero if she is not. Labour market conditions appear to about twice the weight of women's own individual and family characteristics in determining whether she is employed or not. If the metropolitan area in which she lives contains industries with a good number of female jobs and if there are high female wages, married women in that area are more likely to work but if the cost of household help is high and there is a high female ratio in the population, their changes are less favorable. The lower her husband's income and the more her own schooling the greater the likelihood that married women will work. However if she has pre- school age children, she is deterred from working. If she is block but all the other characteristics are the same as a white women's she is also more likely to work.

Katherine Mckee, (1999)[55] in her study found that as a consequence of implementation of land reforms, the lives of women have changed. They were less sub-ordinate of the land lord

[53] Cherian, J. & Prasad K.V. (1999) *Women, work and inequality: The reality of gender.* New Delhi: National Labour Institute.

[54] Jhabvala, Renana and Sinha, Shalini (1999): "Liberalisation and the Women Worker".Economic and Political Weekly; Vol. 37, Nov.18- Dec.26 , Pp.2037-2044.

[55] Katherine Mckee, (1999), in her paper "Micro Level Strategies for Supporting Livelihoods", Journal of the Society for International Development

and more sub-ordinate to the men of their own groups. They were also more economically valuable helping with showing weeding and harvesting. A few of them also worked in the homes of land lords, while the women among the agricultural laborers tend to benefit from land reforms legislation, they are not placed on equal footing with men in the sphere of social relations. This is more due to the impact of the dominance of patriarchal family structure in the Indian society. Gough is of the view that through agricultural labour women constitutes a substantial proportion of the membership of parties and mass movements. They are hardly associated in maters of decision making.

Talwar Sabanna (2001)[56] says that the new economy offers a plethora of opportunities to educated and trained women workers who compete on par with mew for jobs in the IT, telecom and other technology sectors. The process of structural adjustment hits unorganized and unskilled women workers. The hardest coping mechanisms must include retraining, orientation towards service industry sectors and focus on market trends for traditional products. The social stales of women have been considerably increased in the country during the post-reform period. The women population has been gradually enabling itself to overcome the shackles of a custom ridden, basically orthodox society. This could be observed from the increasing enrolment of female population in educational institutions at all levels, increasing number of female job–seekers on the live registers of employment exchanges, steadily rising rate of women employment–in public and private sectors, growing rate of female participation in voluntary organizations promoting women welfare and social service activities etc. Thus the post–reform period has been associated with growing employment opportunities for women. However, these claims of increased employment generation are generally supplemented with information on the nature of employment and the terms and conditions under which labour is employed in the emerging women lobour market.

Koran Prasad (2002)[57] reveals that women carry a disproportionate and growing share of economic and domestic responsibility for the family. Inspire of this they do not have the decision making power to determine when they start a family and at what time intervals they have children. Access to information and means for enhancing their reproductive health and family planning choices has been demonstrated to be a major tool forth empowerment of women. The first formal definition of women's reproductive rights at the Teheran conference

56 Talwar Sabanna (2001): "The Service Sector for Growth and Employment" The Indian Journal of Labour Economics; Vol. 38 , No. 4, Oct- Dec, Pp. 673-680.

57 Koran Prasad (2002) Indian Women: Their Health and Productivity; World Bank Discussion Paper 109; Washington DC

generated intense debate on this issue at all consequent international conferences and conventions. These conferences also arrived at several policy measures which world improve the lives of girls and women including better education and economic opportunities ,equality before the law, an end to gender based violence access to high quality and family planning information and services and greater participation by men in family planning and family life. Achieving these objectives will increase women's freedom to take their own reproductive decisions which is not only a basic human right but will also help to reduce unwanted pregnancy, improve reproductive health and slow population growth. the human rights campaign to reinforce women's reproductive rights will not only improve girls and women's lives but will not only improve girls and women's lives but will be the key to any strategy for empowering women and achieving national development. It is well established that women carry a disproportionate and growing share of economic and domestic responsibility for family members

Raka Sharan (2005)[58] conducted a survey on women workers employed in industrial and non-industrial organizations in Kanpur city. The main objectives of her study were to analyze the working conditions of women workers to measure there socio– conditions states and to study their participation in trade union activities. She had selected 100 samples in the industrial sector and 100 samples in the non-industrial sector and collected the necessary data from them. Socio-economic status of women workers we one measured with the help of kappasamy's method of rating scale. Various economic and social indicators were used to measure the socio-economic status. Her study revealed some important aspects of women labour. Among the industrial and non-industrial women workers 80 percent were from the young category that is between 20 and 35 years. The non-industrial workers were more qualified. Them the industrial workers. The working conditions of the women workers were far from satisfactory. There was sluggish participation in trade union activities among women workers. The bulk of the respondents adopted middle life style and value orientations.

2.6 Studies pertaining to Globalization and its impact on Women workers

Horton (1996)[59] points out that while in most Asian countries women move to regular jobs, in the case of India, they move to the less advantageous status of casual employees.

[58] Raka Sharan (2005), Labour Reform and Social Safety Net, Indian Journal of Labour Economics, Vol.40, No.3. pp 74-89.

[59] Horton, Susan (1995): "Women and Industrialization in Asia"; Routledge, London Human Development Report 2001

Moreover, compared to countries like South Korea, Indonesia, Philippines, and Thailand, women's work participation in India is marked by relatively low and stagnant rates. Women's workforce participation has been increasing in many developing countries. This could have occurred due to increasing education levels of women, new opportunities of employment in the industrial sector or increasing migration to urban areas. Falling household real incomes and income insecurity boosting the "additional worker" effects, may also force the women to enter in the labour market. One of the reasons that could be attributed to the increase in female workforce participation is the increasing globalization trend which the world witnessed since the late eighties. Women's employment has gone up significantly in every region of the world, with the exception of Africa (UN Report, 1999).Informalization of work has stimulated growth of female employment across the countries (as casual, contract worker, outsourcing, home-working). The drop in female unemployment rates relative to men has also been noted by scholars, to be recent phenomena.There are many economists who say that female work participation has declined during post reform period.

Artecona & Cunningham (2001)[60] examined the change in the gender wage gap in the manufacturing sector in urban Mexico over the trade liberalization period (1987-1993). Trade liberalization was found to be associated with higher gender wage gaps in the Mexican manufacturing sector, but this is likely due to an increased premium to men's higher (experience) skills; the discrimination component of wage differentials seems to fall with competition that is brought about by international competition. A comparison of men's and women's wages before and after Mexico's trade liberalization period shows that the wage gap in the manufacturing industry increased. However, the increase in the wage gap appeared to be due to general movements in the economy over the period and an increased premium to skills, as found by Hanson and Harrison (1999). Suggestive evidence was found (significant at the 20 percent level) that trade liberalization leads to a decrease in wage discrimination. In particular, those industries that were forced to become competitive due to trade liberalization saw a fall in the gender wage gap. These findings indicate that trade may be beneficial to women by decreasing wage discrimination, but an improvement in women's relative wages will depend on improving women's skills to better compete in the newly competitive markets.

---

[60] Artecona & Cunningham (2001) The status of women in the States - Women's economic status in the States: Wide Disparities by Race, Ethnicity, and Region. Washington, Dc: Institute for Women's Policy Research.

Giri, A.K. (2002)[61] has the view that the pattern of employment observed in percentage contribution of different sectors during the post- reform period was not very much significantly different from that observed during the pre-reform period. In rural areas the primary sector and in the urban areas the tertiary sector was the most important sources of employment both for males and females. The trend observed in the change of employment over the period of time was that the proportion of person employed in the tertiary sector both in the rural and urban areas was seen to increase for both males and females; and this increment was more pronounced during the post-reform period than pre-reform period. On the other hand, employment in the primary sector in urban as well as rural areas was seen to decline over the rounds; and this decline was again more conspicuous during the post- reform period than during the pre-reform period particularly in the rural areas. Regarding employment in secondary sector, it was observed that in the urban areas, it gradually declined over the rounds but in the rural areas it increased during the post-reform period (1993-94 to 1991-2000) despite a decline during the pre- reform period (1987-88 to1993-94).

Ramya Vijaya (2003)[62] explores the impact of trade openness on gender divergence in skills in developing economies. This study combines the Heckscher-Ohlin trade perspective with the evidence of the increasing feminization of the low-skilled export labour force. she analyzes the trends in gender differentiated skills data, school enrolment ratio and the average years of schooling in the adult population, the study carries out a cross-country regression analysis using the available data. The OLS method is used to estimate the empirical equation for a group of 50 countries. It is found that higher growth rates of GNP and public education expenditure lead to a narrowing of the gap between male and female enrolments. The coefficient on the trade variable is not statistically significant which indicates that the impact of higher trade on the enrolment gap is not significant. The results also highlight that countries which start out with a gap between adult male and female skills, trade has a positive impact on the change in the enrolment gap i.e. the enrolment gap increases further. The regression analysis supports causality between trade participation and gender divergence in education investments. Larger trade volumes cause the secondary school enrolment gender gap to increase further in countries that have larger gaps between the average levels of male and female adult education. This research concludes that in low-skilled

[61] Giri, A.K. (2002): " A Post –Modernist Enquiry Into Women's Workforce Participation"; "; The Indian Journal of Labour Economics, Vol. 42 , No. 4,Jan – March, Pp. 557-564

[62] Ramya Vijaya (2003)): "Female Labour Participation in Productive Work"; Man and Development; Vol XXVI, No. 1, March. Pp. 167-173

developing countries where a gender gap in education exists, trade related employment trends have the potential to establish an employment structure that lowers women's incentives to invest in higher education while allowing more opportunities for skills up gradation for men. Therefore, existing gender gaps in education are reinforced and widened.

Berik, Rodgers & Zveglich (2003)[63] explored the impact of competition from international trade on wage discrimination by sex in two highly open economies, Korea and Taiwan. The study explicitly tests Becker's theory that discrimination is incompatible with rising competitiveness. In both economies, trends in international trade were accompanied by structural changes in manufacturing. Two decades of structural change in both economies also saw major changes in the labour market. Labor force participation rates for men fell and for women rose. Despite women's relative gains in labour-market qualifications, Taiwan (China)'s average female-male wage ratio in manufacturing dropped from 66% in 1981 to 60% in 1993, with a reversal to 67% by 1999. Korea's female to male wage ratio rose fairly steadily throughout the period, from 47% in 1980 to 58% by 1998.The residual wage gap in manufacturing changed over time in both economies. Trends in wage gaps are separated by concentrated and less concentrated industries. For Taiwan (China), the residual wage gap was lower in concentrated industries than in non-concentrated industries. In both concentrated and less concentrated industries, the residual wage gap rose sharply until the mid-1990s and diminished somewhat during the late 1990s. Considering the trends in the trade ratios, the period of rising residual gaps coincided with a fairly steady increase in both export and import ratios, while the narrowing in the residual wage gap toward the end of the period coincides with a flattening in trade ratios. In Taiwan (China), greater trade openness in concentrated industries is associated with wider residual wage gaps between men and women, particularly when openness is measured by the manufacturing-sector import ratio. Import competition appears to widen the wage gap by adversely affecting women's relative employment prospects, leading to a loss of bargaining power for women. Women thus appear to be bearing the brunt of employers' competitive cost- cutting efforts. For Korea, the positive relationship between trade openness in concentrated industries and the residual wage gap continues to be evident for exports. Results for both economies imply that concerted efforts to enforce equal pay legislation and apply effective equal opportunity legislation are crucial for ensuring that women's pay gains will match those of men in a competitive environment.

---

[63] Berik, Rodgers & Zveglich (2003) "Globalization Vs Skill based Technological Change: Implications for Unemployment and Wage Inequality";The Economic Journal; Vol. 115, No. 503. April, Pp. 391-393.

Oostendorp (2004)[64] conducted a cross- country study of the impact of globalization on the occupational gender wage gap, based on the ILO October Inquiry. The study analyzes data for the years 1983-1999. 18931 observations are used for a total of 83 countries and 161 occupations. the author conducts a regression analysis to determine the impact of trade and FDI on the gender wage gap, using OLS. Results of the OLS Analysis conducted shows that there is a significant positive impact of GDP per capita on the gender wage gap in poorer countries. The effect of trade is generally negative (although not always significant), that is, the gender wage gap tends to fall with the openness of the economy and as far as the FDI net inflows are concerned, a more ambiguous pattern is found, with a negative and a positive but insignificant effect for the poorer and richer countries respectively. The results state that the occupational gender wage gap appears to be narrowing with increases in GDP per capita. There is a significantly narrowing impact of trade and FDI net inflows on the occupational gender wage gap for low-skill occupations, both in poorer and richer countries, and for high-skill occupations in richer countries. Also there is a lack of evidence of a narrowing impact of trade, but there is evidence of a widening impact of FDI net inflows on the high skill occupational gender wage gap in poorer countries. This shows that, on balance, globalization may not lower, and in some instances may increase gender gaps. This finding complements several other studies documenting an increase in wage inequality after trade liberalization in a number of developing countries. It is also found that wage-setting institutions have a strong impact on the occupational gender wage differentials and may interfere with the impact of globalization on the gender gap.

Reilly & Dutta (2005)[65] in their study "The Gender Pay Gap and Trade Liberalisation: Evidence for India" examine the magnitude of the gender pay gap in India and its relationship to a set of trade liberalization measures. The study focuses on quantification of the magnitude of these effects and eventually assesses whether there is a relationship between industry-specific gender pay gaps and other industry-specific measures that capture the effects of trade liberalization programmes in India. The individual-level data is taken from the National Sample Survey employment surveys and is restricted to males and females in wage employment and aged between 15 and 65 years old. The industry-specific tariff data for 1983-

[64] Oostendorp (2004): "Trade liberalization: Challenges and Opportunities for women in Southeast Asia, UNIFEM and ENGENDER, New York and Singapore.

[65] Reilly & Dutta (2005): "The Pattern of Globalization and Some Implications for the Pursuit of Social Goals"; The Indian Journal of Labour Economics; Vol. 48,No. 1, Jan- March, Pp. 47-61.

84, 1993-94 and 1999-2000 are constructed as simple averages of the basic customs tariff. The finding of a relatively stable average gender pay gap in India and the absence of any obvious trade-related effects represents only a very partial assessment of the effect of trade liberalization on women's relative position in the Indian labour market. The paper suggests that the stability observed in the gender pay gap is attributable to the selective withdrawal of the less able Indian women. Both the unadjusted and the residual gender pay gap appear to have exhibited a degree of stability over a period of very rapid labour market change in India. The role of unemployment and the changing nature of employment contracts through the use of greater informalisation, sub-contracting and out-sourcing have not been explored in this paper. If these issues have a strong gender dimension, they may have had adverse implications for the welfare of those women participating in the labour market.

Menon & Rodgers (2006)[66] in their study "The Impact of Trade Liberalization on Gender Wage Differentials in India's Manufacturing Sector" address the question of whether the increasing competitive forces from India's trade liberalization affects the wages of male and female workers differently. The study demonstrates that although an increase in trade still has a mitigating effect on the gender wage gap, under certain conditions, the net effect may be a widening of the wage gap between male and female workers. The theory is tested by estimating the impact of the trade reforms on gender wage differentials using four cross sections of household survey data from the National Sample Survey Organization between 1983 and 2004. The data has been aggregated to the industry level and merged with several other industry-level data sets for international trade, output, and industry structure. The relationship between the male-female wage gap and variations across industry and time in the exposure to competition from international trade have been examined, while controlling for changes in worker characteristics and domestic concentration. Results show that groups of workers who have weak bargaining power and lower workplace status may be less able to negotiate for favorable working conditions and higher pay, a situation that places them in a vulnerable position as firms compete in the global market place. Rather than competition from international trade putting pressure on firms to eliminate costly discrimination against women, pressures to cut costs due to international competition appear to be hurting women's relative pay. The results are consistent with several previous studies on India that have found negative social impacts resulting from the introduction of trade policy reforms.

---

[66] Menon & Rodgers (2006) "The Challenge of Gender Disparities in India's Economic Development"; The Indian Journal of Labour Economics; LXXXIV (332):123-146.

Sinha, Aseema (2007)[67] indicated that liberalization has increased inequalities in employment opportunities and income. Economic opportunities created by liberalization are highly unequal. For most women workers, quality of employment is poor with very low income returns. In rural as well as in urban areas FWP has declined during 1983 to 1999-2000.In urban India female workers face a marginal decline from 45.8 per cent in 1983 to 45.3 per cent in 1999-2000, Secondly there was a fluctuating trend of regular salaried jobs for rural females whereas it has increased for urban females, the incidence of employment under casual labour basis has increased for rural females and declined for urban females workers. The rural FWPR has decreased from 34.0 per cent in 1983 to 29.9 per cent in 1999-2000, while to their urban counterparts; it has declined feebly from 15.2 per cent to 13.9 per cent during the same period. The gap in worker-population ratio is more pronounced in the urban areas than in the rural areas. The urban female work participation rate in India is lower than the rural. Overall proportion of women workers in the work- force has been declining. Liberalisation has in some sectors caused loss of employment without creation of new employment opportunities.

Yamamoto (2007)[68] assessed the impacts of increases in international trade on gender wage discrimination in Japan. It was found that the residual wage gap increased in concentrated industries relative to competitive industries, or in other words, that gender wage gap declined more in competitive industries than in concentrated industries in absence of import penetration. Results for increased trade competition however, especially the one from Asian neighboring countries, was positively associated with wage discrimination against women in all industries, resulting in wider gender wage gap. In competitive industries, the gender wage gap grew more in industries that experienced greater increases in import penetration than in those that experienced little or no competition from abroad. In contrast to neoclassical theory, the gender wage inequality widens in concentrated industries that experienced greater increase in import penetration than in those that experienced little or no competition from abroad. The results indicate that in competitive industries, increased trade competition adversely affected both male and female wages, but more so for the latter. Among concentrated industries, increased trade competition is positively associated with both male and female wages, but benefiting more for men, thus resulting in widening gender

---

[67] Sinha, Aseema (2007): " Globalization, Rising Inequality, and New Insecurities in India"muse.jhu.edu/journals/journal_of_democracy/.../18.2sinha.html

[68] Yamamoto (2007) The international trade and gender gap : A survey, Tokyo: Asian Productivity Organization.

55

wage gap. As far as the export share is concerned, gender wage gap widened in competitive industries which experienced greater export by suppressing women's wages. Among concentrated industries, increase in export share led to a reduction in gender wage inequality in industries that experienced greater exports. The growth of exports in concentrated industries is negatively associated with residual male wages and positively associated with residual female wages; however both are not statistically significant. Therefore, causes of narrowing export effects on gender wage inequalities are not clear. The high-tech industries experience narrower wage gap relative to low-tech industries. Technological advancement is positively associated with women wages. In other words, that gender wage gap increased more in low-tech industries in absence of import penetration. In low- tech industries, the gender wage gap grew more in industries that experienced greater increases in import penetration than in those that experienced little or no competition from abroad.

Hari Priya (2000)[69] analyzed the problems of women leather workers in Kerala, Her findings are: Majority of the respondents needs to cover a distance of five to ten km, to reach their work place. Majority of the workers have an experience of less than five years and only 18.7 per cent has more than 10 years of experience. Majority of them joined this sector due to circumstantial poverty (husband/parents died) by chance and not by choice. More than half of the respondents (53.3 per cent) are illiterate without attending any formal schooling. Being a politically active and aware state, 68 per cent of the respondents are members of leather union affiliated to either ruling left party or opposition party. The union provides variety of welfare activities such as old age pension, and crisis support. The union also educates its members on entitlement and other rights. At the same time 28 per cent of the respondents felt that the number of women respondents in the union is inadequate and the existing women members are not pro-active. The respondents who have infants and children under 6 years of age is 24.7 per cent. The organisations never provide crèche facility and these women are depending on neighbors, parents and in laws to look after the infants.76.6 per cent are unskilled manual labourers.

Vankar's (2005)[70] survey of women leather workers in Ahmadabad revealed that a majority of workers seek to upgrade their skills. During the survey, 70 per cent of the total workers reported that they are willing to participate in training programmes to help them improve

---

[69] Hari Priya (2000)Quality of women's employment: A focus on the South. International Institute for Labour Studies: Decent Work Research

[70] Vankar (2005). The Economic Status of Women: An Analytical Framework,-in The Role of Women in Contributing to Family Income

their skills. The following findings were reported: 22 per cent of the women workers said that they wanted to be trained in all work, but did not name any specific work,14 per cent of the women workers said that they wanted to undergo training in the work, plaster work and design fitting and that they wanted to participate in such specific training so as to improve their standard of living and increase their income. As many as 83 per cent of the workers claimed that their income and job opportunities would increase and risk in work would be reduced after training.

2.7 Conclusion:

So far plethora of studies have been carried out on the working conditions, safety aspects, awareness of social issues and inclination to upgrade the skill of women workers in the leather industries, the review of the existing literature on the chosen domain enable to formulate the conceptual background for the study.

CHAPTER III

Status of Women, Labour Market, and Leather Footwear Industries- A thematic and Schematic description

3.1 Introduction

Confucius, the philosopher said that subordination of woman to man was the one of the important principles of the society. Aristotle deemed the dominion the male over the female, in our organization of the family, to be natural and necessary. He believe that the head of the household is unmistakably man who rules it, women may be said to be an inferior man[1]. The Hindu sage, Manu, condemned women to eternal bondage. The German philosopher Nietzsche said, when you go to meet a woman, take your whip along. Under the common law, women were treated as chattels. The Greeks, in their period of highest culture imprisoned their women within their houses and denied them all rights. The Spartans often destroyed women who could not give birth to health children. Even the most magnificent and civilized empire of Rome granted it's no legal rights. In Rome, husbands had absolute control over their wives and treated them as slaves. In the end it can be said that women everywhere suffered subordination and were assigned a purely functional role. Aristotle and Rousseau branded qualities like modesty, feminist and meekness as woman and natural for the female sex. Plato did concede them an equal status in his Republic but that is stray example. The socialist thinkers led by Karl Marx, Engel and others believed that women had been transformed from free and equal productive of the member society to subordinate waives and wards. They attributed this transformation to the growth of male-owned property with the family as an institution that appropriates and perpetuates. Even Hobbes and Locke, the advocates of equality, did not assign this equality to women[2].

Social scientists have, in the recent past, shown a very keen interest in studying women's problems due to a wide spread realization of the fact that the position of women in any given society serves not only as an index of its civilization, but it also influences of

---

[1] Adams, Parveen, et al., The Women in Question, Verso Publications, 1990

[2] Hansen, Karen V. and Ilene J. Philipson. eds. 1990. *Women, Class and the Feminist Imagination: A Socialist-Feminist Reader*. Philadelphia: Temple University.

a very large extent socio – economic development. Their position acquires a greater importance in a democratic welfare state like India where huge efforts are underway for its socio – economic development. Unless women are allowed to develop their full potentialities and thereby contribute their might to the developmental efforts, full advantage cannot be derived from the developmental programmes. It is needless to say that women can play their various roles properly only when they possess the necessary awareness, knowledge and skills. But all these depends upon the status that they enjoy in society. This explains the interest of social scientists studying the problems connected with the status of women.

Women all over the world suffer from certain disabilities and possess a status lower than that of men. In both the industrially advanced and less developed countries, women are burdened with cumulative inequalities as a result of socio – cultural and economic discriminatory practices, which until recently, have been taken for granted as though they were part of the immutable scheme of things established by nature[3]. It was only when the status of women was raised by removing their disabilities that they started playing their roles properly in various walks of life and contributing their might to the development of society. The advanced nations of the world were then convinced that the nation's well being as well as that of its women depends upon the developed poeticizing programmes and research that in fully utilized women's potentiality.

It was due to this experience of other countries that our leaders and policy makers wanted to take steps to raise the Status of Indian women. But before any such steps could be taken in a meaningful way, it was necessary to find out what status the Indian women enjoyed and why to pinpoint the areas wherein the changes were needed and above all to point out the directions of such changes. Indian social scientists have studied the problems connected with the status of women from this perspective. Various writers referred to the inferior positions of Indian women before independence. Even Gandhiji admitted that Indian women were subjected to all sorts of injustice at the hands of men

---

[3] Hartmann, Heidi. 1979. "Capitalism, Patriarchy and Job Segregation by Sex". In Zillah Eisenstein, ed. op. cit.: 206-247

and society[4]. It is really shocking to note that our women possessed a very degrading and humiliating position in society before independence. It is necessary to examine their position in the past in order to understand the same in the present context and to take steps to improve it.

The status of women in a given society cannot be assessed in isolation from social framework in which they live. Their status is closely related with social structure, religion, family and kinship, cultural norms and value systems which are important determinants of their position and behaviour pattern society as individual as well as in relation to others inside and outside the family. This is truer in the context to the status of rural women in India where the process of modernization is rather very slow. The whole life and behaviour pattern of the rural women and the attitude of the society towards them is shaped and guided by traditional socio – cultural norms and values which are so deep - rooted in the minds and hearts of the people, that there seems a wide gap between the position they actually hold in the traditional society. Religion, family and kinship, cultural norms, moral values etc. delimit the sphere of women's activities in the family and society. The rural women have yet to come up the traditional norms and taboos and to enjoy a position of 'equality' to men as individual citizen in accordance with the constitution.

3.2 Constitutional Position of Women

The constitution of India radically and deliberately departs from the traditional inferior, the position of woman in the society and treats every woman equal to man as a citizen and as an individual partner of the democratic system. The preamble of the constitution refers to "we the people of India" which means males and female and resolves to 'all' citizens of India equality of Status and opportunity and liberty of thought and expression, besides social economic and political justice. The Constitution does not make any sex – discrimination and treats all men and women as equal in the Indian policy. With this objective, the Constitution 'guarantees' fundamental rights to 'all' citizens including both men and women in positive as well as negative way, The positive rights are equality before law, freedom of speech, movement, profession and occupation,

---

[4] Altekar, Anant,Sadashiv The Position of Women in Hindu Civilization (from historic times to present day), Motilal Banarsidass, Delhi, 1962

association, protection of life and personal liberty etc. The negative rights relate to prohibition of 'discrimination' or 'dental' of equal protection'. The women regardless of the different socio-economic positions they hold in a given system, have been provided these positive and negative rights parallel to their male counterparts[5].

An article 14 of the Constitution ensures equality before law. Article 15 prohibits any discrimination on grounds of sex. Article 16 ensures and guarantees equality of opportunity in matters of public employment. Article 17 abolishing untouchability and making it an offence punishable in accordance with law provides on equal status to all those males and female of the scheduled caste people who were regarded as untouchable since centuries due to socio – religious complex. Article 19 guarantees numerous freedoms to all citizens under some reasonable restrictions. Article 20 and 21 provide protection to every person both male and female in respect of conviction for offences and protection of life and personal liberty.

The Constitution not only declares the objective of equality and opportunity to both males and females of India and guarantees equal fundamental rights to them, but also tries to ensure those necessary conditions which will make the objective and the rights practical and useful. The Directive principles of state policy relating to 'women-specific' concern women directly have a very special bearing on their status. Similarly, articles 40, 41,43,44,35 and 47 related to many welfare activities which are concerned with women indirectly.

In order to achieve the objectives in fundamental rights a number of laws were enacted by the Government of India after independence. Not only were this some special welfare schemes also were initiated for women to better their economic conditions, to increase their earning capacity, to extend the medical facilities and to help them in improving their knowledge etc.

Fundamental Rights furnish individual rights while the Directive Principles of State Policy supply social needs.

Article 39(a) directs the State to direct its policy towards securing the citizens, men and women, equally have the right to have an adequate means of livelihood.

---

[5] ibid

Article 39(d) directs the State to secure equal pay for equal work for both men and women. The State in furtherance of this directive passed the Equal Remuneration Act, 1976 to give effect to the provision.

Article 39(e) specifically directs the State not to abuse the health and strength of workers, men and women.

Article 42 of the Constitution incorporates a very important provision for the benefit of women. It directs the State to make provisions for securing just and humane conditions of work and for maternity relief.

The State has implemented this directive by incorporating health provisions in the Factories Act, Maternity Benefit Act, Beedi and Cigar Workers (Conditions of Employment) Act, etc.

Article 44 directs the State to secure for citizens a Uniform Civil Code applicable throughout the territory of India. Its particular goal is towards the achievement of gender justice. Even though the State has not yet made any efforts to introduce a

Uniform Civil Code in India, the judiciary has recognised the necessity of uniformity in the application of civil laws relating to marriage, succession, adoption, divorce, maintenance, etc. but as it is only a directive it cannot be enforced in a court of law.

Article: 243 T Reservation of seats. (74th Amendment - w.e.f. 1-6-1993) 243T. Reservation of seats provides Not less than one-third (including the number of seats reserved for women belonging to the Scheduled Castes and the Scheduled Tribes) of the total number of seats to be filled by direct election in every Municipality shall be reserved for women and such seats may be allotted by rotation to different constituencies in a Municipality, women Workers

3.3 The Equal Remuneration Act, 1976:-

It was only in 1976, that the equal Remuneration Act, 1976 a landmark enactment was introduced, which provides for payment of equal to both wages to both men and women worked for the same work, or work of similar nature. The Act also prohibits discrimination against women in the matter of recruitment. Yet, studies reveal that wage differentials still exist, and continue to persist.

3.4 The Employees State Insurance Act, 1948 And The Maternity Benefit Act, 1961:-

Maternity benefits are provided under the Employees state Insurance Act, 1948 and the Maternity Benefit Act, 1961. A women employee is entitled to maternity benefits for a period of 12 weeks if she worked in the establishment for 160 days in the 12 months immediately preceding her excepted delivery. Various studies have revealed that only a very small percentage of women workers avail of benefit. Further, the Act only protects the payment of maternity benefits. It nowhere prohibits the dismissal of pregnant women. The service rules of some establishments provide for termination of service of women workers on pregnancy.

The supreme court had struck down a provision whereby an Air Hostess would have deemed to have retired on pregnancy, as being unconstitutional in the case of Air India V. Nargesh Meerza.(1981 (4) SCC 335)[5.3]

3.5 The Dowry Prohibition Act, 1961:-

The Dowry Prohibition Act, 1961 was passed to prevent the evil practice of giving and taking of dowry.

3.6 The Suppression Of Immoral Traffic Act, 1956:-

The suppression of immoral traffic act, 1956 more popularly known as "SITA" was enacted to prohibit exploitation of women with a view of earning money. Subsequently, this Act was renamed as the **Immoral Traffic (Prevention) Act, 1956** wherein sexual exploitation and abuse of the female for commercial gain was made punishable.

3.7 The Pre-Natal Diagnostic (Prevention) Act, 1994

Another landmark enactment is the Pre-Natal Diagnostic (Prevention) Act, 1994 which prohibits the use of pre-natal techniques for the purposes of sex determination. Despite the said enactment having been passed, the tests still continues to take place. The only difference being that they have become more surreptitious. This has come to light from the recent news reports in Patiala, in Punjab, where female fetuses in large numbers were found drowned in a well adjoining a nursing home.

3.8 Protection Of Women From Sexual Harassment At Work Place

The right to bodily integrity is encompassed in the right guaranteed by article 21 of the constitution of India, which guarantees the right to life and liberty.

The Supreme Court defines the term "sexual harassment' as an "Unwelcome sexually determined behaviour (Whether directly or by implication) as:

- ❖ Physical contact and advances:
- ❖ Demand or request for sexual favours;
- ❖ Sexually coloured remarks;
- ❖ Showing pornography
- ❖ Any other unwelcome physical, verbal or non-verbal conduct or sexual nature."

3.9 The Beedi and Cigar workers (conditions of Employment) Act, 1966

Beedi and cigar making is an area where a large number of women and children are employed. They are then subjected to exploitation in terms of wages and working hours. Long hours of work and fewer wage compelled the Government to enact the Beedi and Cigar Workers (Conditions of Employment) Act, 1966 which provided benefits to women workers.

Under Section 25 of the Act it has been laid down that no woman or young person shall be required to work on any industrial premises except between 6 a.m. and 7 p.m. This has been provided to ensure the welfare and safety of women workers.

Even after the enactment of various legislations and implementation of welfare programmmes, the condition of women, particularly of rural women, did not show any improvement. There were several factors responsible for the relative backwardness of Indian women in general and rural women in particular. Some of these factors were illiteracy, traditional values and norms, dominant position of the males, superstitions, religious practices, and social evils like child marriage, dowry etc., and above all economic dependence of women on men. Inspite of constitutional and legal provision, Indian women, particularly in rural areas, continued to suffer from these constraints.

3.10 Changing Role of women

The history of this early period is also the systematic undermining of women's autonomy as agricultural producers in many parts of the globe. The process by which the shift from autonomy to dependence took place was complex. With the advent of the plough cultivation and the emergence of private property, there was a shift of autonomy. "The diverse social structure and supporting ideologies created by men confine as well as define by restricting them (women) to roles and activities described as 'feminine. "The contributions of women however have not been acknowledged quantitatively or qualitatively. Women's work as producers is grossly neglected by economic statistics and analysis of labour and capital

Women are growing in number and are spending and increasing proportion of their time for remunerative jobs; their lives continue to be significantly different from those of men and much of their time is spent in the non-economic sector. The 'double burden' of responsibility for home and market work has made it difficult for women to achieve substantial equality in the public sphere. "Neither the role of 'housewife' nor that of 'working woman' is without significant problems for women." Men's work in the public sphere has usually enjoyed higher status than women's domestic work within the family circle. "But even when women have succeeded in entering the world beyond household to a greater or lesser extent, men have not shown much inclination to share in household work." It is true that child-bearing absorbs an increasingly smaller proportion of a woman's adult life and can, for the most part, be timed at will. "It is the unequal distribution of labour in at home, rather than women's lesser ability to perform other types of work that is the main obstacle of equality."[6]

However there have been some significant changes in women's work scenario in the last two decades, especially during 1980s, both in the developed and developing countries. Women's workforce participation has considerably increased in most countries of the world. At the same time, male participation rate has either stagnated or declined; the change in labour market conditions is so perceptible that of

---

[6] Bhalla, G.S (2008): "Globalisation and Employment Trends in India"; The Indian Journal of Labour Economic;, Vol. 51, No.1, Jan- Mar, p. 2

'marginalization'. The process of global feminization' is said to have been occurring. While this process of feminization has diversified the work opportunities of women, it also brought several adverse consequences for women workers in terms of earning and working conditions. It is important to understand the process of change concerning women's work and its implications in a correct perspective for an appropriate policy intervention as well as for giving input to the ongoing voluntary action and movement for the betterment of the work scenario of women.

3.11 Factors Which Facilitated The Change In Women's Role

❖ There are some social and economic factors, which brought about changes in women's role and elevated them to the status of a 'worker.

❖ A series of technologically advanced innovations provided cheaper appliances to perform the manual work of women in the home. "Market goods have become more substitutable replacing home made products, making women capable enough to option for employment outside the household."

❖ The changes in the concept of family also facilitated the emergence of women labourers. Number of children decreased; there is a reduction in infant mortality, which means that fewer births are needed to achieve a family of desired size.

❖ Mortality of women is also lower now.

❖ The decline in fertility appears to have strengthened their commitment to labour force activity.

❖ With the completion of child bearing at a younger age, a woman can engage in economic activities.

❖ Expanding job opportunities offered by urbanization and industrialization also paved the way for more sphere of activities for women outside the home.

3.12 Factors which prompt Women to work

❖ It may be stated that the families income are low so that women are compelled to work in order to add their own share to the family purse.

❖ Low wages of their husbands also drive women to seek employment.

❖ High rate of literacy among women and the desire for financial independence are also other important factors which prompt women to take up employment.

3.12.1 Occupational Difference between Men and Women

- ❖ The difference in the occupational distribution of women and men leads to the concentration of women in particular fields of employment and job categories.
- ❖ Generally, men dominate the supervisory and managerial positions and women engage in non-supervisory, middle and lower grades.

3.12.2 Reasons for the Differences in Occupation between Men and Women

- ❖ The differences in role identification which begin in infancy result in women following a track where home management is the primary activity and work as secondary.
- ❖ Those women who follow dual careers are likely to seek occupations and work situations which will be complementary with home responsibilities.

3.12.3 Factors Responsible for the Lower incomes of Women Workers

There are some factors responsible for the lower incomes of women.

- ❖ In many employment sectors, a division is seen separating work into jobs for men and women to which the individual worker must adjust. This separation in job arrangement reflects discrimination and lower pay for women.
- ❖ The length and continuity of time spent in the labour force are important influence on earnings. Generally men accumulate more skills and experience through formal and on-the –job training due to their greater involvement in profession.
- ❖ The problem of unequal opportunity for women in the labour market is related to the social view that a woman's first responsibility is to her home. This social attitude finds its full expression in the division of role and responsibilities in the family- a division that is far from equal between husband and wife. The fact that a wife and mother is working seems to have a little effect upon her expected performance at home as cook, chauffeur, laundry helper, cleaner, nurse, child attendant, teacher and an amateur psychologist. Women who take or continue thier work after marriage and the birth of children, assume a second work load, bearing the major weight of the double burden of job and family. They are also exposed to two sets of conflicting demands-the paying job requires attendance at

fixed hours during the week, while home and family exert diverse pressures at all hours of the day.

❖ As a result a woman continues to have a different economic status in her occupations. She remains exploited, oppressed and takes advantage from the management and trade union.

❖ Another reason for lower payments even for the same tasks are due to the assumption (usually shared by both employers and workers) that women are less productive than men.

❖ There is a great deal of absenteeism among women workers, rendering their work unsteady and irregular due to their household involvement.

3.12.4 Women's work and Wages

❖ Labour legislation, as far as the workers are concerned is inadequate. It does not fully safeguard their interests wherever they are employed.

❖ The essential principle of labour legislation should not only prevent employers from taking advantage of workers' helplessness and weaker position but should also to compel them to adopt measures which ensure the rights of the workers especially women to overcome handicaps peculiar to them.

❖ But too many demands and restrictions on the employers are bound to affect the employment of women adversely by making it difficult from the point of view of the management.

❖ Women are usually employed in lighter occupations compared to men who are employed in heavier occupations. Even when they work in similar occupations, distinctions are made sometimes. There is no reason why women are not are paid equal wages for equal work.

3.12.5 Problems of Women Workers

Certain problems are common to women workers. A study of the problems of women workers will indicate the need of welfare measures to be adopted along with proper lines of approach.

❖ Woman is physically weaker than man. In addition, she has to bear the child which requires her to take rest before and after delivery. Where there is no coverage of maternity benefits, it may sometimes become as occasional disability.

❖ Then she has the burden of the growing child; its care takes much of her time. She has also to function as a housewife with all household responsibilities.

❖ The family is a grave concern for the women in our country than her western sister. Her social and economic status is very low.

❖ There are several additional gender-specific dimensions which affect women's work situation. The gender based inequalities in the family in the provision of basic necessities also create health problems for women.

❖ Further they are exposed to health hazards arising from the nature of their work. There exist several types of exploitation by employers and money lenders also.

3.13 Women's Work and Housework

Economists view the gender division of labor as central to the differentiation between men and women. Scholars maintain that the gender division of labor, and not sexual differences alone, create a difference between men and women. Each racial/ethnic group has a historically distinct division of labor. The gender divisions of labor and family systems of people of color have been systematically disrupted and re-organized by racial/ethnic and class processes. Thus, racial/ethnic divisions operate in conjunction with gender differences in the economy.In the economy, gender is manifested in the categories of breadwinner and housewife that anchor the invisibility--the non-recognition--of women's work. Meera analysis indicates that the relationship between these two categories defines women as non-workers, which makes possible the definition of men as workers and breadwinners. Traditional patriarchal ideologies are thus harnessed to develop capitalist production. These norms are based on the fundamentally masculine concept of work. A feminist concept of work would include both biological and social reproduction, and not be confined to the production of goods and services[7]. The presence and legitimacy of the ideology of the housewife, which defines women in terms of marriage and their place in the home is central in this study as well.

---

[7] Desai, Meera and Krishna Raj, M., Women and Society in India. New Delhi:Ajantha Publications, 1987.

The current understanding of gender and work stems in part from the political economy of domestic labor debate of the 1970s. This debate centered around arguments that women's unpaid labor reproduced the labor force and therefore contributed directly and indirectly to the production of surplus value and the accumulation of capital. Only when all household labor is shared equally between men and women can this appropriation of surplus value be stemmed.The terms of this debate are not centrally concerned with race/ethnicity. The analyses focus on the material aspects of gender, which include economic contributions. They do not address the non-material aspects of gender, which include how people think about themselves and their activities. Nor do they address the crucial association between non-material aspects of gender and decision-making that determines access to joint resources.

The social constructionist framework, which gained prominence in the 1980s, posits that gender is fundamental to the way in which work is organized and that work is central in the social construction of gender.The general consensus among a broad range of feminist scholars within the social constructionist framework is that gender hierarchy is perpetuated because women are denied employment opportunities and income relative to men,According to this logic, changing women's relationship to employment and domestic responsibilities is the means to gender equity. However, other feminist scholars have long pushed for a change in "what is recognized and socially legitimated as work" (Zimmerman, 1997; Waring, 1988). The latter group of scholars refers to the dichotomy of work and housework.Women have always worked, but much of the work they perform does not officially count as work . Because people are largely defined by the work they do, the work people do eventually has an impact on how people think about themselves .Work casts a long shadow on the person doing it. If a person's contribution is valued, then work enhances self-worth. Housework, however, is under-valued as is evident in the phrase, "I'm just a housewife" (Ward, 1990). Work leads to empowerment when it makes survival easier for women, increases women's access to resources, gives women more respect, or more opportunities to get together and build networks, or tools for resistance. Relative earnings and perceived contributions of spouses affect the distribution of decision-making in families Work--formal, informal, and housework--also affects the socio-economic empowerment (Sen,1990; England, 1997; Dunn, 1997). When women's

70

contributions are unrecognized, it also likely constrains women's access to decision-making. Therefore, it would follow from this logic that when women's contributions are not recognized or are devalued, there is no challenge to gender hierarchy.

3.14 Women Workers-Some Conceptual Issues and Problems of Measurement

A closer look at the structure of women's labour force participation in various regions of India throws light to the determinants as well as the consequences of their entry into the labour force."The relatively low levels of work participation rates among women in India can be explained in relation to the conceptual and measurement related problems implicit in the identification of women within the labour force. In our subsistence economy, there is deliberate exclusion of a whole range of activities performed by women from the purview of gainful employment."[8] It should be emphasized that apart from their contributions in terms of earnings, there is 'time contribution' of poor rural women workers to a complex range of unpaid tasks-fetching, gathering, cooking, processing, conserving, ministering and building up of kin networks and intra-household relationships in the society. The large amounts of time and energy expended on these domestic chores, however, remain invisibles and no productive economic value is attached to these tasks.

Moreover, there are cognitive problems in identifying women workers which arise from the cultural biases of traditional societies. Women are reckoned primarily as housewives and the economic activities they may perform along with their domestic chores tend to remain under-reported either by women themselves or more often by proxy respondents. The principal data input in framing the of development policies is the national level statistics. But the accuracy of it is severely impaired by biases which lead to an undercounting of women, both as workers and as those available for work. Hence many of the schemes which are instituted to help the poor are misdirected in their very conceptualization. A look at the methodology followed by the National Sample survey

---

[8] Bhalla, Sheila. (1993): "Tests of Propositions about the Dynamics of Change in the Rural Work Force Structure"; The Indian Journal of Labour Economics; Vol. 36(3),July-August Pp. 428-439.

(NSS) and the census organization in India suggests that there are significant deviations from the standard international practice for the measurement of labour force.

"Moreover, neither the 'pull factors', which draw women for employment into non-agricultural sectors of the economy nor the 'push factors' which facilitate their release from the precincts of the household are adequately present in the Indian context. Hence female participation in economic activities has a pronounced tendency to remain clustered around agriculture and allied activities." When compared to men, women are bumped in low paying or unpaid work. They are excluded from most skilled jobs. Rate of unemployment is also more among women than men. Indian evidence shows a manifestation of women in the process of development. Women are increasingly excluded from productive work, and they are pushed into and concentrated in marginal occupations and they are increasingly casualised in terms of employment[9].

Hence the potentially significant role of public policies in facilitating an improved labour force participation of women is the need of the hour. In particular, public investment in the field of health, education and utilities have a vital role to play in setting the stage for the development of vigorous labour market for the women in the country. Then only the full potential of the reserve army of female labour in India can be harnessed without relegating as wasted assets or utilized only by half measure.

3.15 Labour Market discrimination in India

Women in India have traditionally been restricted to the household, but formal labor force participation rates of women have improved just as observed in other countries across the world. Trade theory predicts that relative wages of unskilled labor will rise in the long run in an unskilled-labor abundant country that opens up to trade. It was expected that labor-intensive industries in labor abundant economies would become export competing and women who tended to dominate labor-intensive industries would stand to gain. It is expected that opening up to trade benefit women in a low-skill

---

[9] Devi, D.R., M. Ravindram (1983): "Women's Work in India"; International Social Science Journal; 35(4); Pp. 683 – 701

abundant country like India. (Joseph, Gloria. 1981) in her review of the literature on gender effects of trade reforms found a positive Wage inequalities among race, gender and social groups have been extensively studied in both developed and developing countries. The explanations provided for such wage differences are several, including the human capital theory, compensating differentials, search models, and discrimination. Human capital is the embodiment of productivity in people[10]. The human capital theory predicts that earnings are higher for those with higher education and experience. Even after controlling for all observable factors such as education, age, experience, marital status, occupation and industry in earnings regressions developed by the human capital theory, wage differentials between workers may not be fully explained. The segment of the wage gap that is not explained by observable differences in worker characteristics is typically attributed to discrimination in the Blinder-Oaxaca (1973) decomposition technique. Discrimination in the labor market has been studied extensively, particularly in developed countries. The main economic theory to study discrimination was developed by Gary Becker, in the 1950s. Becker developed a neoclassical model, with typical neoclassical assumptions of perfect competition in labor markets and utility maximization, using the concept of a taste for discrimination on the part of employers, employees or customers to examine the consequences of discrimination, where it exists. Becker proposes that this taste for discrimination creates a wage differential in the short run, as a result of the willingness on the part of discriminators rates than men. Females and lower castes in India have lower levels of education and experience than males and higher castes. This difference in human capital can be one explanation of wage gaps between gender and caste groups. However, studies (Sambamoorthi, 1984; Banerjee and Knight, 1985) have found the existence of wage and job discrimination against female workers.

3.16 Globalization and women workers

Globalization is a multi-dimensional process of economic, political, cultural and ideological change. It has led to increasing violations of women's economic,

---

[10] Joseph, Gloria. 1981. "The Incompatible Menage à Trois: Marxism, Feminism and Racism". In Lydia Sargent, ed., op. cit.: 91-108.

political and cultural rights in large measure due to withering away of the welfare/ Development list state, the feminization of poverty, the expansion of religious fundamentalists and new form of militarism and conflict. Often being unorganized, facing recurrent inequality in employment and harassment at work and violation of their human rights, with low levels of education, limited technological skills, women workers easily become marginalized and hardly derive any benefits from the ever new opportunities emerging in an open and competitive world trade.

Globalization has drawn millions of women into paid employment across the developing world. Today, supermarkets and clothing stores sources the products that they sell form farms and factories worldwide. At the end o their supply chains, the majority of workers-picking and packing fruits, sewing garments, cutting flowers- are women. But these women workers are systematically being denied their fair share of the benefits brought by globalization.

Commonly hired on short-term contracts-or with no contract at all women are working at high speed for low wages in unhealthy conditions. They forced to put in long hours to earn enough to get by. Most have no sick leave or maternity leave, few are enrolled in health or unemployment schemes, and fewer still have saving for the future.

Instead of supporting long-term development trade is reinforcing insecurity and vulnerability for millions of women workers. The harsh reality faced by women workers highlights one of the glaring failures of the current model of globalization. Now we will have a look at the impact of globalization on women working in various sectors.

Globalization has affected women workers in both agricultural as well as no-agricultural sector in India. Because of export promotion in this sector. Many women have lost their jobs as the newer export friendly system of cash crop cultivation and especially aquaculture required much less input from women. Instead of harvesting paddy crops, they have to collect snails for feeding fish. This is not only a hazardous and more dangerous task but it also means much lower pay.

In non-agriculture sector, due to unemployment, many women have been force to turn to prostitution or to work in informal sectors like construction where they are sexually exploitation by contractors. The belief by many that there will be large-scale

74

feminization of labour in a post-globalization situation has also been found to be completely false in case o India.

In a scenario where government wants to reduce the workforce in our country, the first target are women as reflected in the way the voluntary retirement schemes target women. In Export Processing Zones (EPZ), dominance of women workers is a characteristic feature, and India EPZs also follow along the same lines. Women workers constitute 70-80 percent of the work force. Working hours are typically much longer than the specified maximum wages.

According to the PRIA study, "Women do not get maternity leave anywhere; in fact women generally lose their jobs if they get pregnant. Surprisingly, some companies employ women on the condition that they won't get married or pregnant in near future. As per the factories law, employer are prohibited from allowing women to work in night shifts, but the during the survey the contrary was seen women work in nights shifts in many places in EPZ.'

3.17 Employment of Women in Export Processing Zones (Epz) and Export-Oriented Manufacturing Industries

In late nineties, the share of the female employment in total employment in Export Processing Zones (EPZs) and export-oriented Zones manufacturing industries typically exceeded 70 percent. Women workers were preferred by employers in export activities primarily because of the inferior conditions of work and lower pay scales that they were usually willing to accept. Thus, women workers had lower reservation wages than their male counterparts, were more willing to accept longer hours, unpleasant and often unhealthy or hazardous factory conditions, typically did not unionize or engage in others forms of collective bargaining to improve conditions and did not ask for permanent contracts. They were thus easier to hire and fire at will and according to external demand conditions, and also life cycle changes such as marriage and child- birth could be used as proximate causes to terminate employment. The high "burnout" associated with these activities meant that employers preferred work-forces that could be periodically replaced and what better option they can have than to employ female workers who could be easily fired. Average age of women working in these industries is between 20-25 years and they are fired when they cross 30 years of age.

75

3.18 Women Labour and ILO norms

The 1998 ILO booklet on "Giving Women a Voice" makes it clear that in order for women's, and gender, issues to be articulated in the workplace, women should be involved in all processes related to the defense of workers' rights. These include "at the negotiating table, on occupational health, safety and environmental committees, in grievance-handling procedures, as shop stewards, as works council or joint committee members, and on company boards where there is employee representation." For this to happen, unions must also ensure that women have access to the training and re-training necessary to be promoted to senior positions, which will improve representation of women at all levels of the workplace. Such efforts may involve the establishment of an equal opportunities committee, and the use of positive measures. Thus, internal and external measures generally must be considered in a joint fashion.

One of the areas highlighted by the ILO-ICFTU survey is gender equality in collective bargaining. Women may have special concerns in this regard because of their reproductive functions and tasks, past discrimination, lack of implementation of legislation about women's issues, and women's position in the labour force. These concerns (which also are important for men) include:

- ❖ equal pay;
- ❖ maternity, paternity and parental leave;
- ❖ breastfeeding provisions; child care;
- ❖ sexual harassment;
- ❖ night work;
- ❖ family friendly policies; and
- ❖ Positive/affirmative measures.

To encourage women's participation in collective bargaining, the survey reports that some unions have instituted quotas, or proportional representation, for women on negotiating teams, or stipulate that equality or women's officers must be involved in the negotiation process. Others offer guidelines and train female staff in negotiation techniques. One union had enabled its women committee to submit recommendations to the bargaining committee and had provided its negotiating team with a "gender checklist for bargaining" and a model equality bargaining agreement. The report advises that including gender issues in collective bargaining requires the following steps:

❖ promoting awareness and understanding of gender issues;
❖ involving women in the negotiating teams;
❖ consulting women and ensuring that their voices are heard;
❖ making special efforts to get the views of all workers;
❖ being well-prepared for negotiations; and
❖ Following up by publicizing and monitoring implementation and collecting sex-disaggregated statistics.

Other trade union activities to promote gender equality in the workplace focus on:

❖ improving equal pay through job evaluation schemes;
❖ learning schemes; action against sexual harassment; facilities, campaigns and tools to promote greater gender balance in family responsibilities;
❖ workplace improvements such as benefits and facilities;
❖ Awareness rising on gender equality at the workplace.

Gender-based discrimination is a universal phenomenon. Women comprise half of the world's population and perform two thirds of the work, but earn only a third of the total income and own less than a tenth of the resources. The most discriminated people in the world are usually the ones who lack economic power.[11]

3.19 Human Rights of Women workers need special Attention

It has been rightly said that 'Human Development. If not engendered, is endangered'. So equal enjoyment of human rights by women and men was universal accepted principle, reaffirmed by the Vienna Declaration, adopted by 171 states at world conference on human rights in June 1993. But in the current economic turmoil with the winds of changing blowing all over the world bringing about fundamental changes in

---

[11] ILO. (2002): "Decent Work in the Informal Economy"; Report VI, International Labour Conference 90th Session, Geneva.

global trade, diminishing role of the state and rapidly changing work environment, the human rights of the vulnerable women workers seem to be getting sidelined. While new opportunities for economic growth are opening up for national and global economic growth are opening up for national and global economies, an ILO Report has found "a bias against women in all these categories' with some significant following findings.

(a) Women constitute an increasing share of the world's labour force- at least, one third in all regions of the world barring Northern Africa and Western Asia.

(b) The informal sector employs more than men.

(c) Self-employment and part-time and home based work have led to expanded opportunities for women's participation in the labour force but have also resulted in lack of work security, lack of benefits and low income.

(d) Especially younger women and also women are in general experience more unemployment than men and for a longer period of time as compared to men.

(e) Women still are at the lower end of a segregated labour market and continue to concentrated in a few occupations, hold positions of little or no authority and receive less pay than men.

3.20 International Law and International Instrument relating to the Women workers

The international law concerning women workers have been codified in the form of various international instruments mainly by the ILO since the first quarter of the last century. In this context, a "silent revolution" largely inspired by ILO Conventions, had been taking place for decades and continued even, now. No doubt, ILO's international labour standards and the principles they enshrine proved to be a source of inspiration and provided strength and legitimacy to those espousing the human rights of women workers and they have been pace setters in the promotion of equality of opportunity and treatment in education, training, employment and improving working conditions.

The Declaration of Philadelphia adopted by the international Labour Conference in 1994 and a part of the ILO Constitution, emphasizes that " all human beings, irrespective of race, creed or sex, posses, the right to pursue both their material well -being and their spiritual development in conditions of freedom and dignity of economic security and equal opportunity". Equality at work has been the subject of two most widely ratified ILO convention 1958 (No. 111), and the equal Remuneration Convention, 1951(No 100).

The ILO Convention No. 100 stressed the importance of equality between men and women workers in respect of remuneration, which included the basic wage and any additional cash or in kind remuneration or benefits arising out of worker's employment. A pioneering feature of this Convention was its guarantee of equal pay for " work of equal Value" and not just for the same or similar work. This took care of gender biases in the way labour markets are structured, because most women did different jobs from most men. Other important conventions and declarations pertaining to women's rights are: Convention on Elimination of all forms of discrimination against women (CEDAW), Beijing platform for Action and ILO Convention on non-discrimination such as maternity Protection Convention.

The international Labour Conference also promoted gender equality through the adopted of other international instruments, including, in 1975, the ILO Declaration on equality of Opportunity and Treatment for Women Workers and the resolution concerning a plan of aimed at promoting equality of opportunity and treatment for women workers. The Workers and family Responsibilities, 1981 (No. 156), was another step in furthering gender equality at work and in other spheres. Last but not the least, the Millennium Development Goals (MDGs), adopted by the United Nation General Assembly in 2000, has been another landmark in this direction which pointed out the importance of women's access to paid jobs in sectors other than agriculture for improvement of their economic and social status and achieving the goals of gender equality.

3.21 Workforce participation of women

Since the 1980s there has been a near-consistent decline in workforce participation rate (WPR) of women. Even more remarkably, in the latter half of 2000s (i.e. between 2004-05 and 2009-10) both the labour force participation rate (LFPR) and workforce participation rate (WPR) of women has declined sharply, as a result of which the total LFPR and WPR of the population has declined. Male LFPR and WPR has pretty much remained constant over the same period (LFPR for males was 55.1% and WPR was 55%). The sharp decline in female labour force participation has happened in both rural and urban areas, though the decline is much sharper in rural compared to urban areas. This suggests strongly that in both urban and rural areas girls over 14 years of age (i.e. of working age) are remaining in school, more than ever before. As a result, the LFPR of women in India, which is already low by Asian standards, has fallen further. However, this decline should be seen in a positive light precisely because it suggests that girls, after completing elementary schooling are making the transition to secondary schooling in much larger numbers than ever before. In other words, these girls will be available to enter the workforce at a slightly later age better qualified than an earlier cohort. Since they will be better educated they are likely to make the transition out of agriculture into non-agricultural employment, even though it may be in the unorganized sector. Given the fact that the female employment is even more concentrated in informal work than male employment outside of agriculture, their greater participation in schooling indeed is a positive development. However, the much higher rate of education participation of girls augurs well for improvement in their labour force participation. The most serious problem that women in the work force face is that it is not 'decent work'. For the vast majority of women in non-agricultural employment they tend to work from home in home-based work, usually subcontracted to them by male contractors in a variety of low-productivity work (e.g., bidi-making, zari-making, etc) in 1999-2000 the NSS Round had estimated that 29 million in the country were making as home-workers; assuming that such women live in a family of five members, a total of 150 million persons are at least part-dependent upon this kind of work[12].

As per UPSS approach, 104.5 million women in rural areas and 22.8 million in urban areas were in the workforce in 2009-10. This implied decline in women workforce vis-à-vis 2004-05 when 124 million rural and 24.6 million urban women were working. The NSS 66th round has indicated that an estimated 84.79 million women in rural areas were neither working nor available for work as they attended

---

[12] NSS 66st Round: Report No. 515(61/10/1), Part II, (2009-2010):"Employment and Unemployment Situation in India

educational institutions (as per the UPSS approach) in 2009-10. Similarly, in urban areas, 33.88 million women were neither working nor available for work as they attended educational institutions. In the rural areas, women are mainly involved as cultivators and agricultural laborers. In the urban areas, almost 80 per cent of the women workers are working in the unorganized sectors such as household industries, petty trades and services, buildings and construction. The khadi and village industries are one of the largest employers of women workers. Casualisation among women workers is rising. During the period 2004-05 to 2009-10, the proportion of casual workers among rural females increased from 32.6% to 39.9% and among urban females from 16.7% to 19.6%. The corresponding figures are 32.9% and 38% for rural males and 14.6% and 17% for urban males for the years 2004-05 and 2009-10 respectively.[13]

3.22 Indian Leather Footwear industry

The leather footwear industry occupies a place of prominence in the Indian economy in view of its massive potential for employment, growth and exports. In fact, backed by a strong raw-material base and a large reservoir of traditionally skilled and competitive labour force, the Indian leather footwear industry has made significant strides during the past two decades. Not only that, this industry has undergone a dramatic transformation from a mere exporter of raw materials (like tanned hides and skins) in the 1960s to that of value added finished products from the 1970s. Policy initiatives taken by the Government of India (GOI) since 1973 have been quite instrumental to such a transformation. The structure of the Indian leather industry is quite interesting. It is spread in different segments namely tanning and finishing, footwear and footwear components, leather garments, leather goods including saddlery and harness etc. The industry uses primarily indigenous natural resources with little dependence on imported resources. Hides and skins are the basic raw materials for the leather industry, which originate from the source of livestock. India has a very large share of the world bovine animal population further, an overwhelming proportion of the total production of this industry comes from the unorganised sector, i.e., small scale, cottage and artisan sector. The

---

[13] ibid

major production centres are spread over selected areas in a few states, e.g., selected places in Tamil Nadu, Kolkata in West Bengal, Kanpur and Agra in Uttar Pradesh, Jalandhar in Punjab and Delhi. And the major export market for Indian leather goods is Germany, with an oftake of about 25 percent of India's domestic production, followed by the USA, the UK, France and Italy. The important export items are leather handbags, footwear and leather garments. Official policies/programmes undertaken to facilitate the growth of the leather industry include de-reservations of 11 items (particularly semi-finished hides and skins, leather shoes and leather accessories for leather industry) in 2001, abolition of the license system in case of manufacture of most of the leather items. Some items are still reserved for exclusive manufacture by the small-scale sector, but non-small scale units can also obtain approval for the manufacture of these items provided they meet an export obligation of 50 per cent of their annual production

Governments at both the central as well as state levels are in a way to promote formation of more leather manufacturing clusters in different parts of the country to get reap of the benefits from such clustering in both the cost reducing and quality enhancing dimensions. For instance, the Kerala Industrial Infrastructure Development Corporation (KINFRA) is setting up a footwear park at Vazhakkat, near Ramanattukara, in Malappuram district. The Cabinet Committee on Economic Affairs, Government of India recently gave its nod for development of a leather park under Indian Leather Development Programme (ILDP) and earmarked INR3000 million for it. The aim of the sub-scheme is to provide the industry with infrastructure facilities for setting up leather units across product categories and to attract large domestic joint venture and foreign investments into the Indian leather industry. A leather park set up under this sub-scheme would cover all sectors of leather industry – tannery, all products categories and leather machinery; some intrinsic problems affect the leather firms also. Prior to its detailed discussion we can briefly present the nature of the production chain of the industry. The entire production process can be sub-divided into three segments: leather tanning (i.e., raw to semi-finished stage), leather finishing (i.e., semi-finished to finished stage) and making of leather goods/products (i.e., the final stage). Each of these segments has six to eight processes. Tanning is basically converting animal hides (outer covering of cow, buffalo and calf) and skins (outer covering of sheep and goat) into leather. The quality of leather products

82

critically depends on the quality of tanning. However, the activities relating to the processing of leather generate pollution, particularly in the tanning and finishing stages of the production chain and hence, the firms have to bear increasing costs of production for undertaking pollution abating activities and/or relocating their establishments. There are however, some favourable factors also. As we have already explored to some extent in footnote, major world tanning firms are in the process of shifting their manufacturing base to developing countries due to high wage levels and strict environmental norms in the developed countries. Factors such as sufficient availability of raw leather and cheap skilled labour with their long experience in the technical know-how of production and processing of leather items-all work in India's favour. Further, given that the Indian leather footwear industry is still dominated by household and small- scale sectors, more corporate presence may enhance the possibility of turning out quality leather products at smaller unit cost. All this presents a large scope of expansion before the Indian leather industry. The Leather Industry holds a prominent place in the Indian economy. This sector is known for its consistency in high export earnings and it is among the top ten foreign exchange earners for the country. With an Annual turnover of over US$ 7.5 billion, the export of leather and leather products touched US$ 4.86 billion in 2011-12, recording a cumulative annual growth rate of about 8.22% (5 years).The Leather footwear industry is bestowed with an affluence of raw materials as India is endowed with 21% of world cattle & buffalo and 11% of world goat & sheep population. Added to this are the strengths of skilled manpower, innovative technology, increasing industry compliance to international environmental standards, and the dedicated support of the allied industries.

The leather footwear industry is an employment intensive sector, providing job to about 2.5 million people, mostly from the weaker sections of the society. Women employment is predominant in leather products sector with about 30% share. Though India is the second largest producer of footwear and leather garments in the world, India accounts for a share of close to 3% in the global leather import trade of US$ 137.96 billion (2010).The major production centers for leather and leather products in India are located in Tamil Nadu - Chennai, Ambur, Ranipet, Vaniyambadi, Vellore, Pernambut, Trichy, Dindigul and Erode ; West Bengal – Kolkata ; Uttar Pradesh – Kanpur, Agra,

Noida, Saharanpur; Maharashtra – Mumbai ; Punjab – Jallandhar ; Karnataka – Bangalore ; Andhra Pradesh - Hyderabad ; Haryana - Ambala, Gurgaon, Panchkula, Karnal and Faridabad; Delhi; Madhya Pradesh – Dewas ; Kerala – Calicut and Ernakulam / Cochin

3.23 Production Trend of Leather products

Tanning Sector – Annual production 2 billion Sq.ft. Accounts for 10% of world leather requirement. Indian colors continuously being selected at the MODEUROPE Congress

Footwear Sector – Second largest footwear producer after China. Annual Production 2065 million pairs. Huge domestic retail market 1950 million pairs (95%) are sold in domestic market. Footwear export accounts for 42.67% share in India's total leather & leather products export. The Footwear product mix Gents 54%, Ladies 37% and Children 9%

Leather Garments Sector – Second largest producer with annual production capacity of 16 million pieces. Third largest global exporter. Accounts for 11.76% share of India's total leather export

Leather Goods & Accessories Sector including Saddlery & Harness – Fifth largest global exporter. Annual production capacity – 63 million pieces of leather articles, 52 million pairs of Industrial gloves & 12.50 million pieces of Harness & Saddlery items. Accounts for 24.56% share of India's total export

3.24 Major Leather Exports Nations

The major markets for Indian Leather & Leather Products are Germany with a share of 15.01%, UK 11.15%, Italy 10.85%, USA 9.02%, Hong Kong 7.38%, France 6.25%, Spain 6.08%, Netherlands 4.07%, Belgium 2.32%, China 2.54%, U.A.E.2.24%, Australia 1.39%,

Table 3.1 Leather Industries in India: Small Scale and Large Scale

	Small Scale	Large Scale	Total	Percentage
Tamil Nadu	536	41	577	53.3
West Bengal	227	6	233	21.5
Uttar Pradesh	140	7	147	13.6
Andhra Pradesh	18	5	23	2.1
Maharashtra	27	3	30	2.8
Karnataka	15	1	16	1.5
Punjab	8	3	11	1
Other States	37	9	46	4.2
Total	1,008	75	1,083	100

The annual output of the tanning industry grew to 1,800 million sq. ft (162 million sq. m) of finished leathers by 1995. A considerable portion of this was exported. Table gives the export volume of the industry. Of the 1,083 tanneries in India, more than half, i.e. 577 are in Tamil Nadu and of the 577, Chennai City and the North Arcot district account for as many as 397 tanneries. The production in Tamil Nadu is 44% of the total all-India production. Over 66% of the total production in Tamil Nadu is from the Chennai and North Arcot regions. The data regarding the number of tanneries relates to the year 1990. Since most of the tanneries are in the small-scale sector, they are often not registered with any statutory authority. Authentic figures later than those given here were not immediately available.

Table:3.2 Export Volume of the Leather Industry in India

	2007-08	2008-09	2009-10	2010-11	2011-12
Finished Leather	807.19	673.37	627.95	841.13	1023.21
Footwear	1489.35	1534.32	1507.59	1758.67	2077.27
Leather Garments	345.34	426.17	428.62	425.04	572.54
Leather Goods	800.46	873.44	757.02	855.78	1088.09
Saddlery & Harness	106.18	92.15	83.39	87.92	107.6
Total	3548.51	3599.46	3404.57	3968.54	4868.71
% Growth	15.99%	1.44%	-5.41%	16.57%	22.68%

3.25 Changes in women work participation in India and Tamil Nadu from 1983-84 to 2009-10- A overview

The politico-legal, social and economic changes that have taken place during the past decades have definitely brought about perceptible changes in the status of women in the country. Many of these changes have been strongly in a positive direction, such as rapid increase in female literacy rate, participation in political and social activities, and increasing awareness about rights and access to productive resources. Some developments have been retrograde in nature, such as declining trend in sex ratio and increasing violence against women, while many other changes, mainly the role of women in the household and in economy, has not been adequately captured in the statistical system of the country. Most of these changes have also not been uniformly dispersed in the country. Wide ranging variations are existing between and within states which cannot be explained simply by any single factor like economic standards or better governance or delivery of services.

The role of women in and outside the home has become an important feature of the social and economic life of the country. Women in our country share too many responsibilities and perform a wide variety of duties in running the family, maintaining the household, attending to labour and domestic animals and extending a helping hand in artisanship and handicrafts. But most of the times her participation in works is considered as unpaid. Her role has never been evaluated as such in real economic terms.

An important reason for neglecting female employment as a specific category either in research or policy is the 'invisibility' of their economic contribution, especially in the rural areas, and traditional interpretations of such concepts as 'work', 'economic activities', productivities, and work place. At different points of time the data collecting agencies have introduced changes in concepts related with female work participation. Thus now a number of jobs, which were earlier unnoticeable and unpaid, are now considered as paid jobs. Women in large numbers have joined the labour force and taken up paid employment. Though the trend was first visible in western industrialized nations, many of the developing nations have also witnessed significant growth in female labour force participation. Participation of women in the labour force has increased world-wide during the past few decades. In developed countries it increased from around 38 percent in 1970's to around 45 percent in 1990's and in developing countries it increased from around 20 percent to around 30 percent. Women face major challenges as a result of changes in the world economy arising from rapid globalisation, fast-paced technological progress and a growing informalisation of work. As a result, women's labour market status has greatly altered. Although women's representation in the labour force is increasing all over the world still it is much lower to that of men's, and they are disproportionately represented in non- standard and lower-paid forms of work, such as temporary and casual employment, part- time jobs, home-based work, self-employment and work in micro enterprises. They are characterized by lack of security, lack of benefits and low income. The informal sector is a larger source of employment for women than to men. More women than before are in the labour force throughout their reproductive years, though obstacles to combining family responsibilities with employment persist. Women, especially younger women, experience more unemployment and for a longer period of time than men .Women remain at the lower end of a segregated labour market and continue to be concentrated in a few occupations, to hold positions of little or no authority and to receive less pay than men. Available statistics are still far from providing a strong basis for assessing both quantitative and qualitative changes in women's employment. (United Nations Report,2000).[14]

---

[14] UNDP (2003): Human Development Report

3.26 Women work force participation Rate

Since the 1980s there has been a near-consistent decline in workforce participation rate (WPR) of women. Even more remarkably, in the latter half of 2000s (i.e. between 2004-05 and 2009-10) both the labour force participation rate (LFPR) and workforce participation rate (WPR) of women has declined sharply, as a result of which the total LFPR and WPR of the population has declined. Male LFPR and WPR has pretty much remained constant over the same period (LFPR for males was 55.1% and WPR was 55%). The sharp decline in female labour force participation has happened in both rural and urban areas, though the decline is much sharper in rural compared to urban areas. This suggests strongly that in both urban and rural areas girls over 14 years of age (i.e. of working age) are remaining in school, more than ever before. As a result, the LFPR of women in India, which is already low by Asian standards, has fallen further. However, this decline should be seen in a positive light precisely because it suggests that girls, after completing elementary schooling are making the transition to secondary schooling in much larger numbers than ever before. In other words, these girls will be available to enter the workforce at a slightly later age better qualified than an earlier cohort. Since they will be better educated they are likely to be able to make the transition out of agriculture into non-agricultural employment, even though it may be in the unorganized sector. Given the fact that the female employment is even more concentrated in informal work than male employment outside of agriculture, their greater participation in schooling indeed is a positive development. However, the much higher rate of education participation of girls augurs well for improvement in their labour force participation. The most serious problem that women in the work force face is that it is not 'decent work'. For the vast majority of women in non-agricultural employment they tend to work from home in home-based work, usually subcontracted to them by male contractors in a variety of low-productivity work (e.g., bidi-making, zari-making, etc) in 1999-2000 the NSS Round had estimated that 29 million in the country were making as home-workers;

assuming that such women live in a family of five members, a total of 150 million persons are at least part-dependent upon this kind of work.

As per UPSS approach, 104.5 million women in rural areas and 22.8 million in urban areas were in the workforce in 2009-10. This implied decline in women workforce vis-à-vis 2004-05 when 124 million rural and 24.6 million urban women were working. The NSS 66th round has indicated that an estimated 84.79 million women in rural areas were neither working nor available for work as they attended educational institutions (as per the UPSS approach) in 2009-10. Similarly, in urban areas, 33.88 million women were neither working nor available for work as they attended educational institutions.In the rural areas, women are mainly involved as cultivators and agricultural labourers. In the urban areas, almost 80 per cent of the women workers are working in the unorganized sectors such as household industries, petty trades and services, buildings and construction. The khadi and village industries are one of the largest employers of women workers. Casualisation among women workers is rising. During the period 2004-05 to 2009-10, the proportion of casual workers among rural females increased from 32.6% to 39.9% and among urban females from 16.7% to 19.6%. The corresponding figures are 32.9% and 38% for rural males and 14.6% and 17% for urban males for the years 2004-05 and 2009-10 respectively.

One of the major aims of implementation of economic reforms was to generate higher rates of economic growth. Economic growth does not necessarily lead to reduction in gender inequalities. The female work force participation rate in India is not only low, but also has remained near-stagnant over the past several decades. Moreover, there still exists a large difference between the work participation rates of males and females, which is an important aspect of gender inequality. Besides, differences in the nature of work performed also bear evidence to gender inequality. Women are largely confined to unpaid work (at home or in the field) and casual labour, while men concentrate on more valued forms of remunerative work.

3.27 Industry-WiseClassificationofFemaleEmployment

Over the time women's work participation in primary sector has declined but still it is much higher than that of secondary and tertiary sectors. The loss of FWP in primary sector is the gain of secondary and tertiary sectors. In developing countries, changes in employment opportunities for women in the service sector are linked to globalization. New employment created in service sector spreads across both low and high skilled works. This has a two-fold effect on women's employment opportunities. One, new jobs are being created in information-based industries which use telecommunications infrastructure. They employ cheap, educated female workers in developing countries for operations such as data processing; and two, globalisation has facilitated the establishments of branches of service sector multinational corporations in developing countries, such as banks and insurance companies catering to the needs of consumers, and specialist producer services (e.g., accounting, legal services). The rapidly expanding international financial service sector employs a high proportion of female workers in particular with respect to lower skill application as such as data entry. Higher skill services such as software design, computer programming and financial services (banking and insurance) are also being relocated to developing countries and employ a relatively high proportion of women even at a higher grade (Rodgers Janine, 2001). The rapid expansion of trade and foreign investment flows has also an impact on the circulation of people. Nearly as many women as men migrate across international borders. This increase has been driven by a growing demand for a few activities such as domestic services, tourism etc. The international demand for unskilled labour has been partly filled by educated women. The important indicator of empowerment of women is their participation in economic activities. The female work participation rate in the work-force has been changing in India overtime. This can be highlighted by referring to the comparative situation of the female work-force in those sectors of the economy which have traditionally been the prerogative of the females rather than of the males. The focus of this section is on the level of female work participation in economic activities, diversification of female employment in agriculture, industry and service sector, and to examine the growth rates of female employment in different sectors over the pre- and post-reform periods in both the rural and urban areas.

The analysis is based on entirely on the data on occupational structure of population of the 1983 to 2009-2010 Here the two periods are covered, viz., 1983 to 1993-94 (pre-reform period) and 1993-94 to 2009-10 (post-reform period). The post-reform period is further divided into two sub-periods i.e. 1993-94 to 1999-00 (first sub period), 1999-00 to 2009-10 (second sub period). The changes have been observed on the basis of pre-reform and post-reform WPRs in All India and Tamil Nadu, chosen on the basis of their ranks in Human Development Report 2001.

3.28 An Industry-Wise Classification of Usual Status Female Workers in India:

Globalisation and trade liberalization has provided greater avenues of employment in general; at the same time it has changed the structural scenario of employment. Globalisation and other related developments have been accompanied by marginalization and casualisation of female workforce, and it has pushed them in relatively less paid and part time work conditions. Increasing mechanization has dampening impact on female employment; as whenever labour becomes surplus and the process of retrenchment starts the first casualty is child labour and then axe is on female labour. Rural, poor and lower cast females placed in relatively lower hierarchy and suffer the most in the process. On the demand side, the structural transformation of the economy, wherein agriculture, which is the major source of employment for females, has been losing importance and have reducing the demand for female labour. Changing sectoral composition of the workforce particularly that of females has been attributed to various reseasons. Table demonstrates the distribution of usual status female workers in India by region during 1983 to 2004-05.A perusal of the data shows that in India, rural female work participation (RFWP) in primary sector declined from 87.8 per cent in 1983 to 86.6 per cent in 1993-94 and further to 81.1 per cent in 2009-10.

Sector Description	Rural					Urban				
	1983	1993-	1999-	2004	2009-	1983	1993-	1999-	2004-	200*
Primary Sector	87.8	86.6	85.7	83.6	81.1	31.6	25.3	18.1	18.3	18.6
Agriculture	87.5	86.2	85.4	83.3	80.2	31	24.7	17.7	18.1	17.1
Mining and	0.3	0.4	0.3	0.3	0.3	0.6	0.6	0.4	0.2	0.2
Secondary Sector	7.1	8	8.7	9.9	10.3	30	28.5	29	32.2	33.9
Manufacturing	6.4	7	7.6	8.4	8.2	26.7	24.1	24	28.2	29.1
Public Utilities	_	0.1				0.2	0.3	0.2	0.2	0.2
Construction	0.7	0.9	1.1	1.5	1.9	3.1	4.1	4.8	3.8	3.4
Tertiary Sector	5	5.4	5.8	6.6	6.9	37.6	46.3	52.9	49.5	51.3
Trade, Hotelling, etc	1.9	2.1	2	2.5	2.9	9.5	10	16.9	12.2	13.1
Transport,	0.1	0	0.1	0.2	0.2	1.5	1.3	1.8	1.4	1.6
Financial,	0	0	0.1	0.1	0.1	1.3	1.9	2.5	3.2	3.6
Community, Social	3	3.3	3.6	3.8	4.2	25.3	33.1	31.7	32.7	33.7

Source: N.S.S.O Reports of 38th, 50th, 55th 61st and 66st Rounds

With the development of agricultural economy and other economic activities, the demand for women's labour in both the agricultural and non-agricultural industries has been on the rise. Women may work on the farms owned by them or on family farms or as tenants or wage earners and as such they form a large proportion of agricultural workers. In recent times, in agriculture sector, men have taken over women those activities in which technology has substituted machinery for manual labour. All other labour intensive tasks are left to women. One of the reasons of decline in FWP in agriculture is the changes in the cropping pattern that have displaced a large number of female workers from agriculture, and as a result, the share of female workforce in the agriculture sector has declined (Mazumdar 2006)[15]. The decline in agricultural activities in urban India is more than that of rural India. In rural India the proportion of female workers in mining and quarrying has remained almost same over the period 1983 to 2009-10 at 0.3

---

[15] Mazumdar, Deepak (2006): "Impact of globalization on women workers in garment exports: The Indian experience"; Mimeo, Centre for Women's Development Studies, New Delhi.

per cent. The loss of primary sector female workers is gained by secondary and tertiary sectors in both the periods. In rural secondary sector, FWPR increased by 0.9 percentage points and in tertiary sector by 0.4 percentage points during pre-reform period and in post-reform period further secondary sector FWPR increased by 1.9 percentage points and tertiary sector by 1.0 percentage points. It is clear that in both the periods rural female workers have shifted from primary sector to more in secondary sector and less in tertiary sector. On the other side during the period of 1983 to 1993-94 dependence of urban female workers in primary sector reduced from 31.6 percen t to 25.3 per cent and in secondary sector from 30.0 per cent to 28.5 per cent for the staid period. It makes clear that in pre-reform period declined percentage of urban female workers in primary and secondary sectors absorbed by tertiary sector only but in post-reform period (1993-94 to 2009-10) declined percentage of primary sector female workers shared by both the secondary and tertiary sectors with a small difference. Although women in urban areas enjoy better health and better education than their rural counterparts, but their participation in work force is much lower to rural areas. Some of this rural/urban discrepancy is due to the greater importance of subsistence production and the potential of women to work as unpaid family labour in the agrarian society.

Fewer women are economically active in the urban areas because the barriers to be crossed to enter the urban labour force need mobility, modern skills and the ability to line into non-traditional work situations. Since women are at a disadvantage in all these areas; this may well constraint to their work force participation.

Diversion of female work participation from the primary to other sectors is visible, which indicate that women are able to take advantage of the increased employment opportunities in secondary and tertiary sectors. The analysis shows that in post-reform period percentage increase in female work participation is higher in secondary sector than to tertiary sector in both the areas.

One reason for high difference in rural and urban FWPRs is that in rural areas women are generally engaged in household activities such as bearing and rearing of children and in the production of goods and services for self household consumption. Therefore, women's work at home remains unrecognized unless it produces something for sale. But due to the changes in the definition of FWP, now females considered as worker who make significant contribution in the agricultural operations like sowing, harvesting, transplantation, tending cattle and even cooking and delivering food to the farm during the agriculture operation. Therefore, work force participation rate in rural areas has increased. However, in urban areas women do not have any opportunity for such work.

Rural female work participation in manufacturing shows increase by 2 percentage points from 6.4 per cent in 1983 to 8.2 per cent in 2009-10.Female participation in public utilities and in construction, in 2004-05 increased to double that of 1983. It expanded from 0.7 per cent in 1983 to 1.5 per cent in 2009-10. Community services and trade show some increase in FWPR. One can easily find out that in rural India, during the period 1983 to 2009-10, FWPR has declined in agriculture only by 4.2 percentage points. Whereas an increase has been observed in manufacturing sector and followed by construction, trade and community services. Rest of the activities have shown no or negligible increase. On the other hand in urban India, FWP in agriculture declined near to half during 1983 to 2009-10. In both the periods the percentage decline has remained almost same. It declined from 31.0 per cent in 1983 to 18.1 per cent in 2009-10.Rest of the industries show increase in urban FWPRs. FWPR in pre-reform period does not show any change in mining and quarrying and in public utilities. In secondary sector manufacturing is the most important activity in urban areas. Secondary sector has shown consistent increase in FWPR i.e. from 28.5 per cent in 1993-94 to 29.0 per cent in 1999-00 and then to 33.9 per cent in 2009-10, Manufacturing sector shows a decline from 26.7 per cent in 1983 to 24.1 per cent in 1993-94 but after that there was sharp increase in this from 24.0 per cent to 29.1 per cent in 2009-10 and transportation shows negligible decline during the same period. Community services show increase from 25.3 per cent in 1983 to 33.1 per cent in 1993-94 but in post- reform period it declined to 32.7 per cent. Post-reform period shows decline in FWP in mining and quarrying, public utilities, construction, and community services. The industries where FWPR has moved up are manufacturing, trade, transportation and financial services.

It explains that in pre-reform period rural females were moving from agriculture to manufacturing mainly and in post-reform period shift is towards manufacturing, construction, trade and in community services. In urban India, in pre-reform period trend in FWP was from agriculture to community services, and little bit towards construction, trade and financial services. But in post-reform period the trend observed is from agriculture, mining and quarrying, construction and community services to manufacturing, trade and financial services. However, there are immense possibilities for diversification in agricultural sector towards more value added activities such as food processing. This is an area, which has by and large remained unexploited, because reforms in agriculture sector having been very slow, resources have not yet started flowing into food processing industries. Involvement of state governments in implementing reforms in agriculture and food processing sectors is of crucial importance. Economic returns from states initiatives in transforming the rural economy from traditional agriculture to more value added activities in horticulture, etc. has been demonstrated well in some of the states, such as Maharashtra and Himachal Pradesh. Besides the diversification of agriculture into processing activities, the small and medium industries can provide work opportunities to replace those lost in agriculture. But in manufacturing sector there are two extremes in regard to size of establishments. Either there are very large establishments, highly organised, or there are very small establishments, which are in the informal sector. Rural poor females of the poor states cannot afford to be out of job market. Since they supplement their family income by seeking self employment. On the other hand in the richer states as the income level goes higher, they withdraw their females from low paid and other agricultural activities and join non-farm job and activities, which tend to be generally regular. It is hereby suggested that skill formation, rather than literacy can positively contribute towards increasing female work participation in formal and organized sector

Workers in India by Residence:

Table .3.4 Annual Compound Growth Rate of Usual Status Female Workers in India by Place of Residence and Industry: 1983 to 2009-10

(per cent)

Sector Description	Rural					Urban				
	1983 to 1993-94	1993-94 to 1999-2000	1999-00 to 2009-10	1993-94 to 2009-10	1983 to 2009-10	1983 to 1993-94	1993-94 to 1999-2000	1999-00 to 2009-10	1993-94 to 2009-10	1983 to 2009-10
Primary Sector	1.53	0.04	2.16	1.49	1.96	1.32	-3.5	4.34	0.28	1.01
Agriculture	1.52	0.05	2.16	1.5	1.96	1.27	-3.48	4.51	0.4	1.07
Mining and Quarrying	4.64	-3.49	2.52	-0.91	2.27	3.59	-4.38	-5.44	-6.81	-2.44
Secondary Sector	2.89	1.27	4.39	3.9	4.44	3.06	1.01	5.72	4.6	5.02
Manufacturing	2.58	1.25	3.96	3.6	4.04	2.54	0.73	6.56	4.95	4.91
Public	-	-	-	-	-	7.88	-4.38	4.18	-0.49	4.55

Utilities										
Construction	4.26	2.82	7.06	6.87	7.3	6.53	2.87	0.84	2.66	5.9
Tertiary Sector	3.06	0.87	4.39	3.6	4.34	5.77	2.54	3.22	4.06	6.38
Trade, Hotelling,etc	2.69	-0.46	5.77	3.52	4.05	4.13	7.88	-0.46	5.37	6.21
Transport, Communicati on	-	-	12.95		6.83	2.12	5.13	0.59	4.13	4.1
Financial,	-	-	2.52	-	-	7.6	4.44	7.84	8.63	10.65
Community,	2.64	1.31	3.3	3.2	3.81	6.42	0.22	4.64	3.28	6.25

Table 3.4. shows the compound growth rates of female employment by region for the overall period, viz. 1983 to 2009-10 and for the sub periods viz, 1983 to 1993-94, 1993-94 to 1999-00, 1999-00 to 2009-10 and 1993-94 to 2009-10. It shows that annual compound growth rate of female workers in primary sector in case of both the rural and urban India in post-reform period was 1.49 per cent and 0.28 per cent respectively, which are lesser than that, observed in the pre- reform period i.e. 1.53 per cent and 1.32 per cent.Growth rates in secondary sector increased in both the areas by greater margins in post-reform period. But in tertiary sector, the increase in average annual compound growth rates observed was only in rural areas. It increased from 3.06 per cent to 3.60 per cent in post-reform period. But at urban level it declined from 5.77 per cent to 4.06 per cent for said period.

A notable feature of the first half of the post-reform period (1993-94 to 1999-00) is the very less growth rates of female employment in all the three sectors in both the rural and urban India. The second-half has shown very good growth rates as compared to first-half. The rates increased to 2.16 per cent, 4.39 per cent and 4.39 per cent respectively in rural areas and 4.34 per cent, 5.72 per cent and 3.22 per cent respectively for urban areas.Annual compound growth rates of employment in primary sector in both the areas have remained less as compared to secondary and tertiary sectors during all the periods. It may be due to the very slow speed of implementation of policies in agriculture sector. Secondly this sector by and large has remained unexploited. Women are worst affected by mechanization in agriculture. The employment of manual workers is reduced and is displaced by workers who run the machines. In these cases the total number of jobs is reduced drastically. Moreover women are generally replaced by men. But diversification of agriculture into processing activities up to some extent has increased the employment opportunities in primary sector in post-reform period. The compound growth rates of rural female workers in agriculture in pre and post reform periods have remained almost same i.e. 1.50 per cent and 1.52 per cent but it declined in urban areas from 1.27 per cent in pre-reform period to 0.40 in post-reform period. In mining and quarrying, compound growth rate was high i.e. 4.64 per cent in pre- reform period but entered in negative territory (-0.91 per cent) in post-reform period.

Among manufacturing, construction, trade and community services, construction industry shows maximum growth from 4.26 per cent in pre-reform period to 6.87 per cent in post-reform period. Rest of the three industries show increase of almost 1 percentage point. In rural India, in pre-reform period construction and mining and quarrying were showing highest growth rates but in post-reform period only construction activity has shown good results. But in urban India, construction sector growth rate of female employment declined from 6.53 per cent during 1983 to 1993-94 to 2.66 during 1993-94 to 2009-10 and the other industries where highest decline in post-reform period in urban areas have been recorded are community services and mining and quarrying. The compound growth rate of mining and quarrying, manufacturing, trade has increased to almost double. It has been seen that the process of structural transformation of the rural work force that was steadily tilting in favor of non-agricultural jobs during the decade preceding economic reforms, for both regions in most of the states, got reversed in some states. Secondly irrespective of the structural shifts that took place during pre-and post 1993 periods, in most of the states, agriculture continued to be the main stay for rural female workers. Work opportunities that are lost in traditional agriculture have to be replaced by work opportunities in some other sectors. In the normal course it is the secondary sector (manufacturing, electricity and construction) that grow much faster than agriculture during transition of an economy. However, in the post reform period the growth of manufacturing industries has been constrained by opening up of trade and removing the quantitative restrictions on imports. There by the local producer could not compete with the unprecedented inflow of imports from abroad.

3.29 An Industry Wise Classification of Usual Status Female Workers in Tamil Nadu:

In Tamil Nadu, where economic growth rate is higher than all India and where women are relatively more educated, experience the lowest female work participation among the major states in India, especially among the educated. The work participation rate indicates to a great extent the economic empowerment of women in the society. The status of women is intimately connected with their economic position, which in turn depends on opportunities of participation in economic activities.

Within India, the state Tamil Nadu has carved out a separate position for itself in development discourse due to its impressive performance over the years on the demographic and social development front. Much has been written about Tamil Nadu's high level of female literacy, high level of life expectancy, low infant mortality and cohesive social structure promoting effective interpersonal channels of communication. However it is certainly paradoxical that, in such a society well acknowledged for according higher status and position to women, participation of the women in the labour force has not been satisfactory. Such a paradox deserves close scrutiny.Tamil Nadu is a state that reports for the highest level of unemployment in the country and the incidence of unemployment is particularly seen among women. A careful examination of the employment structure, sectoral and gender composition, and occupational distribution would better reflect the well-being of the economy.

Table :3.5 Nine- Industry Classification of Usual Status Female Workers in Tamil Nadu by Area of Residence: 1983 to 2009-10 (per cent)

	Rural					Urban			
	198	1993	1999	2004-	2009-	1983	1993-	1999-00	2004-05
Primary Sector	71	63.4	60.6	51.9	48.2	42.9	33.7	14.8	19.8
Agriculture	70.	63	59.8	51.7	46.1	42.5	33.3	14.6	19.8
Mining and Quarrying	0.6	0.4	0.8	0.2	0.2	0.4	0.4	0.2	0
Secondary Sector	17.	21.4	22	22.8	23.9	23.1	28.7	29.3	26.5
Manufacturing	17.	19.2	19.3	20.9	22.1	20.7	25.1	27.2	23.4
Public Utilities	-	0.1	0	0.2	0.2	0.8	0.6	0.2	0.2
Construction	0.5	2.1	2.7	1.7	2.1	1.5	3	2.1	2.9
Tertiary Sector	10.	15.1	17.5	25.3	28.2	33.4	37.5	55.7	53.6
Trade, Hotelling,etc	2	3.6	3.7	5.2	6.1	4.9	6.5	25.1	11.5
Transport,	0.6	0.4	0.2	1.4	1.8	3.1	1	1.8	1.7
Financial,	0.2	0.5	1.1	1.6	1.9	1.2	1.6	3.7	5.2
Community, Social	7.8	10.6	12.5	17.1	19.2	24.2	28.4	25.1	35.2

Table 3.4 demonstrates the distribution of usual status female workers in Tamil Nadu during 1983 to 2009-10. In Tamil Nadu the female workers dependence for employment on the primary sector witnessed a steady decline during all the periods. Comparatively more decline has been observed in post-reform period. The rural female work participation in primary sector declined from 71.0 per cent in 1983 to 63.4 per cent

in 1993-94 and further to 48.9 per cent in 2009-10. In rural secondary sector FWP accelerated from 17.8 per cent in 1983 to 21.4 per cent in 1993-94 to 22.8 per cent in 2004-05 and further to 20.1 in 2009-10 the corresponding values in tertiary sector have been continuously increasing since 1983.It increased from 10.6 per cent to 15.1 per cent 25.3 per cent and 28.1 for said period. It is clear that as compare to post-reform period, secondary sector was more favorable for female employment in pre- reform period. In post-reform period, most of the female workers have been shifted to tertiary sector. Same trend has been observed at the urban level.

Urban female work participation in primary sector declined from 42.9 per cent in 1983 to 19.8 per cent 1n 2009-10, total decline of 23.1 percentage points which were gained by both the secondary and tertiary sectors. But major share of 20.3 percentage points absorbed by tertiary sector. In urban tertiary sector more increase in FWP has been recorded in post-reform period. Changes in the sectoral distribution of female work force in Tamil Nadu clearly shows that the structural transformation of women's economic activity has indeed taken place in the state with primary sector losing its importance and tertiary sector taking up its place. These had further led to the intensification of unemployment in the state, more so among the educated females.

As analysis shows, limiting of options has been more severe for the women in Tamil Nadu. The decline of traditional industries in Tamil Nadu, which were dominated by women, has also contributed to the loss of female jobs. The increase in the number of women workers in the service sector in Tamil Nadu has largely occurred in the teaching and clerical occupations, which can, however, absorb only the higher educated among the female labour force.

Tamil Nadu, which ranks third among the Indian States in terms of Human Development Index (HDI) and Gender Development Index (GDI), presents, however, a poor picture in terms of female work participation. Radha Devi (1981) studied the extent of female participation in economic activity in the state and the occupational pattern among them. She found that women in Tamil Nadu are primarily engaged in skilled or semi-skilled vocations and level of education among working-women is much higher than the rest of the women. Again, marriage and family was found not to affect the work participation rate but family disruption due to divorce or separation did. Kumar (1994)

101

had pointed out the nature of the economic structure in the state, which has shown reduced demand for female labour, and losses in the primary and secondary sector that has not been offset by the service sector.

Theoretically, it is natural for economic activity among women to follow a U-shaped curve along the course of development. In the initial stages of development, when society is primarily agrarian, increased demand of female labour leads to higher workforce participation among women. Industrialization gives rise to greater demand for skilled labour, and as a consequence involves displacement of women labour and its substitution by male labour. It is only in the later stages of development, as a consequence of the emergence and expansion of tertiary sector; demand for women labour is renewed. However, it is felt that it is not going to follow exactly the same pattern in Tamil Nadu. Although women labour has been systematically displaced from agriculture and household industry, their traditional sectors of employment, growth of tertiary sector, mainly manifest in the proliferation of service sector, has not been able to entirely absorb the redundant female labour.

There has also been significant change in perceptions about jobs among the educated women, even in rural areas also. As a natural corollary of spread of education and social progress, an increased number of women now aspire for salaried jobs, preferably government jobs or even economically less rewarding private jobs, as compared to getting employed in either fields or factories. According to NSS round 1999-00 data the percentage of women in paid jobs in the state is slightly less than 23 percent. This is much less than the work participation rate of women in other Indian states with far lower levels of literacy. For example states like Madhya Pradesh, Gujarat, Karnataka and Maharashtra with around 50 percent female literacy rate, report double the female work participation rate of Tamil Nadu. Data from NSSO survey (1999-00) show that the proportion of jobless women in Tamil Nadu is ten times the national average.

Marked improvement in the educational and training accomplishments of women in Tamil Nadu enables them to compete effectively in the labour market. Secondly due to high qualifications, women's aspirations and job expectations have changed, which induces the women to wait for better jobs than to unwanted casual works. In Tamil Nadu rural FWP in agriculture has been continuously declining since 1983. It declined from

70.4 per cent in 1983 to 63.0 per cent in 1993-9 to 51.7 per cent in 2004-05 further deteriorated to 46.1 in 2009-10. In all the industries where FWP has declined is remained higher in post-reform period except transportation and community services. Maximum increase in rural FWP in pre-reform period was observed in manufacturing and community services. Those have increased from 17.3 per cent and 7.8 per cent to 19.2 per cent and 10.6 per cent respectively. In post-reform period, FWP in mining and quarrying further declined to 0.2 per cent, and in trade FWP increased from 3.6 per cent to 5.2 per cent. In urban Tamil Nadu in pre-reform period share of agricultural female workers declined from 42.5 per cent to 33.3 per cent (1983 to 1993-94). In mining and quarrying, public utilities and in financial services share of female workers have shown very negligible changes for said period. But in manufacturing, construction, trade and community services FWP shows good increase in the range of 2 to 5 percentage points. In pre-reform period in urban Tamil Nadu, maximum increase in FWP took place in manufacturing and community services. But most of the sectors which were showing increase in FWPR in pre-reform period have shown decline or no change in post-reform period. In post-reform period trade, financial services and community services have shown higher increase in FWP as against manufacturing in pre-reform period. Thus it has seen that in post-reform period, urban female workers have been shifted from agriculture and manufacturing to trade, transport and other services.

The female workforce in the state has felt most of the damages because women have historically dominated in industries like coir, leather garments, cashew, beedi, and handloom and to some extent fish-processing. In connection with the fall in female employment in the household industry it is apparent that increase of capital-intensive technologies even within the domestic industries has forced out women workers gradually. High cost of labour on account of higher than national average labour wages, and resistance to technological up gradation due to fear of retrenchment, had paralysed both industrial and agricultural sectors alike, and uneconomic returns had caused industries to close down or migrate out of the state and shifting of cropping pattern in agriculture. In most of the cases, it was the women worker who was worse hit by these changes in Tamil Nadu.

3.30 Annual Compound Growth Rate of Employment for Usual Status Female Workers in Tamil Nadu by Residence:

One reason behind the paradox of low female employment and high social development is the development process in the state, which has remained largely irresponsive to the transition in the quality of the women workforce, as well as the overall occupational transformation in the state..

Table 3.6: Annual Compound Growth Rate of Usual Status Female Workers in Tamil Nadu by Place of Residence and Industry: 1983 to 2009-10

Sector Description	Rural					Urban				
	1983 to 1993-94	1993-94 to 1999-2000	1999-00 to 2009-10	1993-94 to 2009-10	1983 to 2009-10	1983 to 1993-94	1993-94 to 1999-2000	1999-00 to 2009-10	1993-94 to 2009-10	1983 to 2009-10
Primary Sector	-3.28	0.24	-	-0.1	-2.14	0.79	-9.53	4.55	-4.2	-2.33
Agriculture	-3.25	0.15	-	-0.08	-2.11	0.77	-9.55	4.75	-4.09	-2.27
Mining and	-6.06	10.31	-	-4.6	-6.86	0.98	-7.99			
Secondary Sector	-0.4	1.25	2.72	2.76	1.57	5.52	0.93	-1.01	-0.01	3.43
Manufacturing	-1.15	0.89	2.91	2.63	1	5.26	1.72	-1.7	0.08	3.34
Public Utilities	-	-	-	8.71	-	0.33	-12.71	0.38	-9.21	-6.03
Construction	12.92	4.17	-4.6	-0.21	7.8	10.67	-3.89	5.02	0.42	6.89
Tertiary Sector	1.35	2.77	7.15	6.9	5.43	4.49	5.96	-0.15	4.21	5.66
Trade, Hotelling,	3.75	1.18	6.73	5.41	6	6.21	19.94	-9.99	6.34	8.2
Transport,	-6.06	-7.84	33.5	14.63	5.28	-7.79	8.64	-0.41	5.93	-1.26
Financial,	7.21	11.68	7.25	13.66	13.7	6.27	12.22	5.28	12.64	12.46
Community, Social	0.87	3	6.33	6.52	4.86	4.92	-0.94	5.38	2.81	4.99

Table 3.5 depicts that in primary sector female employment growth rates in both the periods in both the areas remained negative except at urban level in pre-reform period, Rural secondary sector female employment growth rate increased from -0.40 per cent in 1983 to 1993-94 to 2.76 per cent during 1993-94 to 2009-10 and in rural tertiary sector from 1.35 per cent to 6.90 per cent but urban secondary sector growth rates of female employment declined from 5.52 per cent in pre-reform period to -0.01 per cent in post- reform period. Tertiary sector growth rates had shown a marginal decline from 4.49 per cent to 4.21 per cent. It is clear that growth rates of FWP in Tamil Nadu in post-reform period have improved in rural areas only and urban areas performance has shown a robust decline. Structural changes in the Indian economy, initiated under the New Economic Reforms in 1991, has set in motion of a transitory force within the economic system of the country but Tamil Nadu had not been immune to such forces. Much of these changes are believed to have profound implications for the levels and nature of employment or participation in economic activities, particularly for the women. It is apparent from available data that agriculture is no longer the surest channel of employment among the Kerallite women. In Tamil Nadu a structural transformation manifest in declining employment in agriculture, more pronounced for females, has been in process during the last decade, it appears that redundant female work force from rural areas might have joined the informal sector in urban areas, construction sector being the most important channel of such alternative employment. It also found that the negative compound growth rate of rural female workers in agriculture and mining and quarrying in both the periods. In pre-reform period at rural level the maximum growth took place in construction sector i.e. 12.92 per cent which entered into negative territory in post-reform period. At urban level the observed growth rates in construction was 10.67 per cent in pre-reform period which dropped to 0.42 per cent in post-reform period. Female workers compound growth rate in trade has remained same in both the periods around 6.25 per cent.It makes clear that in both the areas in pre-reform period construction industry was attracting the females more and in post-reform period transportation at rural level and financial services at urban level were more favourable for female employment.

106

3.31 Conclusion

The chapter laid a conceptual background of the study and further substantiated the same with some empirical verification which pertains to India and Tamil Nadu context. Further the chapter also demonstrated the various dimensions of the women workers in the Global and Indian scenario and the existing protective measures for women worers across the world.

CHAPTER IV

Profile of the study area

4.1 Introduction

This Chapter illustrates the profile of Chennai, which includes the socio, economic, climate, demographic, industrial information of the study area. As Chennai is the capital of the Tamil Nadu, the rich source of transportation, medical facilities and educational institutions and other well developed facilities are available, this chapter elaborately illustrates these facilities.

4.2 Location and Area

Tamil Nadu constitutes the south-eastern extremity of the Indian peninsula. Chennai is the capital city of the State, besides being an important district. The district city is one of the metropolises of India and serves as the gateway of the culture of South India. In spite of being the capital of a Tamil speaking State, it has emerged as a cosmopolitan city playing an important role in the historical, cultural and intellectual development of India, representing still the distinct components of the highest form of Dravidian Civilisation. In addition, it holds out an interesting fare of South Indian architecture, music, dance, drama, sculpture and other arts and crafts. Chennai is situated on the north-east end of Tamil Nadu on the coast of Bay of Bengal. It lies between 12* 9' and 13* 9' of the northern latitude and 80* 12' and 80* 19' of the southern longitude on a 'sandy shelving breaker swept beach'. It stretches nearly 25.60 kms. Along the bay coast from Thiruvanmiyur in the south to Thiruvottiyur in the north and runs inland in a rugged semi-circular fashion. It is bounded on the east by the Bay of Bengal and on the remaining three sides by Chengalpattu and Thiruvallur Districts.

4.3 Significance of Chennai

The city of Chennai came into being due to a strategic necessity and historical accident. It symbolizes the rise of British power in South India by setting up and consolidation of the East India Company in the seventeenth century with its headquarters at Fort St. George in Chennai as a trading centre. Within 350 years, a few scattered villages (important being Mylapore, Triplicane and Chennai Patnam) have developed into a modern metropolitan city without shedding its traditional customs, religious outlook and other traditions. It can be proudly remarked that the greatness of ancient Chennai is mostly religious due to the preservation of the old famous Saivaite and Vaishnavite shrines signifying the antiquity of the place. The growth of the city is significant and closely linked with the development of British Institutions and administration. In short, Chennai city was the chief centre from which the British rule expanded in the sub-continent and it remains a standing monument of British contribution to India. Chennai city has acted as an important centre of culture and education in South India and has been the cradle of many movements which have played an important role in the history of the sub-continent.

A large number of institutions which are known in India and abroad are found located in the city, of which mention may be made of the Theosophical Society, the Kalakshetra and colleges of Arts and Crafts. The establishment of professional colleges like Medical, Veterinary, Law and Teaching, the location of the Indian Institute of Technology and the establishment of Central Leather Research Institute have added to the development of the city. Chennai is one of the leading cities in India today from the point of view of trade and commerce, with the fourth largest port in the country and the first to have developed a full-fledged container terminal to international standards.

The city of Madras has now been renamed as Chennai. It is stated that the name Chennai traced its origin to "some other language". The rechristening of the city is part of the steps announced for the "growth of Tamil in various fields". There are different versions about the name of this once sleepy coastal village. When the British landed here in 1639 A.D. it was said to be part of the empire of the Raja of Chandragiri. The British named it Chennapattinam, after they acquired it from Chennappa Nayakar. Gradually, it became Chennai. The first instance of the use of the name Chennai is said to be in the Vestiges of Old Chennai, the sale deed of August 1639 to Francis Day, an agent for the British. There it has been referred to as Chennaipatnam. The British are said to have built Fort Saint George, the present seat of power, in 1640. It was named after the patron saint of England. The Vestiges of Old Chennai infer that the original village of Madraspatnam lay north of the proximate to Chennapattinam. In course of time and with rapid growth, the two virtually became one. It is also inferred that the English preferred the name Madraspatnam, while Indians chose Chennapattinam.

4.4 Geographical and Physical Features

Chennai is a low-lying area and the land surface is almost flat like a pancake. The even topography of the land throughout the district renders sub-divisions into natural regions rather difficult. It rises slightly as the distance from the sea-shore increases but the average elevation of the city is not more than 22' above mean seal-level, while most of the localities are just at sea-level and drainage in such areas remains a serious problem. From very early times, Chennai was known for its pleasant scenery and was said to be a town open to sky and full of garden of mangoes, coconuts, guavas, oranges, etc.

In earlier days when the city was not so congested, gardens and groves were a common feature and most of the roads were flanked by frequent groves of palm and other trees. Even a number of houses too had gardens displaying fine trees canopied by green bough and creepers, Chennai city today is devoid of any forest areas but can still be proud of some of the well maintained green belts found in the Peoples park, the Napier park, the Horticulture-gardens, My Lady's Park, Children's Park Guindy, Snake Park, Nehru Park, Nageswara Rao Park, Independence Park, Anna Square Park, the Raj Bhavan, the Theosophical Society Campus, and a number of bungalows and newly developed colonies where provisions of public parks, etc. have been provided. The indigenous trees found include among others neem, mango, tamarind, rain-tree, vagai, banyan, coconut, palm and pipal. Stretches of casuarina plantations are available on the sea-coast beyond the mouth of the Adyar in the South and Tondiarpet in the North, supplying firewood to the city. House gardening is not very common these days due to shortage of water and lack of space.

4.5 Rivers

The city is intersected by two languid streams, the Cooum and the Adyar. Cooum runs through the heart of the city and enters the sea in-between the university buildings and the Fort. St. George underneath the Napier Bridge, while the latter wends its way through the southern part of the city and enters the sea near Adyar. These two rivers are almost stagnant and do not carry enough water except during rainy seasons. Cooum River starts from Kesavaram Anicut in Kesavaram village built across Kortaliyar River. The surplus from Cooum tank joins this course at about 8 kms. Lower down and this point is actually the head of Cooum River which is located at 48 kms. West of Chennai. The river receives a sizeable quantity of sewage from its neighbourhood for disposal. Though the river Adyar can be traced to a point near Guduvancheri village, it assumes the appearance of a stream only after it receives the surplus water from the Chembarambakkam tank as wells as the drainage of the areas in the south-west of Chennai. The river has no commercial importance, but the fishermen in the neighbourhood make their living by fishing in the river.

4.6 Canals

The Buckingham canal which runs through the states of Tamil Nadu and Andhra Pradesh is a navigation canal. This canal runs almost parallel to the Coromandal coast within the limits of 5 kms. From the coast. It joins up a series of natural backwaters and connects all the coastal districts from Guntur to South Arcot. Entering the city at Tondiarpet in the north and running along the western outskirts of George Town, it joins the new canal, south-west of General Hospital. The other canal worth mentioning in the city is the Otteri Nullah which commences from the village Mullam, runs eastwards upto Purasawalkam and then passes through Buckingham and Carnatic Mills and finally joins the Buckingham Canal, north of Basin Bridge Railway Station. Chennai has 25.60 kms. of sea coast which is flat and sandy for about a km. from the shore. The bed of the sea is about 42' deep and slopes further in gradual stages for a distance of about 5 kms. from the coast attaining a depth of about 63'. The two principal currents, first from the north and second from the south flow parallel to the coast. The former sets in about the middle of October and continue till February while the latter starts by about August and continues till the burst of the north-east monsoon in the middle of October. These two principal currents must be caused by the winds.

4.7 History of Chennai

Chennai, originally known as Madras Patnam, was located in the province of Tondaimandalam, an area lying between Pennar river of Nellore and the Pennar river of

Cuddalore. The capital of the province was Kancheepuram.Tondaimandalam was ruled in the 2nd century A.D. by Tondaiman Ilam Tiraiyan, who was a representative of the Chola family at Kanchipuram. It is believed that Ilam Tiraiyan must have subdued Kurumbas, the original inhabitants of the region and established his rule over Tondaimandalam. Subsequent to Ilam Tiraiyan, the region seemed to have been ruled by the Chola Prince Ilam Killi.The Chola occupation of Tondaimandalam was put to an end by the Andhra Satavahana incursions from the north under their King Pulumayi II. They appointed chieftains to look after the Kancheepuram region. Bappaswami, who is considered as the first Pallava to rule from Kancheepuram, was himself a chieftain (of the tract round) at Kancheepuram under the Satavahana empire in the beginning of the 3rd century A.D., The Pallavas who had so far been merelyviceroys, became independent rulers of Kancheepuram and its surrounding areas.Pallavas held sway over this region from the beginning of the 3rd century A.D.to the closing years of the 9th century except for the interval of some decades when the region was under Kalabharas. Pallavas were defeated by the Chola under Aditya-I by about 879 A.D. and the region was brought under Chola rule.Pandyas under Jatavarman Sundara Pandya rose to power and the region was brought under Pandya rule by putting an end to Chola supremacy in 1264 A.D.Pandya's rule over this region lasted a little over half a century followed by Bahmini kingdom with the extension of Delhi Sultanate under Khilji dynasty especially under the rule of Alauddin Khilji, a pioneer of all revenue works. During 1361, Kumara Kampana II, the son of Vijayanagar King, Bukka I conquered and established Vijayanagar rule in Tondaimandalam.

The Vijayanagar rulers appointed chieftain known as Nayaks who ruled over the different regions of the province almost independently. Damarla Venkatapathy Nayak, an influential chieftain under Venkata III, who was in-charge of the area of present Chennai city, gave the grant of a piece of land lying between the river Cooum almost at the point it enters the sea and another river known as Egmore river to the English in 1639. On this piece of waste land was founded the Fort St. George exactly for business considerations. In honour of Chennappa Nayak, father of Venkatapathy Nayak, who controlled the entire coastal country from Pulicat in the north to

112

the Portuguese settlement of Santhome, the settlement which had grown up around Fort St. George was named after Chennapatanam.

The older area called the Madraspatnam lay to the north of it. Later on, the intervening space between the older northern site of Madraspatnam came to be quickly built over with houses of thenew settlers (as the two expanded) and that the two villages became virtually one town. While the official centre of the settlement was designated Fort St. George, the British applied the name Madras Patnam to the combined town. Golkonda forces under General Mir Jumla conquered Madras in 1646 and brought Chennai and its immediate surroundings under his control. On the fall ofGolkonda in 1687, the region came under the rule of the Mughal Emperors of Delhi.

Firmans were issued by the Mughal Emperor granting the rights of English company in Chennai. In the later part of the seventeenth century, Chennai steadily progressed during the period of Agency and under many Governors. During the regime of Governor Elihi Yale (1687-92), the most important event was the formation of the institution of a mayor and Corporation for the city of Chennai. In 1693, a perwanna was received from the local Nawab granting the towns Tondiarpet, Purasawalkam and Egmore to the company. Thomas Pitt became the Governor of Chennai in 1698 and governed for eleven years. This period witnessed remarkable development of trade and increase in wealth.

The important events during this period were the blockade of Chennai by Daud Khan and its repulsion and the acquisition of additional suburban villages by the English. Thiruvottiyur, Vysarpadi, Kathivakkam, Nungambakkam and Satangadu were made as a free gift to the English in 1708. In 1735, Chintadripet was taken over and in 1742 Vepery, Perambur and Periamet were presented to the British. Nicholas Morse was the Governor from 1744 to 1746. The most important event during his time was the outbreak of war between England and France and the consequent struggle for supremacy between the French and the English in South India. Chennai was captured by the French in 1744 but consequent on the treaty of peace of Aix-La-Chapelle, Chennai was restored to the English in 1749.

George Pigot was the Governor for the period from 1755 to 1763. The period is remarkable for the fact that the Company form a trading corporation, owning isolated towns, forts and factories, became a ruling power controlling vast territories. Charles Bourchier became Governor in 1767. During his period Hyder Ali who usurped the Sovereignty of Mysore joined hands with the Nizam and began an offensive on Chennai. In 1761, a treaty was signed between Hyder Ali and the Company for an alliance and mutual restitution of the conquests. The Governance of the Carnatic became the responsibility of the Chennai Government which could not maintain a large army without the revenue of Nawabs. In 1763,the English got the district of Chengalpattu known as Chennai Jagir for the maintenance of the army.Lord Macartney took charge of the Chennai Government in 1781.

During his period, Chennai was turned into an important naval base. Major General Medows became Governor in 1790. The position of the English was made secure in South India. The elimination of other foreign power and settlement of the limits of native territory gave stability and paved the way for an era of commercial development. In 1792, in a new treaty Mohammed Ali handed over the entire management of the Carnatic to the English and accepted in return a pension. Another important event of this period was the outbreak of Mysore war. Tippu was killed in 1799 and the whole of Carnatic ceded to the British.

Thus the supremacy of the English in South India was established. The present day territorial limits of the city existed in the shape of scattered villages for centuries before the advent of the British. In the process of growth, many villages got agglomerated into a single unit. The shape and extent of the city which existed during 1939-40 was reached even during the opening years of 19th century. The period in between 1803 to 1827 represents consolidation and development of institutions.

Sir Edward Elliot was the important Governor of Chennai during this period. He appointed a Judicial Commission with Munro as its President in 1814. Several reforms in the administrative system were made by the Commission. Sir Thomas Munro became the Governor in 1820 and continued till 1827. He tried his best to improve literacy. He initiated English education in Chennai and established a body called Board of

Public Instructions to improve and direct public education. Important improvement made to Chennai city during the first half of the 19th century was the progress made in the establishment of institutions for professional and technical education.

School of Industrial Art was started in 1850, Civil Engineering College in 1834 and Madras Medical College in 1835, etc. The Madras University was started in September 1857. The Chennai High Court was created in June 1862. The Railway Company in Chennai was formed in July 1845. The first construction work began on 9th June 1853 and in 1858; South Indian Railway was formed having Chennai as the Railway Headquarters. Lord Hobart who was the Governor from 1872 to 1875 initiated Chennai Harbour project. The Congress party came to life during the period 1881-90. The Indian National Congress held its session in 1887 at Chennai.

The First Governor of Chennai in the 20th century was Lord Ampthill (1901-06). Sir Arthur Law-by was the Governor from 1906-1911 and Lord Pentland from 1912-19. The important Landmarks during this period were the establishment of Chennai Electric Supply Corporation in 1906 and opening of Indian Bank in 1907. During 1934 and 1936 for a short period, two Indians Sir M.D. Usman Sahibs and Sir K. Venkatareddy Naidu acted as Governors of Chennai. In 1937, the Ministry of Shri C. Rajagopalachari came into power for two years. The influence of the Governors on the administration considerably diminished. The British departed on 15th August 1947 but Chennai remained as a standing monument of what the British have done to India.

4.8 Demographic Structure of Chennai City

Chennai with current population of 5,008,763 (5 million) is one of the largest cities of South India. The Population density of Chennai is 26903, which is currently largest in the state of Tamil Nadu. Chennai has witnessed a tremendous growth in its manufacturing, retail, health care and IT sector in the last 10 years. It is regarded as India's fourth largest city after Delhi, Mumbai and Kolkata. Being a major business hub of the state, the population of Chennai has witnessed a rapid growth in its Population. Chennai has become an important destination for trade and tourism in recent years. It has evoked as a city with tremendous potential for industrial growth because of its economic viability and available infrastructure. The state government departments are geared towards increasing trade and commerce links with other countries and developing greater industrial growth. This entire boom in the trade and business of Chennai city accounts largely for its rapidly growing population. More business and job opportunities in the city lure people from in and around Chennai to come and settle here. Major multinationals have already set up there branch offices in Chennai leading to more people being hired by this companies. So Population of Chennai has grown rapidly in the last 20 years due to its major industrialization and tremendous growth.

In 2011, Chennai had population of 4,681,087 of which male and female were 2,357,633 and 2,323,454 respectively. In 2001 census, Chennai had a population of 4,343,645 of which males were 2,219,539 and remaining 2,124,106 were females. Chennai District population constituted 6.49 percent of total Maharashtra population. In 2001 census, this figure for Chennai District was at 6.96 percent of Maharashtra population. There was change of 7.77 percent in the population compared to population as per 2001. In the previous census of India 2001, Chennai District recorded increase of 13.07 percent to its population compared to 1991.

4.8.1 Density of Chennai

The initial provisional data released by census India 2011, shows that density of Chennai district for 2011 is 26,903 people per sq. km. In 2001, Chennai district density was at 24,963 people per sq. km. Chennai district administers 174 square kilometers of areas.

4.8.2 Growth of Population in Chennai

According to 2001 census, Population of Chennai was 4.3 million (4,343,645). The population density in the city was 24,682 per km, making it one of the most densely populated cities in the world. **Chennai** has a good sex ratio of 951 females per 1000 males in the last census which currently stands at 986. Also Literacy rate in the City has improved a lot as compared to last census. Average literacy rate in the city is also very higher at 80.14% as compared to overall literacy rate of India which is only 64.5%.

116

Chennai is rated at fourth position in terms of slum population of India. The city is home to 820,000 slum people (Census 2001) living in slum conditions. There was change of 7.77 percent in the population compared to population as per 2011. In the previous census of India 2001, Chennai District recorded increase of 13.07 percent to its population compared to 1991.

Table 4.1 Growth of Population in Chennai

Year	Population	Growth Percent
1951	1,416,056	
1961	1,729,141	22.1
1971	2,469,449	42.8
1981	3,266,034	32.3
1991	3,841,398	17.6
2001	4,343,645	13.1
2011	4,681,087	7.8

Source: Census Reports of India (various issues)

4.9 Economic Profile

The tendency to ascribe failure of development policy to bad or inadequate governance has become nearly universal. It seems development of finance institutions, multilateral agencies like World Bank, Asian Development bank, policy makers have all come to the Chennai holds immense attraction to investors from all over the country and world in industry and trade and commerce, technology and education on account of its advantage location, availability of skilled manpower, finance institution, communication network and institution of higher learning, management and research. In addition to this amicable and tolerant nature of the inhabitants of Chennai is also the factor. The information technology had given more job opportunities to the younger generation in Tamil Nadu during the last half decade. Most of the software units in Tamil Nadu are ideally located in Chennai itself due to its vast number of educated and skilled labour force, availability of institutions for higher studies etc.

117

4.10 Work Participation

Work participation rate plays a very important role for analyzing the economic status of any state or district. It gives an idea about the percentage of people worked; the Census of India classified the work participation rate in two forms called main workers and marginal workers. As per the Census of India, main workers means number of workers engaged in various activities more than 180 days in a year, while marginal workers means people engaged in various economic activities less than 180 days in a year. Non-workers are another category mainly consisting of children below 14 years of age and old age people.

4.2 Main & Marginal Workers of Chennai & Tamil Nadu in 2011

No.	Details	Tamil Nadu	Chennai
1.	Main Workers	23684611	1343578
2.	Marginal Workers	4127036	97804
3.	Total Workers	27805347	1441382
4.	Work Participation Rate	44.76	34.19

Source: *District Statistical Abstract of Chennai Government of Tamil Nadu, Chennai.*

No.	Category	Workers	
		Chennai	Tamil Nadu
1.	Cultivators	788 (0.05)	5114384 (18.39)
2.	Agricultural Labourers	715 (0.05)	8665040 (31.16)
3.	Workers Engaged in Household Activities	22108 (1.54)	1458546 (5.24)
4.	Other Workers	1417771 (98.36)	12573677 (45.21)
5.	Total Workers	2882764 (100.0)	27811647 (100.0)

Source: *District Statistical Abstract of Chennai Government of Tamil Nadu, Chennai.*

4.11 IT development in Chennai

Chennai holds immense attraction to investors from all over the country and world in industry and trade and commerce, technology and education on account of its advantage location, availability of skilled manpower, finance institution, communication network and institution of higher learning, management and research. In addition to this amicable and tolerant nature of the inhabitants of Chennai is also the factor. The information technology had given more job opportunities to the younger generation in Tamil Nadu during the last half decade. Most of the software units in Tamil Nadu are ideally located in Chennai itself due to its vast number of educated and skilled labour force, availability of institutions for higher studies etc.

Table 4.3 Distribution of Software Units in Tamil Nadu 2010-11.

No	Place	No. of Units	Per cent
1.	Chennai	676	89.30
2.	Tamil Nadu	757	100.00

Source: District Statistical Abstract of Chennai Government of Tamil Nadu, Chennai.

4.12 Small Scale Industries

The SMEs are the important portion of the Tamil Nadu economy which give more employment to the major chunk of the population, In order to understand the position of small Scale industrial units in the state of Tamil Nadu and Chennai district, an analysis has been carried out. A good percentage of the small-scale industrial units in Tamil Nadu existed in Chennai district itself.

Table 4.4 Registered Small Scale Industrial Units in Chennai District & Tamil Nadu

No	Area	2010	2011
1.	Chennai	40094 (10.34)	43664 (10.41)
2.	Tamil Nadu	387597	419524

Source: District Statistical Abstract of Chennai Government of Tamil Nadu, Chennai.

119

4.13 Employment situation of Chennai people

The employment position occupies a pivotal role in the development of society. It gives a vital input for analyzing the position of the particular area, can understand the purchasing power of the people etc. Now most of the urban people think both husband and wife need employment for smooth functioning of their family, especially for meeting the high cost of living.

Table 4.5 Employment situation of Chennai people

Year	Public	Private	Total
2004-05	281274	106529	387803
2005-06	282801	103034	385835
2006-07	275914	107906	383820
2007-08	283533	110572	394105
2008-09	281406	110673	392079
2009-10	281287	102358	383645
2010-11	316553	94674	411227

Source: District Statistical Abstract of Chennai Government of Tamil Nadu, Chennai.

4.14 No of co-operatives shops in Chennai

The co-operatives shops are the important affirmative action of the State through which people requirement could be fulfilled with the subsidized rate and significant portion of the population are slum dwellers, hence ratio shops are important source for the livelihood for the poor people in Chennai.

Table 4.6 co-operatives shops in Chennai

No	Details	Chennai		Tamil Nadu
1.	Fair Price Shops operated by			
	a. Co-operatives	898	(3.44)	26109
	b. Others	354	(26.50)	1336
	c. Total	1252	(4.56)	27445
2.	Card Holders	1618380	(10.42)	15533697

Source: District Statistical Abstract of Chennai Government of Tamil Nadu, Chennai.

120

4.15 Sources of Water Supply

Chennai water supply is the very huge task of the state, the information on the source of the water supply illustrated below

Table 4.7 Sources of Water Supply

No	Sources	Water Supply (mld)		Areas Served
		Available	Supply	
1.	Poondi, Cholavaram, Red Hills	236	195	Ambattur, Avadi and HVF
2.	Tamaraipakkam	148	-	City and Manali, ground water industries
3.	South Chennai Coastal Belt	10	5	Southern part of the city
4.	Palar	25.5	25.5	Alandur, Tambaram Pallavapuram, MFPEZ
5.	Checkdam on Kortalayar	20	20	
6.	Local Borewells	6.5	6.5	Thiruvottiyur, Avadi
7.	Total	426	231	

Source: District Statistical Abstract of Chennai Government of Tamil Nadu, Chennai.

4.16 Financial operation of the Chennai people

Institutional financial operations are the important evidence of the financial wealth of the individuals

Table 4.8 Financial operation of the Chennai people

No	Details	2008-09	2009-10	2010-11
1.	Percapita Deposit (Rs)			
	a. Chennai	52158	61679	73642
	b. Tamil Nadu	8896	10546	12350
2.	Percapita Credit (Rs)			
	a. Chennai	63962	75560	84865
	b. Tamil Nadu	7972	9040	5761
3.	Credit Deposit Ratio			
	a. Chennai	122.6	122.5	115.2
	b. Tamil Nadu	89.6	85.7	46.6

Source: District Statistical Abstract of Chennai Government of Tamil Nadu, Chennai.

4.17 Population of Vehicles in Chennai

Transportation is the important element of any urban centers, increasing vehicle population is the important challenges for the inhabitants

Table 4.9 Population of Vehicles in Chennai

No	Vehicles	2010		2011	
		Chennai	Tamil Nadu	Chennai	Tamil Nadu
1.	Motor Cycles	319419	1142550	362514	1334348
2.	Scooters	195784	684567	212544	752129
3.	Mopeds	415683	2335885	436014	2514088
4.	Tri Cycle Auto	2557	3731	2557	3813
5.	Motor Car	218002	446824	234381	483799
6.	Jeep	8344	35546	8450	36877

7.	Station Wagons	325	2089	326	2146
8.	Tractor	1147	66955	1152	70209
9.	Three Wheelers	3822	8398	4200	11589
10.	Four Wheelers	1280	4575	1283	4833
11.	Road Rollers	58	427	60	471
12.	Others	5388	9170	5605	11689
13	Non Commercial (Total)	1171809	4740717	1269086	5225991
14.	Commercial	85089	421365	86464	432106
15.	Total	1256898	5162082	1355550	5658097

Source:-Commissioner of Transport, Government of Tamil Nadu, Chennai. 5.

4.18 Value of Foreign Trade in Chennai Port, Airport & Tamil Nadu

Chennai is the one of the main place for the foreign trade which induce the development of the state as well as the region

Table 4.10 Value of Foreign Trade in Chennai Port, Airport & Tamil Nadu

Years	Chennai			Tamil Nadu
	Airport	Port	Total	
2005-06	213112	523925	737037	908580
2006-07	246339	771843	1018182	1246009
2007-08	300769	962794	1263563	1583283
2008-09	349661	1082099	1431760	1759627
2009-10	386320	1102178	1488498	1917719
2010-11	568197	1281079	1849276	1877128

Source: Department of Tourism, Government of Tamil Nadu

4.19 Tourists Arrivals in Chennai & Tamil Nadu 2010-11

Tourist's arrivals are also important source of income and the scope for cultural transactions which would enhance the quality of life

Table 4.11 Tourists Arrivals in Chennai & Tamil Nadu 2010-11

No	Years/Tourists	Chennai	Tamil Nadu
1.	2009		
	a. Domestic	4230709	22981882
	b. Foreign	309178	786165
	c. Total	4539887	23768047
2.	2010		
	a. Domestic	4361559	23812043
	b. Foreign	300979	773073
	c. Total	4662538	24585116
3.	2011		
	a. Domestic	4635278	24661754
	b. Foreign	310198	804641
	c. Total	4945476	25466395

Source: Department of Tourism, Government of Tamil Nadu

4.20 Medical and family welfare

Medical facilities and the infrastructure is the prominent factor for the good human capital, Coimbatore district has got very good amount of Medical facilities which enable the inhabitants to hold good position in health status the following table illustrates the Medical infrastructure of Chennai

124

Table 4.12 Medical and family welfare

No	Details	Chennai	Tamil Nadu
1.	Beds		
	a. 2005-2006	14015 (55.21)	23140
	b.2011-12	15015 (53.44)	23742
2.	Doctors		
	a. 2005-2006	2646 (51.21)	4414
	b.2011-12	2736 ((50.54)	4617

Source: District Statistical Abstract of Chennai Government of Tamil Nadu, Chennai.

4.21 Land Use Pattern of Chennai Metropolitan Authority

Land use pattern is indicate the economic profile of the region with respect to Chennai as it is the capital of the state thus it is essential to observe the land use pattern

Table 4.13 Land Use Pattern of Chennai Metropolitan Authority

No	Land use	Area	Per cent
1.	Residential	19277.65	19.40
2.	Commercial	9706.76	9.77
3.	Industrial	7481.50	7.53
4.	Institutional	6543.67	6.59
5.	Open Space & Recreational	332.06	0.33
6.	Water Bodies	11696.33	11.77
7.	Urbanisable	28099.15	28.29
8.	Non- urbanisable	16200.85	16.33
Total		99337.97	100.00

Source: District Statistical Abstract of Chennai Government of Tamil Nadu, Chennai.

CHAPTER V

Analysis and interpretation

Socio-economic groups within regions and between sexes with multiple consequences that continue to erode the equality of people's life. Women are not only affected as part of the family and as a disadvantaged grouped of society, but also a result of their position in the sexual division of work. No doubt, the aspects of globalization have provided women with increasing opportunities to work but on the other hand it couldn't gender wage differentials and marginalization of women which is reflected through segregation of women workers in certain specific jobs which are less rewarding, low in status but have long working hours. Unhealthy working conditions with mostly facilities for their maternity requirements and care of young siblings missing while the mothers are at work, unfavorable working hours, lack of training and skill up-gradation opportunities and lesser career mobility in the formal sector of economy still prevail in almost every country. This section exhibits the primary data analysis consists of information on socio-demographic variables viz, age, education, marital status, religion and caste, followed by the economic activities like income, savings, indebtedness. The next section deals with the working time and the structure of the industries which would be helpful to understand the amenities made available for the workers in the study area, next section of the analysis derives the information on the health conditions of the workers, next segment analyzed the information on the work environment and the job engagement practice of the industry which would enable to assess the job satisfaction and job involvement of the workers, Next section would receive the opinions of the workers on various issues pertaining to the work through which women workers perceptions are at comprehensive manner in gender dimension.

5.1 Socio-demographic variables

The information like age, education, marital status, religion and caste would represent the social status of the society which have ample of impact on the activities of the individuals in the society as the Indian society nebulously inter-woven with lot of value system, thus, these variables are important source for any form of socio-economic analysis.

126

Table: 5.1 - Socio-demographic variables

Variables	Respondent's Category	Nos	Percent
Study Area	North Chennai	100	33.3
	Central Chennai	100	33.3
	South Chennai	100	33.3
Age	Below 30	112	37.3
	31 – 50	174	58
	51 – 60	14	4.7
Religion	Hindu	212	70.7
	Muslim	48	16
	Christian	40	13.3
Caste	BC	75	25
	MBC	78	26
	SC	130	43.3
	ST	17	5.7
Education	Illiterate	34	11.3
	Primary level	34	11.3
	Middle School	90	30
	Higher secondary	68	22.7
	Degree	12	4
	Diploma	43	14.3
	Post Graduation	9	3
	Professional Course	10	3.3
Marital Status	Married	158	52.7
	Unmarried	78	26
	Divorced / Individual	21	7
	Widows	43	14.3
	Total	300	100

Source: Computed from primary data.

Table: 5.1 illustrates the socio-demographic information of the respondents in the study area, this would call for a close examination of the causal relationship of various economic variables and the status of women. Before analyzing the socio-economic situation of the female labourers in the leather sector, the back ground data of the women taken in samples has been given to highlight the general trends noticed with regard to such aspects as their age, caste, education, assets, marital status, with respect to the study area 100 respondents from each zones viz North, central and South were collected, 58 percentage of the respondents fall in the age group of 31-50 years, 37 percentage of the respondents fall in the age group of below 30 years, only 5 percentage of the total respondents fall in the group of 51-60 year and.In the study, age has been taken as one of the important variables for studying the health of women workers, as per the religion as concern 71 percent of the respondents from Hindu religion, 16 percent belongs to Muslim and 13 percent belongs to Christian religion. Thus, majority of the respondents were Hindu in the study area. Religion is one of the important factors determine the socio-economic activity of the individuals, the religious institution are the powerful in the world especially in India which is the important directive mechanism embedded with lot of traditions and belief system, caste is the important phenomenon in the society, around 43.3 percent of the respondents belongs to schedule caste, 5.7 percent of the respondents belong to Tribal community, 26 and 25 percent of the respondents belongs to MBC and BC respectively. In precise, Majority of the respondents belonged to SC, MBC and BC community in the respondents groups, socially marginalized persons are economically weaker as well, and SC and ST people are economically vulnerable in the study area, with regard to educational qualification nearly 11.3 percent of the women were illiterates, while 11.3 percent of the respondents were finished primary education, 30 percent of the respondents have completed middle level education and 22.7 percent of the respondents have completed high school education,4 percent finished their degree, 14.3 percent and 3 percent of the respondents have finished diploma and post graduation respectively and 3.3 percent have done their professional course, as per as marital status as concern, 52.7 percent of the respondents are married, 3.3 percent of the respondents same professional course unmarried, 7 percent of the respondents divorced or individual and 14.3 percent of the women were widows, at the outset socio-demographic variables replicate the conditions of the women leather footwear workers.

5.2 Financial operations

The operations of pecuniary aspects are the important variable manifest the economic status of the individuals, the financial operations could be map-out viz annual income, expenditure pattern, savings pattern and the loans, thus these factors need to be analyzed as the important exercise to understand the economic status of the respondents.

Table:5.2 -Financial operations of the respondents

Variables	Response Category	Nos	Percent
Annual Income	Less than 60,000	151	50.3
	60,001 to Rs. 90,000	123	41
	90,001 to Rs. 120000	18	6
	120001 and above	8	2.7
HH Expenditure	**No Expenditure**	0	0
	0-10000	212	70.7
	10001-20000	25	8.3
	20001-30000	31	10.3
	30001-40000	9	3
	40001-50000	6	2
	50001-60000	7	2.3
	60000 and above	10	3.3
	Total	300	100
Monthly Savings	**No savings**	112	37.3
	0-100	90	30
	100-200	45	15
	200-300	23	7.7
	400-500	19	6.3
	500 and above	11	3.7

	Total	300	100
Source of loan	**Private Money lenders**	121	40.3
	Pawn Broker	90	30
	Co-operative banks	11	3.7
	SHGs	75	25
	Commercial banks	3	1
	Total	300	100
Current outstanding	**0-5000**	31	10.3
	5001-10000	42	14
	10001-15000	79	26.3
	15001-20000	102	34
	20001-25000	27	9
	25000 and above	19	6.3
	Total	300	100

Source: Computed from primary data.

Table 5.2 depicts the variables pertains to the financial aspects of the respondents viz annual income, expenditure pattern, savings and loans of the respondents which would be essential to understand their economic position with regard to income of the respondent 50.3 percent of the respondents annual income is less than 60,000, nearly 41 percent of the respondents income range from 60001 to 90,000, 6 percent of the respondents income constitutes from 90,001 to 1,20,000, and 3 percent of the respondents annual income is above 120000 , nearly 91 % of the respondents annual income were below 90,000 which implies that the women leather workers were paid less and more over the economic status determines the purchasing power, with respect to the expenditure pattern the analysis exemplified that the none of the people falls in no expenditure category, 70.3 percent of the respondents spend on procurement of food and

130

non-food items per annum between 0-10000,8.3 percent of the respondents spends between 10001-20000, 10.3 percent of the respondents spends from the slab between 20001-30000, 3 percent of the respondents spend between 30001-40000, 2 percent of the of the respondents spends from 40001-50000, 2 percent of the of the respondents spends from 50001-60000, and 3 percent of the respondents spends 60,000 and above per annum, with respect to savings pattern 37.3 percent of the people revealed that they haven't made any savings, 30 percent of the respondents were savings 0-100 per month, 15 percent of the respondents were made saving 101-200 per month, 7.7 percent of the people saves between 200-300 rupees per month,6.3 percent of the respondents were saves between 400-500 per month and 3.7 percent of respondents were made savings 500 and above per month, Saving money is a mirage among the labour households,. The SHG has taken the responsibility of collecting some of the earnings of the labourers once in 15 days under chits. So also the labourers organized themselves in groups to collect little money daily, weekly or fortnightly from each labourer who is willing to join the association. The respondents who saved money at home revealed that it was difficult for them to contribute regularly to the chits. Hence they did not join the chits, loans are the important component of the economic activity of the women workers around 40.3 percent of the respondents use to avail the loan from the private moneylenders, 30 percent of the respondents revealed that they mortgage the jewels in the nearby pawn broker shops for the credit requirement, 3.7 person availed loan from co-operative banks, 25 percent of the respondents availed the loan from SHGs and merely 1 percent of the respondents were got the loan from commercial loans, it could be inferred from the empirical investigation that the institutionalized credit facilities are not accessible to the respondents at the large. with regard to current outstanding 10.3 percent of the respondents have the outstanding between 0-5000 rupees,14 percent of the respondents got between 5000-10000, 26.3 percent of the respondents got the outstanding between 10001 - 15000, 34 percent of the respondents having the outstanding between 15001-20000, 9 percent of the respondents got the outstanding between 20001-25000, and 6.3 percent of the respondents got 25,000 and above, Further the above analysis reveals that the majority of workers had not taken any of the loan from any of the institution like Banks.

5.3 Work-situation and number of working days:

The peace and tranquility of the work-spot and the efficiency of labourers depends to a considerable extent upon the wage structure and the amenities provided at the field or work-spot. Further the psychological conditions of the women workers are influenced by the situation prevailing at the work-spot.

Table 5.3: Reason to become leather footwear worker

Response category	Nos	Percent
Low education qualification	90	30.0
Oriented to my qualification	17	5.7
No other jobs	45	15.0
Don't have other infrastructure	12	4.0
To cater the family expenses	95	31.7
Friends persuasion	41	13.7
Total	300	100.0

Source: Computed from primary data.

Table 5.3 illustrates the reasons which make the respondents to became the leather footwear workers, 30 percent of the respondents were opined that they have Low education qualification hence the opt to choose the job for their livelihood,5.7 percent of the respondents have opined that their job oriented to qualification, 15 percent of the respondents have revealed that they have been bound to do the work since they don't have any other job, 12.4 percent of the respondents conveyed that they don't have any other infrastructure which pull them into this work, 13.7 percent of the people told that Friends persuasion is the reason why they became leather worker and 31.7 percent of the respondents opined that they opt the job in order to cater their family expenditure and forced to take up the work for the livelihood subsistence, it could be inferred from the empirical investigation that most of the people opt the job since they don't have formal education, as the area known for industrial cluster which facilitate the people to get the job in the study area.

132

Table 5.4: No of Hours in work per day

Response category	Nos	Percent
8 hrs	102	34.0
9 hrs	90	30.0
10 hrs	67	22.3
Depends on the work	41	13.7
Total	300	100.0

Source: Computed from primary data.

Table 5.4 exemplifies the working hours of the respondents in the study area, 34 percent of the respondents have told that they use to work for 8 hrs per day, 30 percent of the respondents have opined that they worked for 9 hrs per day, 22.3 percent of the respondents were told that they are engaging in the work around 10 hrs per day,13.7 percent of the respondents have told that they use to depends on the condition of the assignment , almost all the respondents have opined that hrs of the work may vary according to the season of the work, however that many women told that women workers have been working more intensively and longer period of time on the office.

Table.5.5: Employment Patterns by Hierarchy

Response category	Nos	Percentage
Managerial Staff	2	0.7
Supervisory Staff	21	7.0
Skilled Workers	100	33.3
Non-Skilled Workers	177	59.0
Total	300	100.0

Source: Computed from primary data.

Table 5.5 indicates that female employees are more concentrated at the lower levels of hierarchy in the organizations. Hence, amongst managers woman only comprise roughly 0.7 % of employees while at the worker level they comprise about 59 % of employees, at the supervisory level 7 % comprise whereas 33.3 percent of the employees constitutes in skilled workers category, This might be because of low level of skill and education amongst women on account of cultural and opportunity barriers.

133

In addition, this could also be the result of women not pursuing a career and leaving the workforce early on accounts of marriage and household management liabilities further the size of the organization plays a role in the employment of women at each level of the organization. Smaller companies exhibit lower female employment at all levels with no woman manager hired in these firms. As the size of the organization increases, female participation also increases for all levels of the hierarchy including management. At the outset it apparent from the empirical findings that major chunk of women workforce comprise of semi-skilled and low paid jobs in the study area.

Table. 5.6: Employment Patterns in Various Departments

Response category	Nos	Percentage
Knitting	27	9.0
Dyeing	21	7.0
Pre-cutting Fabric	31	10.3
Processing/Fusing	22	7.3
Stitching / Sewing	39	13.0
Washing/ Pressing	24	8.0
Inspection/Quality	19	6.3
Folding / Packing	21	7
Helping / Cleaning	76	25.3
Maintenance	20	6.7
Total	300	100.0

Source: Computed from primary data.

Fig. 5.1

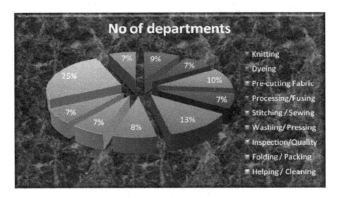

Table 5.6 indicates that women's participation in various departments of leather footwear manufacturing units is fairly different. There seems to be a specialization of work for gender or horizontal discrimination. Hence, looking at the overall column, one notices that female proportions are much less in somewhat more technical areas such as knitting with 9 percent, dyeing with 7 percent, processing and stitching with 7.3 and 10.3 respectively, with regard to washing and inspection with 8 percent and 6 percent respectively, 7 percent and 25.3 percent for folding and helping respectively, and 6.7 percent to maintenance but in the department like managerial and R&D women are fewer in numbers in some administrative areas such as finance, HR and marketing. Many more women are either in stitching or low skill areas as finishing and packing. This specialization seems to be the result of differential skill levels of women and physical and cultural constraints in the study area.

5.4 Challenges and constraints faced by the workers

In the patriarchal soceity women have been structurally oppressed under the cultural domain which totally denied the basic rights as human being, Women workers in the informal economy is associated with low levels of organization, small-scale production, and casual employment, little or no social protection and lack of job security or health insurance, thus it is imperative to analyze the following variables to ascertain the gender based discrimination in the study area.

Table 5.7:Wage discrimination on the basis of Gender

Response category	Male		Female	
	Nos	Percent	Nos	Percent
Up to 3000	34	11.3	114	38.0
3000-6000	45	15.0	98	32.7
6000-9000	112	37.3	46	15.3
9000-12000	67	22.3	21	7.0
12000 and above	42	14.0	21	7.0
Total	300	100.0	300	100.0

Source: Computed from primary data.

Fig. 5.2

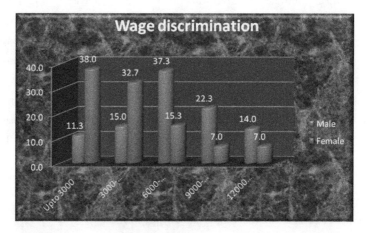

Table 5.7 portrayed the wages entitled for women and men for the same work at the leather footwear industries in the study area. 11.3 percent of male and female 38 percent had availed the wages up to 3000 per month,15 percent of male and female 32.7 percent had availed the wages between 3000-6000 per month 37.3 percent of male and female 15.3 percent had availed the wages between 6000-9000 per month 22.3 percent of male and female 7 percent had availed the wages between 9000-12000 per month14 percent of male and female 7 percent had availed the wages more than 12000 per month,

136

despite of the fact both of them engaging in the same sort of work male workers have entitled to get more remuneration while compare to female counterpart, it could be inferred from the empirical investigation that there was significant discrimination in wage between male and female at leather industries in the study area.

Table. 5.8: Kind of Difficulties in work place

Response category	Nos	Percentage
Health problems	32	10.7
Oppression of the supervisors	23	7.7
Forced to work more time	21	7.0
wage discrimination	20	6.7
Uncertainty of employment	12	4.0
All above five	192	64.0
Total	300	100.0

Source: Computed from primary data.

Table 5.8 explains the kind of difficulties women worker has been facing in the study area, 10.7 percent of the respondents have told that they have health problems, 7.7 percent of the respondents have opined they have been undergoing lot of oppression from the supervisors ,7 percent of the respondents have opined that they had been forced to work more than the entitled time schedule, 6.7 percent person faced wage discrimination even among the women workers on the basis of gender, 4 percent of the people told that uncertainty of employment situation, 64 percent of the respondents have exemplified that they had been facing all the above five problems, hence it is very apparent from the empirical illustration that women have been undergoing lot of problems in the working area.

Table.5.9: Experience of the Respondents

Response category	Nos	Percent
Up to 2 yrs	55	18.3
2yrs -4 yrs	87	29.0
4yrs-6 yrs	46	15.3
Above 6 yrs	112	37.3
Total	300	100.0

Source: Computed from primary data.

Table 5.9 illustrates the experience of the respondents in the leather companies, 18.3 percent of the respondents got the experience up to 2 years, 29 percent of the respondents got the experience between 2 years to 4 years, 15.3 percent got the experience between years to 6 years and 37.3 percent had experience more than 6 years, it could be inferred from the empirical verification that nearly half of the respondents were got the experience more than 5 years and the information regarding the experience pertain to the industries where they are working now as it is essential to assess the work environment in the study area.

5.5 Amenities and entitled privileges in the working places

According to the ILO directive polices companies should provide the basic amenities and the entitled privileges like leave, incentive etc, as the amenities and privileges are the essential component to provide the comfort in the working place

Table.5.10: Perceptions on the amenities available in the company

Response category	Highly satisfied	Percent	Satisfied	Percent	Not Satisfied	Percent
Standard of cleanliness	45	15.0	50	16.7	205	68.3
Ventilation	51	17.0	54	18.0	195	65.0
Lighting arrangements	40	13.3	46	15.3	214	71.3
Protective measures	32	10.7	38	12.7	230	76.7
Drinking water	23	7.7	29	9.7	248	82.7
Sanitation facilities	31	10.3	37	12.3	232	77.4
Rest room	27	9.0	35	11.7	238	79.3
Recreation activities	29	9.7	34	11.3	237	79.0

Source: Computed from primary data.

Fig: 5.3

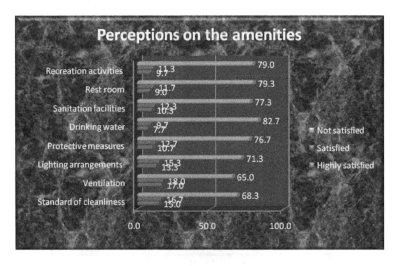

Table 5.10 illustrates the perceptions of the respondents on the amenities made available in their industries, with respect standard of cleanliness 15 percent of the respondents highly satisfied with the cleanliness maintained in the company premises,

16.7 percent satisfied and 68.3 percent of the respondents were not satisfied,with respect ventilation 17 percent of the respondents highly satisfied with the ventilation, 18 percent satisfied and 65 percent of the respondents were not satisfied,with respect to lighting arrangements 13.3 percent of the respondents highly satisfied with the lighting arrangements maintained in the company premises, 15.3 percent satisfied and 71.3 percent of the respondents were not satisfied,with regard to protective measures 10.7 percent of the respondents highly satisfied with the protective measures followed in the company premises, 12.7 percent satisfied and 76.7 percent of the respondents were not satisfied, with respect to provision of drinking water facilities 7.7 percent of the respondents highly satisfied with the drinking water facility available in the company premises, 9.7 percent satisfied and 82.7 percent of the respondents were not satisfied,with respect to sanitation facilities 10.3 percent of the respondents highly satisfied with the sanitation facilities made available in the company premises, 12.3 percent satisfied and 77.4 percent of the respondents were not satisfied,in connection with the availability of rest room 9 percent were highly satisfied,11.7 percent have satisfied and 79.3 percent of the respondents were not satisfied, and in regard to recreational activities in the company premises 9 percent highly satisfied, 11.3 percent were not satisfied and the 79 percent were not satisfied with the facilities, it could be inferred from the empirical findings that majority of the respondents have not satisfied with the provision of the amenities in the company as it has enormous influence on the welfare of the workers and eventually enrich the potentiality of the workers at large, thus, it was apparent from the study that the amenities were inadequate in the study area.

Table. 5.11: Women leather footwear workers perceptions on the leave facilities of the companies

Response category	Highly satisfied	Percentage	Satisfied	Percentage	Not satisfied	Percenta
Allowed to have Medical leave	43	14.3	56	18.7	201	67.0
Deduct Pay for Medical leave	32	10.7	37	12.3	231	77.0
Deduct Pay for Casual leave	17	5.7	20	6.7	263	87.7
Allowed to have Maternity leave	50	16.7	79	26.3	171	57.0

Source: Computed from primary data.

Fig.5.4

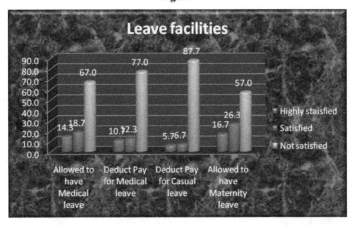

Table 5.11 shows the perception of the respondents on the leave facilities provided by the companies, 14.3 percent of the respondents were highly satisfied with the company's permission to allowed to have medical leave, 18.7 percent were satisfied and 67 percent of the respondents were not satisfied with the entitlement provided by the companies, 10.7 percent of the respondents were highly satisfied with the company's procedure to deduct pay for medical leave, 12.3 percent were satisfied and 77 percent of the respondents were not satisfied with the procedure followed by the companies, 5.7 percent of the respondents were highly satisfied with the company's procedure to deduct pay for casual leave,6.7 percent were satisfied and 87.7 percent of the respondents were not satisfied with the procedure followed by the companies, 16.7 percent of the respondents were highly satisfied with the company's permission to avail maternity leave, 26.3 percent were satisfied and 57 percent of the respondents were not satisfied with the entitlement provided by the companies, generally companies have a specified leave structure for salaried women leather footwear employees most of the companies allow medical and casual leaves to their employees. However, maternity leaves are a question mark with some companies as only 15% provide this facility. What is even more interesting is that even for

few companies, which are relatively more liberal in providing maternity leave; the number of women who had availed maternity leave in the past five years is pretty low. This might be the result of fewer married women working in the industry and also their decision to leave the job after marriage or at the start of pregnancy. This behavior could even be encouraged by the companies as they do not want to incur the costs involved. Thus, it is apparent from the empirical evidence that people have not satisfied with the leave structure followed by the companies in the leather footwear industries in the study area.

Table. 5.12: Perception on Company Policies for Labour Laws

Response category	Yes	Percentage	No	Percentage
Prominent display of labor laws in the factory	38	12.7	262	87.3
Awareness about Voluntary Code of conduct on sexual harassment	21	7.0	279	93.0
Written code of conduct on sexual harassment in	19	6.3	281	93.7

Source: Computed from primary data.

Fig :5.5

142

Table 5.12 illustrates the opinion of the respondents on displaying the labour law in the company premises 12.7 percent of the respondents revealed yes to the statement that prominent display of labour laws in the factory premises, 87.3 percent said no, with respect to the awareness on the code of conduct on sexual harassment 7 percent agreed that their companies followed such guidelines but 93 percent revealed company didn't follow such guidelines,6.3 percent of the respondents told that their company got the written code of conduct on sexual harassment in the factory but 93.7 percent revealed their company didn't have such guidelines, Labour laws have been designed to create a healthy working relationship amongst labour, employers and the government and to make sure that labour is not exploited by the more powerful management. Consequently, the government also advises companies to make sure labor laws are properly displayed with the objective being that workers are aware of their rights and obligations, but empirical evidence revealed the contrast situation where legislative measures have not been followed by the company authorities to ensure the protection of the women workers.

Table.5.13: Facilities available for women workers in the companies

Response category	Highly satisfied	Percentage	Satisfied	Percentage	Not satisfied	Percentage
Medical facility inside the Factory	45	15.0	54	18.0	201	67.0
Medical Facility in the Factory	23	7.7	17	5.7	260	86.7
Separate bathrooms for Female	78	26.0	98	32.7	124	41.3
Separate Rest Area for Female	40	13.3	65	21.7	195	65.0
Separate Working Places for Male and Female	27	9.0	40	13.3	233	77.7
Transportation/Pick and Drop facility provided	54	18.0	73	24.3	173	57.7
Concession given for heavy work to	28	9.3	46	15.3	226	75.3
Day-care facility in the factory for small kids	21	7.0	26	8.7	253	84.3
Flexible working hours to women for household responsibilities	18	6.0	26	8.7	256	85.3
Workers Union	28	9.3	38	12.7	234	78.0

Source: Computed from primary data.

144

Fig: 5.6

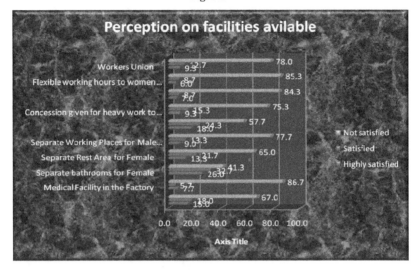

Table 5.13 illustrates the perception of the respondents on the facilities provided by the leather footwear factories to women workers in the study area, with regard to availability of medical facilities adjoined to companies 15 percent of the respondents were highly satisfied, 18 percent were satisfied and 67 percent were not satisfied with the availability of the medical facility in the nearby area, with regard to availability of medical facilities inside the companies 7.7 percent of the with respondents were highly satisfied, 5.7 percent were satisfied and 86.7 percent were not satisfied with the availability of the medical facility in the company, with respect to availability of separate bathrooms for female 26 percent of the with respondents were highly satisfied, 32.7 percent were satisfied and 41.3 percent were not satisfied with the availability of the medical facility in the company,13.3 percent highly satisfied with the separate working place for separate rest area for female,21.7 percent satisfied and nearly 65 percent of the respondents were not satisfied with the separate rest area for female, with regard to transportation facilities 18 percent of the respondents were highly satisfied, 24.3 percent were satisfied and 57.7 percent were not satisfied, with respect to concession given to the women workers during pregnancy 9.3 percent of the respondents were highly satisfied, 15.3 percent were satisfied and 75.3 percent were not satisfied with the availability of the medical facility in the company,

with regard to flexible working hrs for women 6 percent of the with respondents were highly satisfied, 8.7 percent were satisfied and 85.3 percent were not satisfied with the availability of the medical facility in the company, it could be inferred from the analysis that companies appear to provide little care about the health of their employees as most of the companies are providing some form of medical facilities on the premises for their employees but not adequate level. As far as special facilities for woman workers are concerned most companies seem to be providing separate bath rooms, prayer and rest areas for women. Female mobility is a big issue and companies interested in employing female workers need to provide this facility. At the outset respondents have not satisfied with the facilities provided by the companies as either in adequate or inappropriate to the women workers in the study area.

5.6 Work environment

Work environment have strong influence on the productivity and comfort level of the employees, good ambience would always enrich the quality of work life, thus the information regarding the work environment is important tool to evaluate the work culture of the companies or organization.

Table. 5.14 Work Environment of the respondents

Response category	Yes	Percentage	No	Percentage
Determination of wage and incentive	45	15	255	85
Women were Underpaid	234	78.0	66	22.0
Sexual harassment in the work place	260	86.7	40	13.3
Male chauvinism is high	220	73.3	80	26.7
Long working hours for women	244	81.3	56	18.7
Malice attitude of management	256	85.3	44	14.7
No cordial relation with women workers of the management	231	77.0	69	23.0
Discriminated performance appraisal	221	73.7	79	26.3

Source: Computed from primary data.

Fig: 5.7

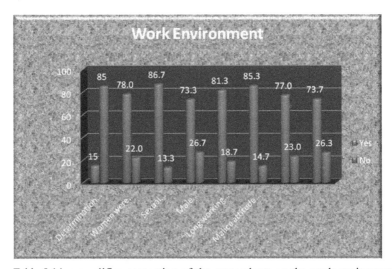

Table 5.14 exemplifies perception of the respondents on the work environment in the study area, 15 percent of the respondents opined that men and women are given equal opportunity 85 percent revealed didn't in determine wage and incentive, 78 percent of the respondents opined that women were underpaid, 22 percent revealed that women were given equal payment ,86.7 percent of the respondents revealed that sexual harassment exsist in their work place but 13.3 percent sexual harassment didn't taken place,73.3 percent of the respondents revealed that male chauvinism is high in their comapany,26.7 percent revealed no such things happened, 81.3 percent of the respondents revealed that working hours for women workers were long and nearly 18.7 percent revealed that women workers have entitled working hours, 85.3 percent of the respondents revealed that malice attitude of management manifested in many activities and nearly 14.7 percent revealed it was not so,77 percent of the respondents revealed that No cordial relation with women workers of the management prevails in their company and nearly 23 percent revealed cordial relationship maintained with the women workers by the management in their company,73.7 percent of the respondents revealed that

147

discriminated performance appraisal executed in their company and nearly 26.3 percent revealed it was not so, the empirical investigation suggests that there seems to be a congenial work environment for woman workers in the industry in general. almost all managers, irrespective of designation, seem to agree that men and women have not given an equal opportunity of being hired and promoted in the company. Both genders seem to be getting almost equal pays for comparable jobs. On top of it all sexual harassment was also not considered a problem in the industry. At the outset work environment seems unfavour to the women workers in the study area.

Table. 5.15: Perception of the respondents on factory environment

Response category	Strongly Agree	Percent	Agree	Percent	Undecided	Percent	Disagree	Percent	Strongly disagree	Percent
Conducive for women to work	23	7.7	36	12.0	40	13.3	112	37.3	89	29.7
Gender discrimination is high	19	6.3	34	11.3	51	17.0	109	36.3	87	29.0
Late working hours	39	13.0	50	16.7	21	7.0	100	33.3	90	30.0
Discriminated payment	100	33.3	123	41.0	27	9.0	30	10.0	20	6.7
Sexual harassment	102	34.0	121	40.3	21	7.0	31	10.3	25	8.3
Hazardous work	98	32.7	121	40.3	18	6.0	35	11.7	28	9.3

Source: Computed from primary data.

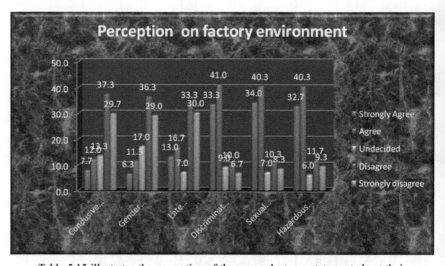

Table 5.15 illustrates the perception of the respondents on statement about their factory environment, with respect to the statement conducive for women to work merely 7.7 percent of the workers strongly agreed the statement, 12 percent of the agreed the proclamation, 13.3 percent of the respondents have no opinion, 37.3 percent of respondents disagree and 29.7 percent of the respondents strongly disagree the statement, , with respect to the statement gender discrimination is high, only 6.3 percent of the workers strongly agreed the statement, 11.3 percent of the agreed the proclamation, 17 percent of the respondents have no opinion, 36.3 percent of respondents disagree and 29. percent of the respondents strongly disagree the statement, with regards to statement late working hours 13 percent of the workers strongly agreed the statement, 16.7 percent of the agreed the proclamation, 7 percent of the respondents have no opinion, 33.3 percent of respondents disagree and 30 percent of the respondents strongly disagree the statement, with regards to statement discriminated payment 33.3 percent of the workers strongly agreed the statement, 41 percent of the agreed the proclamation, 9 percent of the respondents have no opinion,10 percent of respondents disagree and 6.7 percent of the respondents strongly disagree the statement, respondents opinion on the statement sexual harassment revealed that 34

percent of the workers strongly agreed the statement, 40.3 percent of the agreed the proclamation, 7 percent of the respondents have no opinion,10.3 percent of respondents disagree and 8.3 percent of the respondents strongly disagree the statement, with regards to statement hazardous work 32.7 percent of the workers strongly agreed the statement, 40.3 percent of the agreed the proclamation, 6 percent of the respondents have no opinion,11.7 percent of respondents disagree and 9.3 percent of the respondents strongly disagree the statement, it could be inferred from the empirical verification that majority of the statement contains the working environment for women workers in leather footwear industries that lot of constraints exists in the environment, however, women converting the constraints into comfortable situation for the more effective working environment in the study area.

Table.5.16 Perceptions on the comparison of skills between male and female workers

Response category	Strongly Agree	Percent	Agree	Percent	Undeci ded	Percent	Disagree	Percent	Strongly disagree	Percent
Female workers are highly productive than	97	32.3	112	37.3	41	13.7	30	10.0	20	6.7
Female give more quality than male	85	28.3	90	30.0	53	17.7	41	13.7	31	10.3
Female workers are work alcoholic	105	35.0	121	40.3	21	7.0	30	10.0	23	7.7
Female are more loyalty towards work	100	33.3	119	39.7	32	10.7	28	9.3	21	7.0
Female worker are honest	101	33.7	119	39.7	28	9.3	27	9.0	25	8.3

Source: Computed from primary data.

152

Fig.5.9

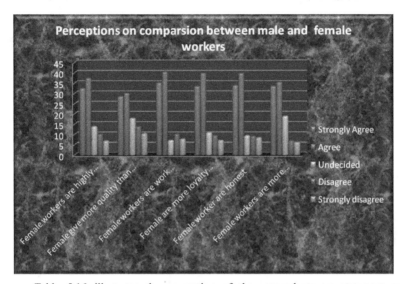

Table 5.16 illustrates the perception of the respondents on statement on comparison of skills between male and female workers in their factory, with respect to the statement Female workers are highly productive than male merely 32.3 percent of the workers strongly agreed the statement, 37.3 percent of the agreed the proclamation, 13.7 percent of the respondents have no opinion, 30 percent of respondents disagree and 6.7 percent of the respondents strongly disagree the statement, with respect to the statement Female give more quality than male, only 28.3 percent of the workers strongly agreed the statement, 30 percent of the agreed the proclamation, 17.7 percent of the respondents have no opinion, 13.7 percent of respondents disagree and 31. percent of the respondents strongly disagree the statement, with regards to statement Female workers are work alcoholic 35 percent of the workers strongly agreed the statement, 40.3 percent of the agreed the proclamation, 7 percent of the respondents have no opinion, 30 percent of respondents disagree and 7.7 percent of the respondents strongly disagree the statement, with regards to statement Female are more loyalty towards work 33.3 percent of the workers strongly agreed the statement, 39.7 percent of the agreed the proclamation, 10.7 percent of the respondents have no opinion, 21

percent of respondents disagree and 7 percent of the respondents strongly disagree the statement, respondents opinion on the statement sexual harassment revealed that 34 percent of the workers strongly agreed the statement, 40.3 percent of the agreed the proclamation, 7 percent of the respondents have no opinion,10.3 percent of respondents disagree and 8.3 percent of the respondents strongly disagree the statement, with regards to statement Female worker are honest 33.7 percent of the workers strongly agreed the statement, 39.7 percent of the agreed the proclamation, 9.3 percent of the respondents have no opinion,9 percent of respondents disagree and 8.3 percent of the respondents strongly disagree the statement, it could be inferred from the empirical verification that majority of the statement contains the working environment for women workers in leather industries that lot of constraints exists in the environment, however, women converting the constraints into comfortable situation for the more effective working environment in the study area.

Table 5.17 : Frequency of injury or accidents in work place

Response category	Nos	Percentage
Frequently	30	10.0
Occasionally	60	20.0
Rarely	86	28.7
Never	124	41.3
Total	300	100.0

Source: Computed from primary data.

Fig.5.10

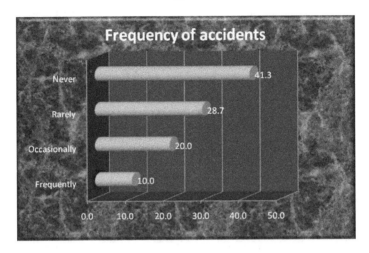

Table 5.17 illustrates the frequent of accidents occurring in the companies of respondents in the study area, 10 percent of the respondents opined that accidents occurred frequently, 20 percent accidents taken place occasionally, 28.7 percent revealed rarely accidents occurred in their companies, 41.3 percent of the respondents were told that accidents never occurred in their companies, generally accidents related with the protective and precautionary measures taken by the companies, Accidents and injuries were reported to be relatively frequent in the industry. Reported accidents/injuries were, however, relatively minor, e.g. scissor cuts or needle pricks on fingers were the most common, while sewing machine injuries on fingers were also reported as occupational injuries. Employers were apparently not very keen on implementing safety measures, especially in the leather footwear industries. In the leather footwear industry, about one-third reported occupational safety and protective equipment were being provided. From the responses of the women workers it was quite apparent that employers commonly ignored the stipulation of the labour law regarding occupational safety measures. Among the illnesses most frequently reported, ulcers on hands and coughing were experienced mostly by leather footwear workers. Although it is difficult to say anything conclusively on the basis of just these observations, it certainly raises questions as to whether generally unhygienic work places and the

155

inhalation of wool dust were behind the observed frequency of illnesses. In the same manner, fainting incidents were reported workers but no obvious explanation could be discerned. It could be due to the stress of working to meet production quotas.

Table 5.18: Facilities and benefits received by workers

Response category	Highly satisfied	Percent	satisfied	Percent	Not satisfied	Percent
Clothing/uniform	56	18.7	80	26.7	164	54.7
Canteen	72	24.0	97	32.3	131	43.7
ESI	71	23.7	84	28.0	145	48.3
Provision of basic needs like	74	24.7	86	28.7	140	46.7

Source: Computed from primary data.

Fig.5.11

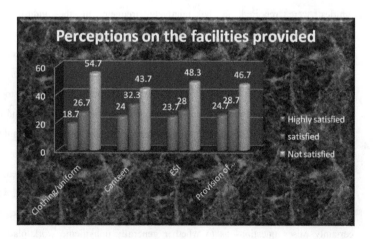

Table 5.18 illustrates the respondent's perception on the facilities provided by the company with regard to the clothing/uniform 18.7 percent were highly satisfied, 26.7 percent have satisfied and 54.7 percent were not satisfied by the provision, with respect to the canteen facilities 24 percent were highly satisfied, 32.3 percent have satisfied and 43.7 percent were not satisfied by the provision, with regard to ESI facility 23.7 percent were highly satisfied, 28 percent have satisfied and 48.3 percent were not satisfied by the provision, in connection with the provision basic needs like soaps and tooth paste etc 24.7 percent were highly satisfied, 28.7 percent have satisfied and 46.7 percent were not satisfied by the provision,it could be inferred from the empirical verification that majority of the respondents have not satisfied with the provision of facilities to the leather workers, even though workers were entitled to certain benefits and facilities from their employer but due to their weaker negotiating power, receiving those benefits depended entirely on the generosity of their employer in the same line Leave entitlements were not usually defined clearly, and nearly one-half said they were not allowed any leave; another one- fourth reported having a few days annual leave during the time of the above-mentioned festivals, The only other benefit that around one-tenth of the domestics received was medical treatment for minor ailments. At the outset workers have not received adequate facilities from the companies in the study area.

Table. 5.19: Problems experienced at work

Response category	Nos	Percent
Long hours of work	66	22.0
No time for rest or leisure	47	15.7
Often reprimanded by employer	46	15.3
Verbally abused	80	26.7
Sexual harassment	61	20.3
Total	300	100.0

Source: Computed from primary data.

157

Fig.5.12

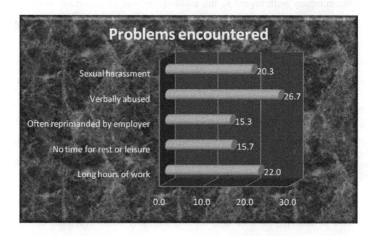

Table.5.19 indicates the various problems encountered by the respondents n their working place, 26.7 percent revealed the magnitude of verbal abuse of the superiors in the office, 22 percent of the respondents opined long hours of work is the important problem, 20.3 percent and 15.7 percent revealed that sexual harassment and non-availability of leisure time were the important problem respectively and 15.3 percent of the respondents noted that reprimand of the superiors was the important problem in the working places, sexual harassment, Harassment at work is usually considered a main reason why women might refrain from working outside the home. Nearly 40 per cent of those interviewed reported facing some kind of harassment but in general, the incidence was very low for all three sectors. The harassment that was reported was verbal abuse by employers or supervisors. There was only one instance of sexual abuse. Women usually refrain from sharing incidents of sexual harassment at the workplace with others, including family members, for fear of shame. It can be considered virtually impossible that any of the women would have spoken of harassment with the interviewer – a complete stranger. The most common types of problems included minor injuries, no proper facilities to cater the menopause period problems, cracked skin in winter was also relatively common, as were reports

of backache - both of which are related to the work (with freezing water and squatting on the floor). Gastric and other stomach disorders, as well as giddiness and tiredness were also commonly mentioned as the consequences of the work environment on health of the respondents in the study area.

5.7 Status of the women workers in their house

Family is the very indispensable element of the human beings especially in India family system is the vital tools which give privileges and also restrictions especially such kind of pressures are poised on women more, it is also imperative to study the women workers role in their family to analyze the socio-economic condition in holistic dimension.

Table 5.20: Distribution of the respondents with the entitlement of decision making in various situations in her family

Response Category	Work related issues	Percent	Domestic issues	Percent	Heirs related issues	Percent
Herself	80	26.7	22	7.3	51	17.0
Brother	23	7.7	10	3.3	9	3.0
Father	23	7.7	15	5.0	13	4.3
Husband	88	29.3	63	21.0	152	50.7
Father in Law	35	11.7	35	11.7	30	10.0
Mother in law	51	17.0	155	51.7	45	15.0
Total	300	100.0	300	100.0	300	100.0

Source: Computed from primary data.

Fig .5.13

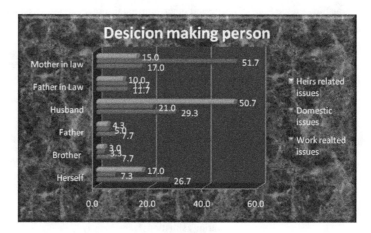

Table 5.20 depicts the decision making power of the respondents. with respect to work related issues 26.7 respondents were have the liberty to take the decision on their own, 7.7 percent rely upon their brother for the decision, 7.7 percent and 29.3 percent of the respondents depends on father and husband respectively, 11.7 percent depend on their father-in-law and 17 percent sought the help of mother-in law,with regard to the issue pertains to domestic issues 7.3 respondents were have the liberty to take the decision on their own, 3.3 percent rely upon their brother for the decisions, 5 percent and 21 percent of the respondents depends on father and husband respectively, 11.7 percent depend on their father-in-law and 51.7 percent sought the help of mother-in law, with regard to the issue pertains to their heir related issues 17 respondents were have the liberty to take the decision on their own, 3 percent rely upon their brother for the decisions, 4.3 percent and 50.7 percent of the respondents depends on father and husband respectively, 10 percent depend on their father-in-law and 15 percent sought the help of mother-in law, In a male dominated society like India and extent of power in decision making enjoyed by women is very important in assessing their status in the family. In order to analyze the role of women in decision making process one would have to assess their influence on all the family decisions. Since a complete record of decision is unobtainable, some important decision making areas were selected like who makes decisions about women, and children's

160

education, employment, marriage, dowry, medical treatment. These areas of decision making in the family include both money centered and children-centered decision making areas. They money centered decision making areas are the most important in assessing the status of women in the family, since traditionally it is the male who takes decisions in the economic spheres of the family. In this background an attempt was made to find out the extent of power in decision making in the context of various matters stated above.

Table. 5.21:Behaviour of husband at home

Response Category	Chastisement to wife	Percent	Abusing to wife	Percent	Insulting wife and family	Percent	Drinking liquor and harassing the family	Percent
Not Applicable	142	47.3	142	47.3	142	47.3	142	47.3
Yes	101	33.7	97	32.3	96	32.0	84	28.0
No	57	19.0	61	20.3	62	20.7	74	24.7
Total	300	100.0	300	100.0	300	100.0	300	100.0

Source: Computed from primary data.

162

Fig.5.14

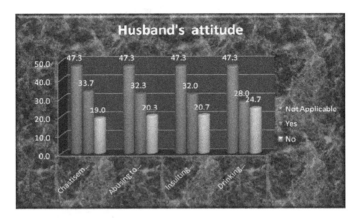

The above table 5.21 depicts that 47.3 % respondents belong to unmarried, widow and divorcee category hence the question is not applicable to them. with regards to chastisement 19 % respondents enjoy high status as their husbands do not indulge in chastisement whereas 33.7 % respondents have low status, as their husband indulge in chastisement. As regards abusing by the husband 22.3 % respondents do agree that their husbands do not indulge in abusing and they feel better status then those women whose husband's indulge in abusing. It is not necessary that if a husband does not indulge in chastisement, he is not involved in abusing his wife. This fact is clear from the table that 32 % respondents accepted abusing by the husband. with regard to drinking liquor and harassing the family 28 percent of the respondents accepted that they have been undergoing the stress whereas 24.7 percent opined that they didn't experienced such a problem, generally the status of women depends by a large on the behaviour of husband at home. If the behaviour of husband is good that the does not indulge in chastisement, abusing, turning out his wife from the house, insulting his wife from the house, insulting his wife and children and drinking liquor and harassing his wife and family, then wife may enjoy a good status within family. If the husbands indulge in any or all of the above activities then the life of his wife and family becomes hell and a woman cannot even think of a high status,The empirical investigation shows that an overwhelming majority of the respondents have not enjoyed a high status in terms of not being turned out from the house by their husbands.

Table 5.22: Distribution of respondents according to their position in family due to their employment

Response Category	Better position in the family due to employment	Percentage
Yes	172	57.3
No	128	42.7
Total	300	100.0

Source: Computed from primary data.

Fig 5.15

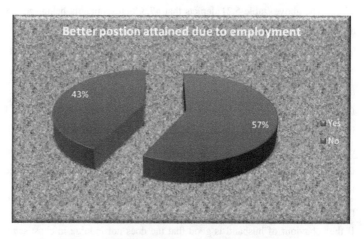

The table 5.22 reveals that near about 57.3 of the respondents agree with the fact that their status has become high due to employment whereas 42.7 % of the respondents do not agree with this fact. According to them there is no correlation between the status and employment in the family. Employment is an important factor contributing to the status of women in the family. If a woman is employed or works outside the family to earn money, she remains absent from the house for a fixed time, this results in narrowing down her role at home. Thus an employed or working woman may exert a pressure for rearrangement of the household management. Sharing

164

of the household responsibilities by the male member makes her traditional housekeeping role. It is, therefore, expected that an employed women or a women working in other fields for earning money has a low participation in housekeeping activities. at the outset it could be inferred from the empirical verification that employment might have not influence the status of the women in the home.

Table.5.23: Age at marriage

Response category	Nos	Percent
Not Applicable	78	26.0
Below 18	38	12.7
18-21	71	23.7
21-23	28	9.3
23-25	34	11.3
25-27	23	7.7
Above 27	28	9.3
Total	300	100.0

Source: Computed from primary data.

Fig: 5.16

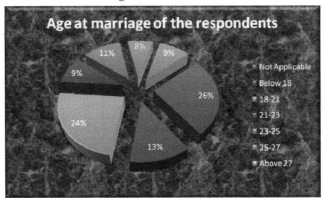

Table 5.23 exemplifies the information on respondents age at marriage in the study area, the question is not applicable to 26 percent of the respondents as they have not got married so far, 12.7 percent got married below 18 age, 23.7 percent of the respondents have got married

165

at the age between 18-21,9.3 percent of the respondents have got married at the age between 21-23,11.3 percent of the respondents have got married at the age between 23-25,7.7 percent of the respondents have got married at the age between 25-27,9.3 percent of the respondents have got married at the age above 27,age at the time of marriage has got significant influence on the working capacity of women workers. Most of the female workers got married at an early age. After the marriage, they are not kept at home, but they are forced to work, These young women workers are found working through out the day in office and at home. Besides the household duties, they have to look after the aged parents and husband. Added to this, poor living environment with poor sanitation and insufficient pure drinking water in the construction premises lead to progressive deterioration in health of women workers.

5.8 Work environment and health

Work environment unleash lot of externalities to the employees both positive and negative such as, low hygienic, protective measures, hazardous working conditions and ignorance causes severe impact on the health of the employees. Especially women workers have suffered lot, it is essential to explore the relationship between work environment and the health deterioration of the women workers.

Table.5.24: Influence of work environment on disease

Response category	Yes	Percent	No	Percent
Work Environment is responsible for Headache	208	69.3	92	30.7
work environment cause Anxiety disorder	187	62.3	113	37.7
Work Environment caused back pain	190	63.3	110	36.7
Work Environment caused any injuries	198	66.0	102	34.0
Work environment causes skin rashes	200	66.7	100	33.3
Work Environment caused Ulcers	185	61.7	115	38.3
Work Environment caused Dust allergy problem	210	70.0	90	30.0

Source: Computed from primary data.

Fig.5.17

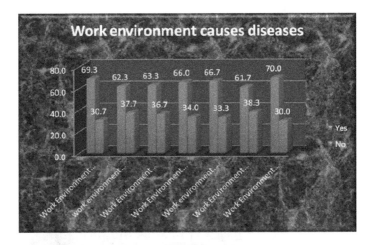

Table.5.24 depicts the opinion of the respondents whether work environment is caused any diseases, 69.3 percent of the respondents opined that the work environment caused headache,30.7 percent of the respondents opined no for the same,62.3 percent of the respondents opined that the work environment caused anxiety disorder,37.7 percent of the respondents revealed it didn't caused, 63.3 percent of the respondents accepted that work environment caused backpain,36.7 percent of the respondents didn't accept the same66 percent of the respondents opined that the work environment caused injuries, 34 percent of the respondents opined no for the same,66.7 percent of the respondents opined that the work environment caused skin rashes,33.3 percent of the respondents didn't accept the statement,61.7 percent of the respondents opined that the work environment caused ulcers,38.7 percent of the respondents opined no for the same,70 percent of the respondents opined that the work environment caused dust allergy problems,30 percent revealed no for the assertion, hence at the outset working environment responsible for diseases of the respondents. Generally the leather footwear industries have negative repercussions on the health status of the human beings and its intensity is more for the people who have been engaging directly with leather works, moreover companies have not followed the adequate safety measures for their workers so health deterioration is that the workers are working in the hazardous environment

Table.5.25: **Slabs of average expenditure on illness caused by job**

Response category	Nos	Percent
Up to 100	27	9.0
100-200	98	32.7
200-300	141	47.0
300 and above	34	11.3
Total	300	100.0

Source: Computed from primary data.

Fig.5.18

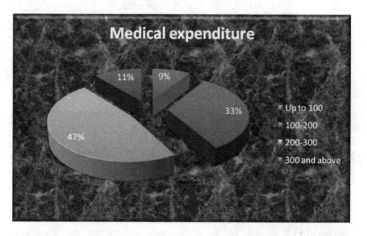

Table 5.25 exemplifies monthly expenditure incurred by the respondents towards treatment for the diseases caused due to work stress, 9 percent of the respondents spent upto Rs 100 per month, 32.7 percent use to spent between 100-200,nearly 47 percent of the respondents spent between 200 -300 per month, 11.3 percent spend more than 300 per month, it could be inferred from the empirical verification that respondents spent around 5 to 10 percent of their salary for the health deterioration occurred due to work environment, Ability implies the capacity of the workers to meet the minimum medical expenses by oneself and to the immediate dependents. When workers are getting only the subsistence income, it would

be highly painful to set apart an amount for meeting medical contingencies. It is also to be noted that the non existence of the health\welfare assistance either from the employer or from the government and the limited income of the informal sector workers limit their affordability of health expenditure. More over the recent hike in medical expenses consequent of the ongoing globalization make the already painful medical needs worse confounded. Hence it is apparent that major chunk of the respondents faced the negative consequences in the study area.

5.9 Perceptions on the nexus between work environment and physical health

This section illustrates the respondents perception on degree of importance of various components of work environment on physical health status of the women leather footwear workers in the study area.

Table 5.26: *Unhygienic work Environment have impact on the health of the workers*

Response category	Nos	Percentage
Strongly agree	126	42
Agree	70	23.2
Undecided	51	17
Disagree	38	12.6
Strongly Disagree	15	5.1
Total	300	100

Source: computed from primary data

Table 5.26 exemplified the opinion of the respondents about the Unhygienic work Environment have impact on the health of the workers 42.0 percent of the workers strongly agreed the statement, 23.2 percent of the agreed the proclamation, 17 percent of the respondents have no opinion, 12.6 percent of respondents disagree and 5.1 percent of the respondents strongly disagree the statement, hence it was apparent from the empirical findings that the nearly 68 percent of the agreed upon the statement which clearly indicates that the work environment and the nature of the work closely correlated with the health status of the respondents in the study area.

169

Table.5.27:*Job stress diminish the health status*

Response category	Nos	Percentage
Strongly agree	22	7.1
Agree	24	8
Undecided	57	19
Disagree	94	31.4
Strongly Disagree	103	34.5
Total	300	100

Source: Computed from primary data.

Table 5.27 exemplified the opinion of the respondents on the statement that Job stress diminish the health status, 7.1 percent of the workers strongly agreed the statement, 8.0 percent of the agreed the proclamation, 19.0 percent of the respondents have no opinion, 31.4 percent of respondents disagree and 34.5 percent of the respondents strongly disagree the statement, hence it was apparent from the empirical findings that the nearly 63 percent of the respondents didn't agreed upon the statement that Job stress diminishes the health status of the workers in the study area.

Table 5.28:Poor didn't night sleep affect the health

Response category	Nos	Percent
Strongly agree	43	14.2
Agree	49	16.8
Undecided	31	10.2
Disagree	100	33.2
Strongly Disagree	77	25.7
Total	300	100

Source: Computed from primary data.

Table 5.28 exemplified the opinion of the respondents on the statement that Poor sleep during night time didn't affect the health , 14.2 percent of the workers strongly agreed the statement, 16.8 percent of the agreed the proclamation, 10.2 percent of the respondents have no opinion, 33.2 percent of respondents disagree and 25.7 percent of the respondents strongly disagree the statement, hence it was apparent from the empirical findings that the nearly 66 percent of the respondents didn't agreed upon the statement that poor sleep during night time didn't affect health status of the respondents in the study area.

Table 5.29:Measures are taken to reduce the intense of occupational hazards

Response category	Nos	Percent
Strongly agree	43	14.2
Agree	57	19
Undecided	43	14.4
Disagree	83	27.7
Strongly Disagree	74	24.8
Total	300	100

Source: Computed from primary data.

Table5.29 exemplified the opinion of the respondents on the statement that measures are taken to reduce the intense of occupational hazards, 14.2 percent of the workers strongly agreed the statement, 19.0 percent of the agreed the proclamation, 14.4 percent of the respondents have no opinion, 27.7 percent of respondents disagree and 24.8 percent of the respondents strongly disagree the statement, hence it was apparent from the empirical findings that the nearly 52 percent of the respondents didn't agreed upon the statement that the measures are taken to reduce the intense of occupational hazards in the study area.

Table 5.30: *Industrial wastages are disposed in healthy way*

Response category	Nos	Percent
Strongly agree	6	2
Agree	8	2.9
Undecided	30	10
Disagree	121	40.3
Strongly Disagree	135	44.9
Total	300	100

Source: Computed from primary data.

Table 5.30 illustrates the opinion of the respondents on the statement that Industrial wastages are disposed in healthy way. Merely 2 percent of the workers strongly agreed the statement, 2.9 percent of the agreed the proclamation, 10.0 percent of the respondents have no opinion, 40.3 percent of respondents disagree and 44.9 percent of the respondents strongly disagree the statement, hence it was apparent from the empirical findings that the nearly 85 percent of the respondents didn't agreed upon the statement that Industrial wastages are disposed in healthy way in the study area which consequently have negative impact on the health among the workers and the inhabitants in the area.

5.10 Protective measures

This section illustrates the protective measures taken by the industries to preserve the employees health in terms of curative and preventable measures, it could be inferred from the empirical verification that the protective measures are not adequate for the employees in the study area.

Table 5.31: Dye chemical didn't affect health of the workers

Response category	Nos	Percentage
Strongly agree	13	4.4
Agree	25	7.5
Undecided	64	21.2
Disagree	108	36.7
Strongly Disagree	90	30.1
Total	300	100.0

Source: Computed from primary data

Table 5.31 illustrates the opinion of the respondents on the statement that Dye chemical didn't affect health of the workers. Merely 4.4 percent of the workers strongly agreed the statement, 7.5 percent of the agreed the proclamation, 21.2 percent of the respondents have no opinion, 36.7 percent of respondents disagree and 30.1 percent of the respondents strongly disagree the statement, hence it was apparent from the empirical findings that the nearly 67 percent of the respondents didn't agreed upon the statement and nearly 22 percent didn't have any opinion which emphatically implies that Dye chemical didn't affect health of the workers in the study area.

Table 5.32: Dust levels emitted within the prescribed intensity

Response category	Nos	Percentage
Strongly agree	16	5.3
Agree	46	15.3
Undecided	67	22.6
Disagree	99	33.0
Strongly Disagree	72	24.1
Total	300	100.0

Source: Computed from primary data

Table 5.32 illustrates the opinion of the respondents on the statement that dust level is emitted within the prescribed intensity. Merely 5.3 percent of the workers strongly agreed the statement, 15.3 percent of the agreed the proclamation, 22.6 percent of the respondents have no opinion, 33.0 percent of respondents disagree and 24.1 percent of the respondents strongly disagree the statement, hence it was apparent from the empirical findings that the nearly 57 percent of the respondents didn't agreed upon the statement and nearly 22 percent didn't have any opinion which emphatically implies that management is emitting the dust level within the prescribed intensity in order to protect the health of the workers of the industries in the study area.

Table.5.33: *Management provided all the protective Equipments for the workers*

Response category	Nos	Percentage
Strongly agree	22	7.5
Agree	28	9.3
Undecided	61	20.4
Disagree	100	33.2
Strongly Disagree	89	29.6
Total	300	100

Source: Computed from primary data

Table.5.33 illustrates the opinion of the respondents on the statement that Management provided all the protective Equipments for the workers . Merely 7.5 percent of the workers strongly agreed the statement, 9.3 percent of the agreed the proclamation, 20.4 percent of the respondents have no opinion, 33.2 percent of respondents disagree and 29.6 percent of the respondents strongly disagree the statement, hence it was apparent from the empirical findings that the nearly 63 percent of the respondents didn't agreed upon the statement and nearly 21 percent didn't have any opinion which categorically implies that management didn't have adequate concern on the protection of the workers and it also didn't comply with the ILO norms to ensure the protection of the workers in the production process.

Table.5.34:Workers get back from the work with aches regularly

Response category	Nos	Percent
Strongly agree	61	20.1
Agree	80	26.5
Undecided	91	30.5
Disagree	44	14.8
Strongly Disagree	24	8
Total	300	100

Source: Computed from primary data

Table 5.34 illustrates the opinion of the respondents on the statement that workers are get back from the work with aches regularly 20.1 percent of the workers strongly agreed the statement, 26.5 percent of the agreed the proclamation, 30.5 percent of the respondents have no opinion, 14.8 percent of respondents disagree and 8 percent of the respondents strongly disagree the statement, Hence it was apparent from the empirical findings that   nearly 47 percent of the respondents agreed upon the statement and nearly 30.5 percent of them didn't have any opinion   which emphatically implies that workers regularly get twinge from the process of working in the industries in the study area.

Table 5.35: Hazardous to wrist and hand in working in the machinery without proper protection

Response category	Nos	Percentage
Strongly agree	68	22.6
Agree	99	33
Undecided	75	25
Disagree	24	8
Strongly Disagree	34	11.5
Total	300	100

Source: Computed from primary data

175

Table 5.35 illustrates the opinion of the respondents on the statement that Hazardous to wrist and hand in working in the machinery without proper protection, 22.6 percent of the workers strongly agreed the statement, 33.0 percent of the agreed the proclamation, 25 percent of the respondents have no opinion, 8 percent of respondents disagree and 11.5 percent of the respondents strongly disagree the statement, hence it was apparent from the empirical findings that the nearly 47 percent of the respondents agreed upon the statement and nearly 25 percent of the didn't have opinion which emphatically implies that workers are aware that it is very dangerous to work in the heavy machines without proper safety measures in the study area.

Table 5.36:Immediate attention given during emergency

Response category	Nos	Percentage
Strongly agree	8	2.7
Agree	16	5.1
Undecided	47	15.9
Disagree	124	41.2
Strongly Disagree	105	35.2
Total	300	100

Source: Computed from primary data

Table 5.36 illustrates the opinion of the respondents on the statement that immediate attention is given during emergency. Merely 2.7 percent of the workers strongly agreed the statement, 5.1 percent of the agreed the statement, 15.9 percent of the respondents have no opinion, 41.2 percent of respondents disagree and 35.2 percent of the respondents strongly disagree the statement, hence it was apparent from the empirical findings that the nearly 76 percent of the respondents didn't agreed upon the statement and nearly 16 percent didn't have any opinion which categorically implies that management didn't have adequate concern on the protection of the workers and it also didn't comply with the ILO norms to ensure the protection of the workers in the production process

Table 5.37: Unhygienic water in the industries didn't affect the health of the workers

Response category	Nos	Percentage
Strongly agree	17	5.8
Agree	22	7.1
Undecided	69	22.8
Disagree	110	36.9
Strongly Disagree	82	27.4
Total	300	100

Source: Computed from primary data

Table 5.37 illustrates the opinion of the respondents on the statement that Unhygienic water in the industries didn't affect the health of the workers, Merely 5.8 percent of the workers strongly agreed the statement, 7.1 percent of the agreed the statement, 22.8 percent of the respondents have no opinion, 36.9 percent of respondents disagree and 27.4 percent of the respondents strongly disagree the statement, hence it was apparent from the empirical findings that the nearly 64 percent of the respondents didn't agreed upon the statement and nearly 23 percent didn't have any opinion which categorically implies that Unhygienic water in the industries affect the health of the workers in the study area.

Table 5.38:Management provide adequate protection measures to the workers

Response category	Nos	Percentage
Strongly agree	14	4.6
Agree	24	8
Undecided	68	22.8
Disagree	104	34.5
Strongly Disagree	90	30.1
Total	300	100

Source: Computed from primary data

Table 5.38 illustrates the opinion of the respondents on the statement that immediate attention is given during emergency. Merely 4.6 percent of the workers strongly agreed the statement, 8.0 percent of the agreed the statement, 22.8 percent of the respondents have no opinion, 34.5 percent of respondents disagree and 30.1 percent of the respondents strongly disagree the statement, hence it was apparent from the empirical findings that the nearly 65 percent of the respondents didn't agreed upon the statement and nearly 23 percent didn't have any opinion which categorically implies that management didn't have adequate concern on the protection of the workers and it also didn't comply with the ILO norms to ensure the protection of the workers in the production.

5.11 Perceptions on Job Involvement of the Respondents

This section of the analysis confine to the perceptions on the job involvement of the respondents in the study area. As job involvement is the prominent criteria for the job satisfaction and the important tool to assess socio-economic conditions of the leather footwear workers

Table 5.39:Job is the first priority rather than the family members

Response category	Nos	Percentage
Strongly agree	28	9.1
Agree	47	15.9
Undecided	28	9.1
Disagree	109	36.7
Strongly Disagree	88	29.2
Total	300	100

Source: Computed from primary data

Table 5.39 demonstrates the opinion of the respondents on the statement that job is the first priority rather than family members. Merely 9.1 percent of the workers strongly agreed the statement, 15.9 percent of the agreed the statement, 9.1 percent of the respondents have no opinion, 36.7 percent of respondents disagree and 29.2 percent of the respondents strongly disagree the statement, hence it was apparent from the empirical findings that the nearly 66

178

percent of the respondents didn't agreed upon the statement and nearly 9.1 percent didn't have any opinion which categorically implies that workers given preference to the family members than the job it is quite obvious that people tend to earn to cater the family members requirements hence job is the means than end.

Table 5.40:Not enthusiastic to take up the responsibility in the company

Response category	Nos	Percentage
Strongly agree	24	8
Agree	35	11.9
Undecided	47	15.7
Disagree	110	36.5
Strongly Disagree	84	27.9
Total	300	100

Source: Computed from primary data

Table 5.40 demonstrates the opinion of the respondents on the statement that job is the first priority rather than family members. Merely 8 percent of the workers strongly agreed the statement, 11.9 percent of the agreed the statement, 15.7 percent of the respondents have no opinion, 36.5 percent of respondents disagree and 29.9 percent of the respondents strongly disagree the statement, hence it was apparent from the empirical findings that the nearly 66 percent of the respondents didn't agreed upon the statement and nearly 15.7 percent didn't have any opinion which categorically implies that workers given preference to the family members than the job it quite obvious that people tend to earn to cater the family members requirements hence job is the means than end.

179

Table 5.41: *Dedication provide promotion and incentive in the job*

Response category	Nos	Percentage
Strongly agree	22	7.3
Agree	31	10.2
Undecided	52	17.5
Disagree	101	33.8
Strongly Disagree	94	31.2
Total	300	100

Source: Computed from primary data

Table 5.41 demonstrates the opinion of the respondents on the statement that dedication in job facilitated to get promotion and incentive in the job. Merely 7.3 percent of the workers strongly agreed the statement, 10.2 percent of the agreed the statement, 17.5 percent of the respondents have no opinion, 33.8 percent of respondents disagree and 31.2 percent of the respondents strongly disagree the statement, hence it was apparent from the empirical findings that the nearly 65 percent of the respondents didn't agreed upon the statement and nearly 17.5 percent didn't have any opinion which categorically implies that dedication in job facilitated to get promotion and incentive in the job.

Table 5.42: *Presently holding interesting job*

Response category	Nos	Percentage
Strongly agree	16	5.8
Agree	27	9.1
Undecided	67	22.1
Disagree	103	34.1
Strongly Disagree	87	29
Total	300	100

Source: Computed from primary data

Table 5.42 demonstrates the opinion of the respondents on the statement that presently holding interesting job. Merely 5.8 percent of the workers strongly agreed the statement, 9.1 percent of the agreed the statement, 22.1 percent of the respondents have no opinion, 34.1 percent of respondents disagree and 29 percent of the respondents strongly disagree the statement, hence it was apparent from the empirical findings that the nearly 63 percent of the respondents didn't agreed upon the statement and nearly 22.1 percent didn't have any opinion which categorically implies that the present employment of the respondents are not interesting one.

Table 5.43:*Hard work acknowledged with incentives in the company*

Response category	Nos	Percentage
Strongly agree	115	38.5
Agree	82	27.4
Undecided	52	17.3
Disagree	29	9.7
Strongly Disagree	22	7.1
Total	300	100

Source: Computed from primary data

Table 5.43 demonstrates the opinion of the respondents on the statement that pay and amount of work is closely correlated.38.5 percent of the workers strongly agreed the statement, 27.4 percent of the agreed the statement, 17.3 percent of the respondents have no opinion,9.7 percent of respondents disagree and 7.1 percent of the respondents strongly disagree the statement, hence it was apparent from the empirical findings that the nearly 66 percent of the respondents agreed upon the statement and nearly 17.3 percent didn't have any opinion which categorically implies that the respondents have perceived the correlation between the payment and amount of the work is very high, thus the people who work more would receive more money in the study area.

Table 5.44: Comfortable environment persuade to work effectively

Response category	Nos	Percentage
Strongly agree	14	4.9
Agree	25	8.4
Undecided	71	23.9
Disagree	102	33.4
Strongly Disagree	88	29.4
Total	300	100

Source: Computed from primary data

Table 5.44 demonstrates the opinion of the respondents on the statement that grievances of the workers are addressed quickly. Merely 4.9 percent of the workers strongly agree the statement, 8.4 percent of them agree with the statement, 23.9 percent of the respondents have no opinion, 33.4 percent of respondents disagree and 29.4 percent of the respondents strongly disagree the statement, hence it was apparent from the empirical findings that the nearly 62 percent of the respondents didn't agreed upon the statement and nearly 23.9 percent didn't have any opinion which categorically implies that the grievances of the employees are not meet out quickly.

5.12 Perceptions on the nexus between work environment and job satisfaction

This section illustrates the respondents perception on the importance of various components of work environment on job satisfaction, as job satisfaction is equally important phenomenon to the physical health status to involve in the production process more effectively.

Table 5.45:*Management given liberty to take decision*

Response category	Nos	Percent
Strongly agree	17	5.8
Agree	50	16.8
Undecided	87	29
Disagree	85	27.9
Strongly Disagree	61	20.6
Total	300	100

Source: Computed from primary data

Table 5.45 illustrates the opinion of the respondents on the statement that Management given liberty to take decision. Merely 5.8 percent of the workers strongly agreed the statement, 16.8 percent of the agreed the proclamation, 29 percent of the respondents have no opinion, 27.9 percent of respondents disagree and 20.6 percent of the respondents strongly disagree the statement. Hence it was apparent from the empirical findings that the nearly 47 percent of the respondents didn't agree upon the statement and nearly 30 percent didn't have any opinion which categorically implies that the management has not given the liberty to the workers to take required levels of official decision independently in the area.

Table 5.46: *Have cordial relationship with the management*

Response category	Nos	Percentage
Strongly agree	14	4.6
Agree	29	9.5
Undecided	65	21.7
Disagree	89	29.6
Strongly Disagree	103	34.5
Total	300	100

Source: Computed from primary data

Table 5.46 illustrates the opinion of the respondents on the statement that workers have cordial relationship with the management. Merely 4.6 percent of the workers strongly agree the statement, 9.5 percent of them agree the proclamation, 21.7 percent of the respondents have no opinion, 29.6 percent of respondents disagree and 34.5 percent of the respondents strongly disagree the statement, hence it was apparent from the empirical findings that the nearly 65 percent of the respondents didn't agree upon the statement and nearly 22 percent didn't have any opinion which emphatically implies that workers doesn't maintain the cordial relationship with the management in the area.

Table.5.47 :Too much constraints and complications exists in the company as well as in home

Response category	Nos	Percentage
Strongly agree	74	24.3
Agree	127	42.5
Undecided	28	9.1
Disagree	34	11.9
Strongly Disagree	37	12.2
Total	300	100

Source: Computed from primary data

Table 5.47 illustrates the opinion of the respondents on the statement that Management has too much authoritative control over the employees . 24.3 percent of the workers strongly agreed the statement, 42.5 percent of them agreed on the proclamation, 9.1 percent of the respondents have no opinion, 11.9 percent of respondents disagree and 12.2 percent of the respondents strongly disagree the statement. Hence it was apparent from the empirical findings that nearly 65 percent of the respondents agree upon the statement which emphatically implies that the management discharge too much of authoritative control over the workers in the study area .

Table 5.48: Felt happy of being associated with leather footwear industries

Response category	Nos	Percentage
Strongly agree	16	5.1
Agree	25	7.7
Undecided	65	21.5
Disagree	100	33.8
Strongly Disagree	94	31.9
Total	300	100

Source: Computed from primary data

Table 5.48 illustrates the opinion of the respondents on the statement that Employees are happy to work with the management. Merely 5.1 percent of the workers strongly agreed the statement, 7.7 percent of them agreed the proclamation, 21.5 percent of the respondents have no opinion, 33.8 percent of respondents disagree and 31.9 percent of the respondents strongly disagree the statement. Hence it was apparent from the empirical findings that nearly 65 percent of the respondents didn't agreed upon the statement and nearly 22 percent didn't have any opinion which emphatically implies that the footwear industries unleash high health deterioration which occurred among the workers engaged in it.

Table.5.49:Management attitude also make to work rather than payment alone

Response category	Nos	Percentage
Strongly agree	28	9.7
Agree	34	11.5
Undecided	49	16.6
Disagree	101	33.4
Strongly Disagree	88	28.8
Total	300	100

Source: Computed from primary data

Table 5.49 illustrates the opinion of the respondents on the statement that Management attitude also make to work rather than payment alone. Merely 9.7 percent of the workers strongly agreed the statement, 11.5 percent of the agreed the proclamation, 16.6 percent of the respondents have no opinion, 33.4 percent of respondents disagree and 28.8 percent of the respondents strongly disagree the statement, hence it was apparent from the empirical findings that the nearly 63 percent of the respondents didn't agreed upon the statement and nearly 17 percent didn't have any opinion which emphatically implies that the management attitude didn't provide conducive environment to the workers in the industries.

Table 5.50: *Satisfied with the shift schedule*

Response category	Nos	Percentage
Strongly agree	90	30
Agree	97	32.1
Undecided	48	16.6
Disagree	34	11.9
Strongly Disagree	31	10.2
Total	300	100

Source: Computed from primary data

Table 5.50 exhibits the opinion of the respondents on the statement that satisfied with shift schedule.30 percent of the workers strongly agreed the statement, 32.1percent of the agreed the statement, 16.6 percent of the respondents have no opinion,11.9 percent of respondents disagree and 10.2 percent of the respondents strongly disagree the statement. Hence it was apparent from the empirical findings that nearly 63 percent of the respondents agreed upon the statement and nearly 16.6 percent didn't have any opinion which categorically implies that the respondents are satisfied with the shift schedule followed in their industries.

Table 5.51: *Satisfied with the salary structure*

Response category	Nos	Percentage
Strongly agree	43	14.6
Agree	52	17.3
Undecided	32	10.8
Disagree	95	31.4
Strongly Disagree	78	25.9
Total	300	100

Source: Computed from primary data

Table 5.51 displays the opinion of the respondents on the statement that salary structure is at satisfactory level. 14.6 percent of the workers strongly agreed the statement, 17.3 percent of the agreed the statement, 10.8 percent of the respondents have no opinion, 31.4 percent of respondents disagree and 25.9 percent of the respondents strongly disagree the statement, hence it was apparent from the empirical findings that the nearly 57 percent of the respondents didn't agreed upon the statement and nearly 10.8 percent didn't have any opinion which categorically implies that employees are not satisfied with the present salary structure.

Table 5.52: There was clear understanding of work tasks which were to be performed

Response category	Nos	Percentage
Strongly agree	90	29.9
Agree	80	26.8
Undecided	37	12.4
Disagree	50	16.8
Strongly Disagree	43	14.2
Total	300	100

Source: Computed from primary data

Table 5.52 exhibits the opinion of the respondents on the statement that There was clear understanding of work tasks which were to be performed in the company, 29.9 percent of the workers strongly agreed the statement, 26.8 percent of the agreed the statement, 12.4 percent of the respondents have no opinion,16.8 percent of respondents disagree and 14.2 percent of the respondents strongly disagree the statement. Hence it was apparent from the empirical findings that nearly 55 percent of the respondents agreed upon the statement and nearly 12.4 percent didn't have any opinion which categorically implies that the team work is essential to demand the legitimate privileges from the authorities. Thus it was apparent that the workers expecting good union would serve better to them.

Table 5.53 : *Management has good concern towards it employee*

Response category	Nos	Percentage
Strongly agree	45	15
Agree	29	9.7
Undecided	55	18.1
Disagree	90	30.1
Strongly Disagree	81	27
Total	300	100

Source: Computed from primary data

Table 5.53 exhibits the opinion of the respondents on the statement that management has good concern towards its employee,15.0 percent of the workers strongly agreed the statement, 9.7 percent of the agreed the statement, 18.1 percent of the respondents have no opinion,30.1 percent of respondents disagree and 27 percent of the respondents strongly disagree the statement, hence it was apparent from the empirical findings that the nearly 58 percent of the respondents didn't agreed upon the statement and nearly 18.1 percent didn't have any opinion which categorically implies that management has good concern towards its employee, thus respondents are not satisfied over the attitude of the management towards employee.

Table 5.54: *Satisfied with the style of my approach according to situation in company*

Response category	Nos	Percentage
Strongly agree	29	9.5
Agree	43	14.4
Undecided	52	17.5
Disagree	103	34.5
Strongly Disagree	73	24.1
Total	300	100

Source: Computed from primary data

Table 5.54exhibits the opinion of the respondents on the statement that employers give adequate incentive to the workers, 9.5 percent of the workers strongly agreed the statement, 14.4 percent of the agreed the statement, 17.5 percent of the respondents have no opinion,34.5 percent of respondents disagree and 24.1 percent of the respondents strongly disagree the statement, hence it was apparent from the empirical findings that the nearly 59 percent of the respondents didn't agreed upon the statement and nearly 17.5 percent didn't have any opinion which categorically implies that employers are not providing adequate incentive to the workers.

Table 5.55: *Work load is challenge not a burden*

Response category	Nos	Percentage
Strongly agree	130	43.1
Agree	81	27
Undecided	43	14.2
Disagree	26	8.8
Strongly Disagree	20	6.9
Total	300	100

Source: Computed from primary data

Table 5.55 exhibits the opinion of the respondents on the statement that work load is a challenge not a burden. 43.1 percent of the workers strongly agreed the statement, 27.0 percent of the agreed the statement, 14.2 percent of the respondents have no opinion,8.8 percent of respondents disagree and 6.9 percent of the respondents strongly disagree the statement, hence it was apparent from the empirical findings that the nearly 71 percent of the respondents agreed upon the statement and nearly 14.2 percent didn't have any opinion which categorically implies that the employers perceived the work load as challenge not as a burden.

Table 5.56 *Grievances of the workers have addressed quickly in the industry*

Response category	Nos	Percentage
Strongly agree	15	4.9
Agree	25	8.4
Undecided	70	23.9
Disagree	101	33.4
Strongly Disagree	89	29.4
Total	300	100

Source: Computed from primary data

Table 5.56 demonstrates the opinion of the respondents on the statement that grievances of the workers are addressed quickly. Merely 4.9 percent of the workers strongly agreed the statement, 8.4 percent of the agreed the statement, 23.9 percent of the respondents have no opinion, 33.4 percent of respondents disagree and 29.4 percent of the respondents strongly disagree with the statement. Hence it was apparent from the empirical findings that the nearly 62 percent of the respondents didn't agree upon the statement and nearly 23.9 percent didn't have any opinion which categorically implies that grievances of the employees are not meet out quickly

190

5.13 Test of Hypotheses

Ho: There is no significant influence of socio-cultural factors on the wage and incentive determination for Women workers in leather industries.

Model summary

Model	R	R Square	Adjusted R Square	Std. Error of the Estimate	Durbin-Watson
1	.786(a)	0.692	0.798	10283.79	1.081

A. Predictors: (Constant),Underpaid, Discriminated performance appraisal, Sexual harassment, Male chauvinism, Long working hours for women, Malice attitude of management, No cordial relation with women workers

B. Dependent Variable: Determination of wage and incentive

ANOVA(b)

		Sum of Squares	df	Mean Square	F	Sig.
1	Regression	64965.612	234	323371.954	58.541	.002(a)
	Residual	9254.78	66	81954.889		
	Total	74220.392	300			

A   Predictors: (Constant),Underpaid, Discriminated performance appraisal, Sexual harassment, Male chauvinism, Long working hours for women, Malice attitude of management, No cordial relation with women workers

B   Dependent Variable: Determination of wage and incentive

191

	Unstandardized Coefficients		Standardized Coefficients	t	Sig.
	B	Std. Error	Beta	B	Std. Err
Determination of wage and incentive	2.876	5678		1.742	0.067
Low payment	0.231	0.021	0.67	0.006	0.04
Discriminated performance appraisal	543.8	32.561	0.22	0.008	0.04
Sexual harassment	0.897	0.235	0.32	0.021	0.002
Male chauvinism	41.89	228.6	0.67	0.003	0.02
Long working hours for women	22.98	78.9	0.34	0.015	0.05
Malice attitude of management	0.052	0.189	0.22	0.002	0.03
No cordial relation with women workers of the management	112.7	129.7	0.024	0.001	0.02

$$Y=\alpha +\beta\ x1+\beta x2+\ldots\ldots\ldots\ldots.\beta xn$$

Determination of

wage and incentive   =**2.876+** (0.67- Low payment) + (0.22- discriminated performance appraisal)

(0.01)   (0.04)

(0.32- sexual harassment)+ (0.67 - Chauvinism) + (0.034-working hours) +(0.22 -Malice)

(0.02)   (0.02)   (0.05)   (0.03)

+(0.024 - No cordial relation among workers)

(0.026)

The Multivariate Regression was applied to find how socio-cultural factors determines the wage and incentive for Women workers in leather footwear industries, The Regression result shows that the calculated F value is 2.876 which is greater than the table value of 1.742 at 5 % level of significance. Since the calculated value is greater than the table value, it is inferred that the independent variables have strong influence on the wage and incentive determination in the study area. Thus, the hypothesis is rejected,

Ho: There is no persuasion of working environment on the worker health deterioration

Model Summary

Model	R	R Square	Adjusted R Square	Std. Error of the Estimate	Durbin-Watson
1	.991(a)	.982	.968	1083.786	2.081

A   Predictors: (Constant), Unhygienic work environment, Job stress, Poor Night sleep, No protective equipments, Emitted dust from leather, Dye chemical, Unhygienic water in the industries.

B   Dependent Variable: Health deterioration

ANOVA(b)

Model		Sum of Squares	df	Mean Square	F	Sig.
1	Regression	58075.632	270	12571.954	18.78	.000(a)
	Residual	10578.895	30	2104.889		
	Total	68654.527	300			

A   Predictors: (Constant), Unhygienic work environment, Job stress, Poor Night sleep, No protective equipments, Emitted dust from leather, Dye chemical, Unhygienic water in the industries.

B   Dependent Variable: Health deterioration

Coefficients(a)

193

	Unstandardized Coefficients		Standardized Coefficients	T	Sig.
	B	Std. Error	Beta	B	Std. Er
Health deterioration	1.578	2475		1.008	0.073
Unhygienic work environment	0.057	0.032	0.15	0.03	0.025
Job stress	4.111	3.461	0.19	0.08	0.114
Poor Night sleep	1.836	0.682	0.76	0.56	0.023
No protective equipments	3.058	4.26	0.41	0.42	0.071
Emitted dust from leather	7.707	60.02	0.31	0.81	0.26
Dye chemical	0.091	0.184	0.10	0.24	0.034
Unhygienic water in the industries	3.29	25.9	0.023	0.45	0.045

$$Y = \alpha + \beta\, x1 + \beta x2 + \ldots\ldots\ldots\ldots \beta xn$$

Physical Health   = 1.578 +(0.015- unhygienic work environment)+(0.19-Job stress)

(0.025)   (0.114)

+(0.76-poor night sleep)+(0.41- No protective equipments)+

(0.23)   (0.71)

(0.31- Emitted dust from leather)+ (0.10-Dye Chemicals)

(0.26)   (0.034)

+ (0.023- Unhygienic water in the industries)

(0.045)

    The Multivariate Regression was applied to find whether the working environment factors persuaded the worker health deterioration of the women leather footwear workers in the study area, The Regression result shows that the calculated F value is 1.578 which is greater than the table value of 1.008 at 1 % level of significance. Since the calculated value is greater than the table value it is inferred that the independent variables have strong influence in diminishing   the health conditions of the women leather footwear workers in the study area. Hence the hypothesis is rejected

Ho: There is no significant influence of work environment variables on job satisfaction and constraints in the job profile

Logistic Regression is a technique used when the dependent variable is dichotomous (0 or 1). Unlike OLS, the methods used to estimate the parameters involve nonlinear approaches such as maximum likelihood. The logistic specification is based on the Cumulative Normal Distribution. One of the more useful aspects of logistic regression is that it outputs the probability of the event which will fall between 0 and 1 (0% to 100%). Therefore, given a set of independent variables, you could predict the probability of the event occurring using specification. For this study, it has been attempted to study factors which might influence the job satisfaction and constraints in the job profile. The variable whether the job involvement and job satisfaction has been identified as the outcome variable (dependent variable) where it has been coded as 1 for 'Yes' and 0 'No'.

To study the factors which are likely to affect the constraints in the job profile and job satisfaction the following predictor variables were identified and used in the logistic Regression Analysis:

Model fitting

Model	-2 Log Likelihood (-2LL)	Chi-Square	df	Sig.
Intercept Only	59.02			
Final	171.2	11.1	300	0

Source: Computed from primary data

The values given against 'Intercept only' and 'Final' are the initial and final estimates of the log likelihood function of the model, which explains how well the model fits the data. "Intercept Only" describes the initial estimates of the model that does not control for any predictor variables and simply fits an intercept to predict the outcome variable. The term "Final" describes the final estimates of the model which includes the selected independent variables. This has been arrived at through an iterative process that maximizes the log likelihood estimate outcome variable. By including the predictor variables and maximizing the log likelihood of the dependent variable, the "Final" model should improve upon the

"Intercept Only" model. This can be seen in the differences in the -2 Log Likelihood values associated with the models. The difference between the 'intial' and 'Final' estimates of the -2LL show that there has been an improvement in the model. The goodness of fit of the $-2LL$ value is 186.62 which was used to test the goodness of fit of the model using chi-square test. The chi-square value is 103.13, which is significant at least at 1% level (given as 0.001 under the column 'Sig.'). The 'df' is the degrees of freedom of the Chi-Square distribution used to test the Chi-Sqare statistic and is defined by the number of predictors in the model.

Pseudo R-Square

Cox and Snell	.552
Nagelkerke	.664
McFadden	.541

Source: Computed from primary data

Link function: logit.

For binary logistic regression all data including ten explanatory variables (Payment, Working hours, Work environment, Cordial management, Safety for women, Less health deterioration, Incentives and promotion, gender sensitive privileges , Medical Facilities) the model prediction was done ten explanatory variables. These variables were selected for model building and further validation of model. A cross-correlation matrix was prepared initially to see if the variables were highly correlated to one another. Overall prediction efficiency of the variables was assessed based on Nagelkerke-R^2 and $-$ Log Likelihood values. Influence of individual variables including categorical variables was assessed using Wald statistics. Hosmer and Lemeshow goodness-of-fit test (chi square test) and concordance analysis (classification tables) were done to understand the fit of the model (Hosmer and Lemeshow,1989). Sensitivity (percentage true positive or presence correctly predicted) and specificity (percentage true negative or absence correctly predicted) were calculated for each cut-off point (0.1 to 0.9) and best cut-off point was chosen on the basis of optimum sensitivity and specificity. The cut-off level would allow categorization of the probability values to represent either 0 if it is below the cut-off point or 1 if it is above the cut-off point. Logistic regression was done using the selected variables and at an appropriate cut-off

196

level and the probability of occurrence was estimated for each of the species using the following formula.

Probability of event (or presence) = 1 / (1 – EXP–z)

where, $Z = a + (b1 \, ' \, X1) + (b2 \, ' \, X2) + (b3 \, ' \, X3) + ... (bk \, ' \, Xk)$,

a =constant, b = coefficients and X = predictor variable.

There are several Pseudo R-Squares. It reveals the logit regression does not have an R squared calculated in OLS regression. However, the Pseudo R-square values are similar to the R square in OLS, but are not equivalent to OLS R squares. These pseudo R squares are only rough estimates of how well the model fits the data. From the above table we can see that the R square values vary between 0.541 to 0.664, which suggest that there is a moderate level of correlation between the dependent and independent variables used in the study. The following table ---gives the estimates of the predictor variables used in the study.

- ❖ Payment
- ❖ Working hours
- ❖ Work environment
- ❖ Cordial management
- ❖ Safety
- ❖ Less health deterioration
- ❖ Incentives and promotion
- ❖ gender discrimination
- ❖ Medical Facilities

Logistic regression for women workers- parameter estimates

Variables	Coefficien	S.E.	Wald	df	Sig.	Exp(B)
Threshold (workers engagement)	1.9269	9.0801	0.4509	1	0.007*	0.0009
Payment	0.0054	0.0054	0.8586	1	0.002*	0.9054
Working hours	0.0036	0.0027	1.1484	1	0.003*	0.8964
Work environment	34.38	17.964	3.2967	1	0.005	0.0153
Cordial management	9.1197	8.28	1.0917	1	0.071	1.3635
Safety for women	41.3631	27.166 5	2.0862	1	0.028	0.0729
Less health deterioration	2.2536	0.8721	6.012	1	0.81	0.0738
Incentives and promotion	0.0045	0.0036	0.6786	1	0.001**	0.0504
gender sensitive privileges	0.0036	0.0027	1.0539	1	0.004*	0.6624
Medical Facilities	1.3815	0.7947	2.7216	1	0.003*	4.1778

(Link function: logistic)

* - Significant at 5% level

** - Significant at 1% level

NS   :Not Significant

The results of the regression coefficients of the predictors are given under the heading 'Estimate'. The predicted probability of workers engagement can be calculated using these coefficients (the first value under this column, the coefficient for "Threshold" is the constant term in the model). For a given household, the predicted probability of workers engagement be calculated as F (1.92+ 0.005* payment +0.003* Education of Family member-1+.........+0.004 *wages as agricultural labour-female) Where F is the cumulative distribution function of the standard normal. However, the coefficients cannot be interpreted as we explain in OLS regression. It is explained in OLS that an unit increase in predictor variable value will result in the corresponding the coefficient times value increase in the dependent variable. But it is not so in Logistic Regression. The increase in probability of outcome variable (here going for workers engagement) for one-unit increase in a given predictor is dependent both on the values of the other predictors and the starting value of the given predictors. For example, if we hold all other predictors as constant at zero except age, then the working hour one hour increase from say from 8 to 9 had a different effect than the one year increase from 9 to 10. However, it could be understood from the regression coefficients that, a positive coefficient will mean that an increase in the predictor leads to an increase in the predicted probability. A negative coefficient means that an increase in the predictor leads to a decrease in the predicted probability. Based on this, from the above regression table it could be seen that the predictors Payment, Working hours, Work environment, Cordial management, Safety for women, Less health deterioration, Incentives and promotion, gender sensitive privileges , Medical Facilities have positive effect on dependent variable(Job satisfaction and Job involvement)engaged in women leather footwear workers. That is, increase in these predictors will result in increase in probability of going influence the work engagement through enhancing the job satisfaction and job involvement. There is also one variable, less health deterioration. This variable had negative regression coefficients and these variables tend to lower the probability of influence the dependent variable. Denomination wise results based on the logistic regression analysis showed that payment (sig. at <0.01 level) was almost 10 times more likely, working hours (sig. at. < 0.05 level) was almost 5 times more likely, With regard to work environment (sig. at 0.01 level) was five times more likely, and cordial management odds significant at (< 0.05 level) was five times more likely safety odds significant at(< 0.05 level) was five times likely, Less health deterioration odds significant (>0.05) which didn't have positive influence, with regard to rest of the variables have positive influence towards the dependent variables.

Ho: Job, education and self confidence are not the determinant of women empowerment

Model Summary

Model	R	R Square	Adjusted R Square	Std. Error of the Estimate	Durbin-Watson
1	.678(a)	0.625	0.691	833.79	1.001

A   Predictors: (Constant), job profile, Income, Self-confidence, Education

B   Dependent Variable: Women empowerment

ANOVA (b)

Mode		Sum of Squares	df	Mean Square	F	Sig.
1	Regression	5663.8	167	1331.21	10.2	.002(a)
	Residual	1211.1	133	675.4		
	Total	6874.9	300			

A   Predictors: (Constant), job profile, Income, Self-confidence, Education

B   Dependent Variable: Women empowerment

Coefficients (a)

	Unstandardized Coefficients		Standardized Coefficients	t	Sig.
	B	Std. Error	Beta	B	Std. Error
Women Empowerment	1.161	234.4		1.012	0.38
Job profile	0.098	1.234	0.001	0.54	0.23
Income	0.032	1.112	0.003	0.31	0.44
Self -confidence	0.083	0.871	0.012	0.61	0.55
Education	0.091	0.773	0.022	0.91	0.71

A   Predictors: (Constant), job profile, Income, Self-confidence, Education

B   Dependent Variable: Women empowerment

$$Y = \alpha + \beta\ x1 + \beta x2 + \ldots\ldots\ldots\ldots\beta xn$$

Women Empowerment=1.161+(0.001-job profile)+(0.003-Income)+(0.012- Self -confidence)

(0.23)   (0.44)   (0.55)

+(0.022- education)

(0.71)

The Multivariate Regression was applied to find whether the job is the determinant of women empowerment, The Regression result shows that the calculated F value is 1.161 which is greater than the table value, of 1.012 at 5 % level of significance. Since the calculated value is greater than the table value it is inferred that the job, education and Income variables have strong influence in determining the empowerment of the women leather footwear workers in the study area. Hence the hypothesis is rejected

5.14 Conclusion

The analysis of the information regarding determinants of physical and Mental health status of the respondents in various perspective, it is also illustrated the degree of influence of number factors on the health status of the leather footwear workers in the study area, Hazards in the workplace are often caused by the use of materials, tools, machinery and chemicals .The leather footwear industries which demonstrates the significant manufacturing activity in the study area is known to display poor and even hazardous working conditions. Even the organized sector is found to be no exception to this sorry state of affairs. The women workers face a variety of problems. like basic hygiene facilities, inadequate exhaust filters, fire prevention and medical facilities (even first aid), emergency transport, waste disposal services, and hazard warning signs. New chemicals have increased the ratio of accidents. Most workers are illiterate and do not know what protective measures should be adopted for their jobs. Not only the ignorance but the financial incapability to adapt such strategy is more prevalence in the study area.

CHAPTER VI

Summary and conclusion

6.1 Introduction

A problem of the women's equality has been and still continues to be raised from time to time. To be specific, systematic and formal studies on women have emerged from the 1970s though movements for the liberation of women in almost all capitalist countries have marked their appearance in the 1960s itself. Though women as equal contributors to the economy are a part of the social system and their role in the society has been an area of constant questioning. It is also evident from the history that no mode of production existed without the participation of women though it was in the latent form. The obvious reason for such treatment towards women's work is the andocentric nature of the whole evolution of the social systems. Patriarchy as an ideology of gender relations, has its concrete implicit presence in different social formations and control over sexuality, productive assets, labour forms can be assigned as the cause of genderisation of sex relations and thereby resulting in subordination of the half of the humanity.

Women do two third of the world's work and receive ten percent of the world's income and own 1 percent of the means of production. This is the present picture of women workers in the era of globalization. The International Labour Organization (ILO) in the year assessed that significant changes in world economy, such as rapid globalization, fast-paced technological progress and growing informalization of work have greatly altered women's labour market status in the recent years. The idea of forced labour conjures up sights of people in shackles being led off to perform hard labour to pay back debts. But this no longer holds true, as the modern picture of forced labour in globalized work is young girls working long hours as indentured servants to cruel employers, or servicing long hours in sweat shops for a mere pittance of what their time is worth. Millions of women throughout the world live in conditions of abject deprivation and are attacked against their fundamental human rights for no other reason than that they are women. From coffee to computers, women workers provide the labour that creates the goods that appear in the world's supermarkets and departmental stores.

203

The intensity of oppression is high among the country like India where the rigid cultural clutches have not recognized the contribution of the women in the production process, physical and mental activities have not duly acknowledged, even though the continuous efforts of the awareness campaign, legislative protection and the affirmative action's couldn't reap the adequate outcome. At this juncture the present work tries to analyze the socio-economic conditions and the role of women workers in the productive function of the leather industries. For the study purpose 300 women leather workers were interviewed and were systematically analyzed. The summary of the important findings and meaningful conclusions drawn on the basis of the statistical tests have been precisely presented in this study. This study was proved to be a valuable and worthwhile one as the inferences drawn through a good deal of light in understanding and gaining meaningful insights in the selected components and aspects pertaining to the profile of the Women leather Workers. Accepting that the universe of the study is limited, taking full cognizance of the fact that the study is limited to selected variables and areas and components and finally realizing the need and scope for further research of areas not covered in this study. A few suggestions have been listed out for further research. However, it must be admitted that a comprehensive attempt have been made such as- extensive and intensive research covering all the aspects of women's career in general and women leather workers.

6.2 Summary of the study

The major thrust of this Thesis is to understand the socio-economic conditions of the women workers of leather industries in Tamil Nadu. The findings of the study could be considered as a replication of the entire Tamil Nadu's structure, since the conditions of the workers are more or less similar across the state. Before illustrating in detail the major findings of the study it could be worth enough to sum up the exercises:

The first chapter contains the basic contextual background of the study and importance of the women workers and various elements of Labour in India. An overview, Economic Significance of Women's Role, Constraints of Women Workers, Gender Disparity and Institutional Economics, Women work situation, Women's work and Wages, Empowerment of Women and work situation, Women Labour in Leather Industries, Selection and justification of the study, significance and the features of the

204

workers in India, changing role of women and significance of the study, selection and justification of the study, methodology, objectives have been structured and illustrated in the introductory chapter.

The second chapter consists of literature's review pertaining to the women workers based on both Indian and international studies. At present gender issue is gaining prominence in Indian labour market. The women labour is characterized by low wages, tedious work environment etc. There are very few studies done on the alternative employment sources for women labourers during off-season and the impact of off season unemployment of women labour on their income, family status etc. Studies conducted on the employment, wages, non-farm employment etc have been reviewed, till recently the theoretical and empirical literature on rural labour markets had completely ignored studies on women labourer. Still the plethora of the studies on the domain has been categorized to have better conceptual and theoretical understanding. Studies conducted on the employment, wages, non-farm employment etc have been reviewed under the following headings. Studies pertaining to Women Labour force in the Economy, Studies pertaining to the constraints faced by the Women workers, Studies pertaining to the Gender based labour market discrimination, Studies pertaining to Globalization and its impact on Women workers, Studies pertaining to Women leather workers. Thus this gives sound understanding about the theoretical nuances of the study.

The third chapter examines the various theoretical insights of the women and their works. It began with the feminist perspective and the women labour position in the productive functional theory: Status of women in Vedic Period, Status of women in Post-Vedic Period, Status of Women in Medieval Period, Status of women in contemporary India, Marxism and women, first wave feminist analyses, second wave feminist analyses, psychological theories of women and work, Women Labour force as a conceptual development, Labour Market discrimination in India, Globalization and women workers, Women Labour and ILO norms, Indian Leather footwear industry. In section II of the chapter, Changes in women work participation in India and Tamil Nadu from 1983-84 to 2009-10 have been exhibited.

Fourth chapter describes the profile of the study area, and it deals with the historic significance of Chennai , climatic conditions of the study area, tropical, demographic situation of Chennai, details of the administrative set-up, Medical and educational infrastructure, rain fall, information on industries and marketing facilities have been illustrated in the chapter.

Fifth Chapter exemplifies the analyses of the primary data and the inferences derived from the analysis have been displayed.

Sixth chapter exemplifies the summary and the conclusion and the major findings of the study, policy recommendations, and scope for future research.

6.3 Major Findings of the study

6.3.1 Socio Demographic information

Age of the Respondents

Nearly 58 percentage of the respondents fall under the age group of 31-50 years, 37 percentage of the respondents fall under the age group of below 30 years and only 5 percent of the total respondents fall under the age group of 51-60 year. In the study, age has been taken as one of the important variables for studying the health of the women workers.

Religion

71 percent of the respondents are from Hindu religion, 16 percent belongs to Muslim and 13 percent belongs to Christian religion.

Caste

Around 43.6 percent of the respondents belong to schedule caste, 5.7 percent of the respondents belong to Tribal community, 26 and 43.3 percent of the respondents belongs to MBC and BC respectively. In precise, Majority of the respondent belongs to SC, BC and MBC community in the respondents groups, socially marginalized persons are economically weaker, and SC and ST people are economically vulnerable in the study area.

Educational Qualification

with regard to educational qualification nearly 11.3 percent of the women were illiterates, while 11.3 percent of the respondents have finished primary education, 30 percent of the respondents have completed middle level education and 22.7 percent of the respondents have completed high school education, 4 percent finished their degree and 14.3 percent and 3 percent of the respondents have finished diploma and post graduation respectively.

Marital Status

Nearly 52.7 percent of the respondents are married, 26 percent of the respondents are unmarried, 7 percent of the respondents are divorcee or individual and 14.3 percent of the women were widows, at the outset socio-demographic variables replicate the conditions of the women leather workers.

6.3.2 Economic status of the Respondents

Annual Income

with regard to income of the respondent 50.3 percent of the respondents annual income is less than 60,000, nearly 41 percent of the respondents income range from 60001 to 90,000, 6 percent of the respondents income constitute from 90,001 to 1,20,000, and 3 percent of the respondents annual income is above 1,20,000 , nearly 91 % of the respondents annual income were below 90,000 which implies that the women leather workers were paid less and more over the economic status determines the purchasing power.

Expenditure pattern

None of the people falls under no expenditure category, 0.3 percent of the respondents spend on procurement of food and non-food items per annum between 0-10000, 30.3 percent of the respondents spend between 10001-20000, 41 percent of the respondents spend from the slab between 20001-30000, 21.7 percent of the respondents spend between 30001-40000, 3.7 percent of the respondents spend from 40001-50000, 2 percent of the respondents spend from 50001-60000, and 1 percent of the respondents spend 60,000 and above per annum.

Savings

with respect to savings pattern 37.3 percent of the people revealed that they haven't made any savings, 30 percent of the respondents savings were 0-100 per month, 15 percent of the respondents made saving around 101-200 per month, 7.7 percent of the people save between 200-300 rupees per month, 6.3 percent of the respondents save between 300-400 per month and 3.7 percent of respondents have made savings of 500 and above per month, Saving money is a mirage among the labored households.

Source of the loan

Around 40.3 percent of the respondents used to avail the loan from the private moneylenders, 30 percent of the respondents revealed that they mortgage their jewels in the nearby pawn broker shops for the credit requirement, 3.7 person availed loan from co-operative banks, 25 percent of the respondents availed the loan from SHGs and merely 1 percent of the respondents got the loan from commercial loans.

Outstanding of Loan

with regard to current outstanding 10.3 percent of the respondents have the outstanding between 0-5000 rupees, 14 percent of the respondents got between 5000-10000, 26.3 percent of the respondents got the outstanding between 10001 - 15000, 34 percent of the respondents having the outstanding between 15001-20000, 9 percent of the respondents got the outstanding between 20001-25000, and 6.3 percent of the respondents got 25,000 and above.

6.3.3 Work-situation and number of working days

Reason to become leather worker

30 percent of the respondents were opined that they have less formal education hence they opt to choose the job for their livelihood, 5.7 percent of the respondents have opined that their job oriented to their qualification, 15 percent of the respondents have revealed that they have been bound to do the work since they don't have any other job, 12 percent of the respondents conveyed that they don't have any other infrastructure which pulled them into this work, 13.7 percent of the people told that they don't know the reason why they became leather workers and 31.7 percent of the respondents opined that they opt the job in order to cater their family expenditure and they forced to take up the work for the livelihood subsistence.

No of Hours in work per day

34 percent of the respondents have told that they use to work for 8 hrs per day, 30 percent of the respondents have opined that they work for 9 hrs per day, 22.3 percent of the respondents told that they are engaging them self in the work for around 10 hrs per day, 13.7 percent of the respondents have told that they use to depends on the condition of the assignment.

Employment Patterns by Hierarchy

Woman comprises of roughly 0.7 % of employees, while at the worker level they comprise about 59 % of employees, at the supervisory level they are around 7 %, whereas 33.3 percent of the employees constitute in the skilled workers category

Employment Patterns in Various Departments

Female proportions are much less in somewhat more technical areas such as knitting with 9 percent, dyeing with 7 percent, processing and stitching with 7.3 and 10.3 respectively, with regard to washing and inspection with 8 percent and 6 percent respectively, 7 percent and 25.3 percent for folding and helping respectively, and 6.7 percent to maintenance but in the department like managerial and R&D women are fewer in numbers in some administrative areas such as finance, HR and marketing.

6.3.4 Work Environment and the Gender inequality

Wage discrimination on the basis of Gender

In about 11.3 percent of the male and female, 38 percent are availing the wages up to 3000 per month, Among 15 percent of male and female, 32.7 percent had availed the wages between 3000-6000 per month. Among 37.3 percent of male and female, 15.3 percent had availed the wages between 6000-9000 per month. Between 22.3 percent of male and female 7 percent had availed the wages between 9000-12000 per month and among 14 percent of the male and female 7 percent had availed the wages more than 12000 per month.

Kind of Difficulties in work place

10.7 percent of the respondents have told that they have health problems, 7.7 percent of the respondents have opined that they have been undergoing lot of oppression from the supervisors ,7 percent of the respondents have opined that they had been forced to work more than the entitled time schedule, 6.7 percent person faced wage discrimination even among the women workers on the basis of gender, 4 percent of the people told that uncertainty of employment situation, 64 percent of the respondents have exemplified that they had been facing all the above five problems

Perceptions on the amenities available in the company.

with respect to standard of cleanliness 68.3 percent of the respondents were not satisfied, with respect to ventilation 17 percent of the respondents are highly satisfied , with regard to protective measures 76.7 percent of the respondents were not satisfied, with respect to provision of drinking water facilities 82.7 percent of the respondents were not satisfied, with respect to sanitation facilities 77.4 percent of the respondents were not satisfied, In connection with the availability of rest room 79.3 percent of the respondents were not satisfied, and in regard to recreational activities in the company premises 79 percent were not satisfied with the facilities such as Women leather workers perceptions on the leave facilities of the companies.

14.3 percent of the respondents were highly satisfied with the company's permission to avail maternity leave, 18.7 percent were satisfied and 67 percent of the respondents were not satisfied with the entitlement provided by the companies, 10.4 percent of the respondents were highly satisfied with the company's procedure to deduct pay for medical leave, 12.3 percent were satisfied and 77 percent of the respondents were not satisfied with the procedure followed by the companies, 5.7 percent of the respondents were highly satisfied with the company's procedure to deduct pay for casual leave,6.7 percent were satisfied and 87.7 percent of the respondents were not satisfied with the procedure followed by the companies, 16.7 percent of the respondents were highly satisfied with the company's permission to avail maternity leave, 26.3 percent were satisfied and 57 percent of the respondents were not satisfied with the entitlement provided by the companies

Perception on Company Policies for Labour Laws

12.7 percent of the respondents revealed yes to the statement that prominent display of labour laws in the factory premises, 87.3 percent said no, with respect to the awareness on the code of conduct on sexual harassment 7 percent agreed that their companies followed such guidelines but 93 percent revealed company didn't follow such guidelines,6.3 percent of the respondents told that their company got the written code of conduct on sexual harassment in the factory but 93.7 percent revealed that their company didn't have such guidelines.

Perceptions on the comparison of skills between male and female workers

perception of the respondents on statement of comparison of skills between male and female workers in their factory, with respect to the statement conducive for women to work merely 37.3 percent of respondents disagree and 29.7 percent of the respondents strongly disagree the statement, , with respect to the statement gender discrimination is high, 36.3 percent of respondents disagree and 29. percent of the respondents strongly disagree the statement, with regards to statement late working hours 33.3 percent of respondents disagree and 30 percent of the respondents strongly disagree the statement, with regards to statement discriminated payment 33.3 percent of the workers strongly agreed the statement, 41 percent of the agreed the proclamation, , respondents opinion on the statement sexual harassment revealed that 34 percent of the workers strongly agreed the statement, 40.3 percent of the agreed the proclamation.

Facilities available for women workers in the companies

with regard to availability of medical facilities adjoined to companies 67 percent were not satisfied with the availability of the medical facility in the nearby area, with regard to availability of medical facilities inside the companies 86.7 percent were not satisfied with the availability of the medical facility in the company, with respect to availability of separate bathrooms for female 41.3 percent were not satisfied with the availability of the medical facility in the company, nearly 65 percent of the respondents were not satisfied with the separate rest area for female, with regard to transportation facilities 57.7 percent were not satisfied, with respect to concession given to the women workers during pregnancy 75.3 percent were not satisfied with the availability of the medical facility available in their company.

Work Environment of the respondents

15 percent of the respondents opined that men and women are given equal opportunity 85 percent denied this , 88.7 percent of the respondents opined that men and women are not given equal payment, 13.3 percent revealed that women and men

211

were given equal payment, 20 percent of the respondents revealed that sexual harassment is not an issue in their company but 80 percent considered it was as an issue, 66.7 percent of the respondents revealed that women workers got harassed by the co-workers and nearly 33.3 percent revealed that they don't mind for that ,81.3 percent of the respondents revealed that women workers are getting harassed by their supervisors and nearly 18.7 percent revealed that women are not harassed by their supervisors.

Frequency of injury or accidents in work place

10 percent of the respondents opined that accidents occurred frequently, 20 percent told accidents takes place occasionally, 28.7 percent revealed rarely accidents occur in their companies, 41.3 percent of the respondents told that accidents never occurred in their companies.

Facilities and benefits received by workers

18.7 percent were highly satisfied, 26.7 percent are satisfied and 54.7 percent are not satisfied by the provision, with respect to the canteen facilities 24 percent were highly satisfied, 32.3 percent are satisfied and 43.7 percent were not satisfied by the provision, with regard to ESI facility 23.7 percent were highly satisfied, 28 percent are satisfied and 48.7 percent were not satisfied by the provision, in connection with the provisional basic needs like soaps and tooth paste etc 24.7 percent were highly satisfied, 28.7 percent were merely satisfied and 46.7 percent were not satisfied by the provision given in their work place.

Problems experienced at work

26.7 percent revealed the magnitude of verbal abuse of their superiors in the office, 22 percent of the respondents opined long hours of work is the important problem, 20.3 percent and 15.7 percent revealed sexual harassment as the major problem and non-availability of leisure time were the important problem respectively and 15.3 percent of the respondents noted that reprimand and of the superiors was the important problem in their working places.

Entitlement of decision making in various situations in her family

26.7 of the respondents have the liberty to take the decision on their own, 7.7 percent rely upon their brother for their decision, 7.7 percent and 29.3 percent of the respondents depends on their father and husband respectively, 11.7 percent depend on their father-in-law and 17 percent sought the help of mother-in law, with regard to the issue pertaining to domestic issues 7.3 respondents have the liberty to take the decision on their own, 3.3 percent rely upon their brother for the decisions, 5 percent and 21 percent of the respondents depend on their father and husband respectively, 11.7 percent depend on their father-in-law and 51.7 percent sought the help of mother-in law.

Influence of work environment on disease

69.3 percent of the respondents opined that the work environment caused headache, 30.7 percent of the respondents opined no for the same, 62.3 percent of the respondents opined that the work environment caused anxiety disorder, 37.7 percent of the respondents revealed it didn't caused them any headache, 66 percent of the respondents opined that the work environment caused injuries, 34 percent of the respondents opined no for the same, 66.7 percent of the respondents opined that the work environment caused skin rashes, 33.3 percent of the respondents responded no to the statement, 61.7 percent of the respondents opined that the work environment caused ulcers, 38.7 percent of the respondents opined no for the same, 70 percent of the respondents opined that the work environment causes problems of dust allergy ,30 percent revealed no for the assertion, hence at the outset working environment responsible for diseases of the respondents Slabs of average expenditure on illness are caused by the job.

27 percent of the respondents spent up to Rs 100 per month, 32.7 percent used to spent between 100-200, nearly 47 percent of the respondents spend between 200 -300 per month, 11.3 percent spend more than 300 per month.

6.3.5 Perceptions on the nexus between work environment and physical health

Work and its Environment have its impact on the health of the workers, 42.0 percent of the workers strongly agreed with this statement, 23.2 percent of them agreed the proclamation

Regular Medical Checkup carried out in the industries

31.4 percent of the respondents disagreed and 34.5 percent of the respondents strongly disagreed the statement, hence it was apparent from the empirical findings that nearly 63 percent of the respondents didn't agreed upon the statement.

Workers take healthy and Nutritive diet

33.2 percent of respondents disagreed and 25.7 percent of the respondents strongly disagree with the statement, hence it was apparent from the empirical findings that the nearly 66 percent of the respondents didn't agreed upon the statement.

Protective measures

Measures are taken to reduce the intense of occupational hazards 27.7 percent of respondents disagree and 24.8 percent of the respondents strongly disagreed with the statement, hence it was apparent from the empirical findings that the nearly 52 percent of the respondents didn't agreed upon the statement.

Industrial wastages are disposed in healthy way

40.3 percent of respondents disagree and 44.9 percent of the respondents strongly disagree with the statement, hence it was apparent from the empirical findings that the nearly 85 percent of the respondents didn't agreed upon the statement that Industrial wastages are disposed in healthy way in the study area.

Noise levels are within the prescribed intensity

36.7 percent of respondents disagree and 30.1 percent of the respondents strongly disagree the statement, hence it was apparent from the empirical findings that the nearly 67 percent of the respondents didn't agreed upon the statement

Dust levels emitted within the prescribed intensity

33.0 percent of respondents disagree and 24.1 percent of the respondents strongly disagree the statement, hence it was apparent from the empirical findings that the nearly 57 percent of the respondents didn't agreed upon the statement.

Management provided all the safety Equipments for the workers

33.2 percent of respondents disagree and 29.6 percent of the respondents strongly disagree with the statement, hence it was apparent from the empirical findings that the nearly 63 percent of the respondents didn't agreed upon the statement.

Immediate attention given during emergency

41.2 percent of respondents disagree and 35.2 percent of the respondents strongly disagree with the statement, hence it was apparent from the empirical findings that the nearly 76 percent of the respondents didn't agreed upon the statement.

Management provide adequate protection measures to the workers

34.5 percent of respondents disagree and 30.1 percent of the respondents strongly disagree with the statement, hence it was apparent from the empirical findings that the nearly 65 percent of the respondents didn't agreed upon the statement.

6.3.6 Perceptions on Job Involvement of the Respondents

Job is given as the first priority rather than the family members

36.7 percent of respondents disagree and 29.2 percent of the respondents strongly disagree with the statement, hence it was apparent from the empirical findings that the nearly 66 percent of the respondents didn't agreed upon the statement.

Not enthusiastic to take up the responsibility in the company

36.7 percent of respondents disagree and 29.2 percent of the respondents strongly disagree the statement, hence it was apparent from the empirical findings that the nearly 66 percent of the respondents didn't agreed upon the statement.

Presently holding interesting job

34.1 percent of respondents disagree and 29 percent of the respondents strongly disagree the statement, hence it was apparent from the empirical findings that the nearly 63 percent of the respondents didn't agreed upon the statement.

6.3.7 Perceptions on the nexus between work environment and job satisfaction

Management given liberty to take decision

27.9 percent of respondents disagree and 20.6 percent of the respondents strongly disagree with the statement, hence it was apparent from the empirical findings that the nearly 47 percent of the respondents didn't agreed upon the statement.

Have cordial relationship with the management

29.6 percent of respondents disagree and 34.5 percent of the respondents strongly disagree with the statement, hence it was apparent from the empirical findings that the nearly 65 percent of the respondents didn't agreed upon the statement.

Too much constraints and complications exists in the company as well as in home

24.3 percent of the workers strongly agreed the statement, 42.5 percent of them agreed the proclamation.

Felt happy of being associated with leather industries

33.8 percent of respondents disagree and 31.9 percent of the respondents strongly disagreed with the statement, hence it was apparent from the empirical findings that the nearly 65 percent of the respondents didn't agreed upon the statement.

Satisfied with the shift schedule

30.1 percent of the workers strongly agreed with the statement, 32.1percent of the agreed the statement

Satisfied with the style of my approach according to situation in company

34.5 percent of respondents disagree and 24.1 percent of the respondents strongly disagree the statement, hence it was apparent from the empirical findings that the nearly 59 percent of the respondents didn't agreed upon the statement.

Work load is challenge not a burden

43.1 percent of the workers strongly agreed with the statement, 27.0 percent of them agreed with the statement.

6.4 Policy Suggestions

Continuous efforts are needed to improve the working conditions of women and some of the policy implications are stemmed below as an outcome of the study.

216

6.4.1 Gender sensitive work environment and health

Gender differences in employment environment have a major impact on gender differences in the work-related health outcomes. Research and interventions must take into account the real jobs that men and women do and the differences in exposure and working conditions.

There is a need to improve research and monitoring by systematically including the gender dimension in data collection, adjusting for hours worked (as women generally work shorter hours than men) and basing exposure assessment on the real work carried out. Epidemiological methods should be assessed for any gender bias. Indicators in monitoring systems, such as national accident reporting and surveys, should effectively cover occupational risks to women.

Work-related risks to women's safety and health have been underestimated and neglected compared to men, both regarding research and prevention. This imbalance should be addressed in research, awareness raising and prevention activities.

Taking a gender-neutral approach in policy and legislation has contributed to less attention and fewer resources being directed towards work-related risks to women and their prevention. Health directives do not cover (predominantly female) domestic workers.

Gender-sensitive interventions should take a participatory approach, involving the workers concerned and based on an examination of the real work situations.

Women are under-represented in the decision-making concerning occupational health and safety at all levels. They should be more directly involved and women's views, experiences, knowledges and skills should be reflected in formulating and implementing OSH strategies.

There are successful examples of including or targeting gender in research approaches, interventions, consultation and decision-making, tools and actions. Existing experiences and resources should be shared.

While the general trends in women's working conditions and situation are similar across the Member States and candidate countries, there are also country with differences within these general trends. Individual countries should examine their particular circumstances regarding gender and OSH, in order to plan appropriate actions.

217

Taking a holistic approach to OSH, including the work–life interface, broader issues in working organisation and employment would improve occupational risk prevention, benefiting both women and men.

Women are not a homogeneous group and not all women work in traditionally 'female' jobs.

The same applies to men. A holistic approach needs to take an account of diversity. Actions to improve work–life balance must be taken into account for both women's and men's working schedules and should be designed to be attractive for both.

Ensure the comfortable work Environment

Women continue to be active participants in the workforce as shown by their increasing employment rates. However, workers with non-standard employment contracts such as part-time employment or non-permanent contracts accounted for most of the increases in employment figures and there is a trend to multiple employments to be observed. Also, the financial downturn may have an impact on the employment prospective especially of younger women.

Occupational segregation, overall, the concentration of female activity in a few sectors seems to be increasing rather than falling over time. The move to service sectors particularly affects women, who work in the growing sectors health care, education and retail. Consequently, if it should be effective, OSH policy should continue to address and enhance its activities for these sectors.

The jobs in which women work and the choices they make still depend largely on their family commitments. This is also true for older women. Inversely, the practices impact on the choices they are given. As this report demonstrates, many women are involuntarily in temporary jobs, on multiple and short-term contracts and this has a high impact on their occupational safety and health.

Women are more likely to suffer from multiple discrimination at the workplace. This may be due to the gender difference, in conjunction with their age, ethnic background, disability and sexual orientation, while migrant women in addition face discrimination based on their origin or class. Some particularly vulnerable groups were identified in this report: young women, women with care obligations in countries where resources are limited, migrant women engaging in informal work, such as cleaning and home care, women in multiple jobs, and very young mothers. The situation of older women is also very variable depending on the country.

Women are increasingly affected by stress. This puts into question the misconception that women's work is less physically and mentally demanding. The combination of work organization and physical risks, links between women's paid and unpaid work, including combined risk exposures and less freedom in time, and the difficulties in finding a stable job, and their impact on the health and safety of women should be further explored.

Violence is a particular issue in service sectors, and is increasing. Additionally, new forms of harassment, such as cyber-harassment are an emerging issue in some sectors, for example in education. Reporting and support procedures are still lacking and female workers in personal services and working at clients premises are particularly vulnerable. Additionally, reports on violence vary considerably between Member States and may be linked to a lack of awareness.

Improving the identification of risks and exposures will be important to 'make the invisible visible', as the improved data documented these risks and exposures, and the related health effects, and a wider range of indicators and more differentiated monitoring instruments to reflect the tasks, occupations and risks specifically faced by women.

Ensure women's participation in policy discussions and when laying out legislation. It will be important to ensure that women participate in the development of occupational safety measure strategies and policies and their implementation in the workplace.

Adapt labour inspection practice to increase number of women in the labour market. The observed shift from industry to services, and the changes in contractual arrangements. A gendered approach to interventions is warranted: resources should be assessed for the contribution they make for an increasingly female workforce, and for how they are adapted to the specific needs in these diverse service sectors.

219

6.4.2 Violence at work:

Measures to target violence and harassment at work and the special committee consists of lawyers, officials from labour Ministry, women activists and the women workers need to be formed and protect the women from the harassment in the work place.

Efficient reporting systems for violence at work should be put in place to address underreporting. These systems need to be linked with quick measures for action, whether to provide immediate support to workers in case of an event or counseling after the event.

6.4.3 Accidents and health effects

Accident rates of female workers are high in the leather industries. To target accident prevention, more information should be gathered about the type of accidents and how women suffer in different segment of works. Factors such as age, sector and occupation, and migration background should be taken into account and formulate and implement the strategy to curb the accidents in the leather industries.

Static work, prolonged standing and sitting, risk factors particularly relevant to female in the work, are not currently monitored and assessed in many workers surveys and the related health effects are underrepresented and explored in the occurrence of lower limb disorder in leather industries. Thus the periodical health checks up, proper rest during the work will diminish the negative consequences of the health.

Women are more susceptible to depression and anxiety than men, and their lower mental health may be linked to the multiple roles they perform on a daily basis which might lead to cardiovascular diseases. So recreation and outlet need to be provided.

Exposures to dangerous substances in the occupations are frequent, but remain under assessed. Women's exposure also involves carcinogens, which would lead to cancer. Gender differences in uptake and metabolisation of dangerous substances should also be further explored and women should be protected from such kind of hazards.

WHO research recommended that specific gender focused research needed to be undertaken in occupational health policies and programmers, to improve training, capacity and the delivery of occupational health services.

6.4.4 *Rehabilitation and reintegration:*

Due to the nature of women within the work force, policy makers and labour organisations should be aware that women with disabilities are at risk of double or multiple discriminations and therefore require special attention, and policies with a focus on gender policies should be aware of this issue in order to reinforce guidelines for disability mainstreaming especially as women with disabilities are discriminated against more than men with disabilities.

Employers should be encouraged to have flexible and effective rehabilitation into work policies, so employers who are able to work only a percentage of the normal hours, are retained in the workforce. The female workers need to be explicitly addressed: rehabilitation measures should also be targeted at temporary workers and part-timers, who are often women, young or migrant workers.

Rehabilitation and back-to-work policies should also address the pattern of work-related health problems, specific to women leading to longer workplace absences and critical for reintegration: the occurrence and distribution of higher prevalence of mental health disorders.

Those responsible for implementing systems need to consider gender issues, and in particular the home life of women and how this affects their rehabilitation. Rehabilitation costs need to include both direct and indirect costs.

There needs to be more research for women on vocational retraining, rehabilitation and re- insertion into work.

6.5 Scope for further research

The outcome of the study unleash the scope for further research in this domain such as

There could be prospective to explore the relationship between women position in informal job market after the globalization.

There could be prospective to explore the relationship between sexual harassment in work environment and the causes and consequences on mental health of the women workers.

Attainment and challenges of working women in the Indian job market.

221

BIBLIOGRAPHY

❖ Vina Mazumdar 'Women workers in changing Economy' (Yojana vol. 19: p.7, 1975)

❖ Delia Davin , 'Women – work' women and the party in Revolutionary China (Oxford university press, 1978), March 8th international working women's Day, p: 212

❖ Gumber, Anil (2000): "Correlates of Unemployment Among Rural Youth in India: An Inter-State Analysis"; The Indian Journal of Labour Economics, Vol. 43(4),October-December, Pp. 657-671

❖ Ghosh, S. K., Women in a Changing Society, Asia Publishing House, New Delhi, 1976.

❖ Kundu, Amitabh (1997): "Trends and Structure of Employment in the 1990'sImplications for Urban Growth"; Economic and Political Weekl;, June 14,Pp.1399-1405.

❖ Papola .T.S and Sharma.N.Alakh (1997): "Employment of Women in India: Some Reseach and Policy Issues"; The Indian Journal of Labour Economic; Vol. 40,No.2, April-June, Pp.348-355

❖ Nirmala, V and Bhat, Sham. K. (1999): "Female Work Participation in the Emerging Labour Market In India"; The Indian Journal of Labour Economics, Vol. 42,No. 4, Pp. 613-624

❖ Ghosh, M., 1996, Agricultural development and rural poverty in India. Indian Journal of Agricultural Economics, 51(3): 374-380.

❖ Tripathy, S. N. and Das, Soudamini, Informal Women Labour in India. New Delhi: Discovery Publishing House, 1999

❖ Agarwal, Bina (1999) "Work Participation of Rural Women in Third World; Some Data and conceptual Biases " Economic and Political Weekly, Vol. 20,No. 51, 1999

❖ Mishra, Bimlesh Kumar, "Women Workers Deserve a Better Deal." Yojana,Vol. 34, No. 12, 1999, p.19

❖ Gumber, Anil (2000): "Correlates of Unemployment Among Rural Youth in India: An Inter-State Analysis"; The Indian Journal of Labour Economics, Vol. 43(4),October-December, Pp. 657-671.

❖ Bureau of Labour Statistics, (2000) U.S. Department of Labor, Current Population Survey Earnings Files, 2000 and earlier years, Washington, D.C.

❖ Greed, C. (2000, July) Women in the construction professions: Achieving critical mass. Gender, Work and Organization, 7(3), pp. 181-196(16)

❖ Mitra and Muopadhyay, (2001), Spatial dimensions of Labour Absorption, Economic and Political Weekly, Bombay.

❖ N.Rajeshwari, "Socio- economic conditions of workers in estate: A survey" southern economist, February 1, 2002, Vol.40.'p.19.

❖ Jha, K. K. (2002) Informal labour in the construction industry in Nepal. Sectoral activities Programme, Geneva: ILO

❖ Elumalai and Sharma (2003) "Measuring women's work in agriculture"; Food and Agricultural Organization Report; Pp. 1-15.

❖ Mohanty, S.K.(2004): "Employment and Unemployment in a Society of Transition"; The Indian Journal of Labour Economics; Vol. 43, No. 2 Pp. 8-17.

❖ Meer Muhammad Parhiar (2005): "Globalization Vs Skill based Technological Change: Implications for Unemployment and Wage Inequality";The Economic Journal; Vol. 115, No. 503. April, Pp. 391-393.

❖ Korinek   (2005)   The Economic Status of Women: An Analytical Framework,-in The Role of Women in Contributing to Family Income (Proceedings of the regional workshop in Bangkok, July, 2005) Friedrich- Ebert Stifling, pp 45-67.

❖ Ahsan, Ahmad (2006))Studies of educated working Women in India Trends and Issues, Economics and political weekly,vol.14 (13)

❖ Kaveri, (1995) Excerpts from women, work and inequity - the reality of gender. Edited by Cherian Joseph and K.V. Eswara Prasad, National Labour Institute.

❖ Deshpande, Sudha, (1996), Changing Structure of Employment in India, The Indian Journal of Labour Economics, Vol.39, No.4.

❖ Sudha Despande, (2001), Informal Sector in India: Perspectives and Policies, Institute for Human Development and Institute of Applied Manpower

❖ Deshpande, A. (2000, May) Does caste still define disparity? A look at inequality in Kerala, India. The American Economic Review, 90(2). Papers and Proceedings of the One Hundred Twelfth Annual Meeting of the American Economic Association, pp. 322-325.

❖ Nirmala Banerjee, (1985), Modernisation and Marginalisation; Social Scientist, Vol.13 and 1997 „How real is the bogey of feminization" Indian Journal of Labour Economics, Vol.40.

❖ Nirmala, V and Bhat, Sham. K. (1999): "Female Work Participation in the Emerging Labour Market In India"; The Indian Journal of Labour Economics, Vol. 42,No. 4, Pp. 613-624.

❖ Ravindar (2003) Avinashilingam Institute for Home Science, Dept. of Economics, Coimbatore.. Labour force participation and time management of women in slums in Coimbatore district. Coimbatore : AIHS-DE. 8 p.

❖ Bhatt, Aparna and Sen, Aatreyee. (2005).Report on domestic workers. New Delhi : National Commission for Women. 98 p.

❖ Singh, D.P. (2005) Women workers in the brick kiln industry of Haryana. Indian Journal of Gender Studies, 12(1) : 83-97.

❖ Vanker, Purushottam. (2005) At the Kadiyanaka : challenges faced by construction workers in Ahmedabad. Ahmedabad : Self Employed Women's Association. 31 p.

❖ Rao, K. Hanumantha (2006): "Female Labour Participation in Productive Work"; Man and Development; Vol XXVI, No. 1, March. Pp. 167-173

❖ Hakim.J(1976),Labour Market Discrimination in a Poor Urban Economy; Journal of Development Studies,Vol.19, No.1.

❖ Usharani et al. (1993) Extent and causes of gender and poverty in India: A Case Study of rural Hayana. Journal of International Women's Studies, 7(2): 182 -190

❖ Jayawardane, A. K. W. & Gunawardena, N. D. (1998, September 1) Construction workers in developing countries: a case study of Sri Lanka. Construction Management & Economics, 16 (5), 521 – 530

❖ Saksena, A. (1999) Gender and human rights. Status of women workers in India. Shipra Publications

❖ Ray and Haque (2000) "Challenges of Decent work in the Globalising World";The Indian Journal of Labour Economic; Vol. 48, No. 1, Jan- March, Pp. 6-7

❖ Solanki and Sharma (2001) : "Impact of Female Work Participation: A Study of Agricultural Labourer Households; The Indian Journal of Labour Economic;Vol. 48, No. 1, Jan- March, Pp. 6-7

❖ Singh (2005): "Economic Reforms and Female Employment: Issues and Challenges"; Man and Development; Vol. XXVII, No. 1, March, p. 1-13

❖ Rana, A.S, Jasbir Singh and Kulwant Singh (2002) "Female Labour Participation in Productive Work"; Man and Develoment; Vol XXVI, No. 1, March. Pp. 167-173.

❖ Muniyandi et al. (2003). Changing Role of Women "A Study of Small Manufacturing Enterprises in India"; Journal of Economics and Social Development; Vol. II,No. 2, July-Dec.

❖ Luke, N. & Munshi, K. (2005, February) Women as agents of change: Female income, social affiliation and household decisions in South India. Retrieved April 20, 2008

❖ Madhok, S. (2005) Report on the status of women workers in the construction industry. New Delhi: National Commission for Women.

❖ Suchitra, J. Y. & Rajasekar, D. (2006, July - September) One size does not fit all: Employment insecurity of unorganized workers in Karnataka. The Indian Journal of Labour Economics, 49(3), 455-473

❖ Sharpe (1979) The dual career family. Human Relations, 22 (10 3 -30.

❖ Rohni Hensman (2004): "Globalization, Women and Work"; Economic and Political Weekly; March 6.

❖ Rosemary (1982), Trends and Prospects for Women"s Employment in 1990"s, European Commission

❖ Jaya Arunachalam (1984). Status and Role Perception of middle class women. New Delhi : Puja Publishers

❖ Lalitha K. Nair (1984) Women's Two Roles. A Study of Role Conflict. Indian Journal of Social Work. 2494), 337-380.

❖ Madula Sherwani (1984): "Women Participation in Labour Force", New Delhi: Rajat Publications, Pp. 46-54.

❖ Kuppuswamy. B (1989). Indian Women From Purdha to Modernity.New Delhi : Vikas Publications

❖ Lalithadevi (2006). Working Couples as parents. In E. Corfman Families Today.Vol. I. Rockville, National. Institute of Mental Health

❖ Manikaramerkar(1995): " Female participation in farm work and non-farm work "; Sociological Bulletin;vol.25, no.2, Pp.105-110

❖ Prakasam, Seepana (2009): "Gender discrimination and inclusive growth in the informal labour market in India"; 51 annual ISLE conference, Punjabi University ,Patiala

❖ Khan and Singh (1994) , Modernisation and Marginalisation; Social Scientist, Vol.13 and 1994 „How real is the bogey of feminization" Indian Journal of Labour Economics, Vol.40

❖ Nischol. (1975). Economically Independent, Emotionally crushed. Social Welfare. 22, (8-7), September -October.

❖ Seta Vaidayalingam (1994): "Development Paradox in Kerala: Analysis of Industrial Stagnation;, Economic and Political Weekly; September 15,

❖ Mangahas M and Jayme-Ho.T, (1977), The Economic Status of Women: An Analytical Framework,-in The Role of Women in Contributing to Family Income (Proceedings of the regional workshop in Bangkok, July, 1976) Friedrich- Ebert Stifling, pp 45-67

❖ Peggy Antrobus, (1996), "Women and Development: An Alternative Analysis"; Journal of the Society for International Development

❖ Senguptha, P.(1998). The Story of Women in India (II edition) , Delhi ;Indian Book Company.

❖ Cherian, J. & Prasad K.V. (1999) Women, work and inequality: The reality of gender. New Delhi: National Labour Institute.

❖ Jhabvala, Renana and Sinha, Shalini (1999): "Liberalisation and the Women Worker".Economic and Political Weekly; Vol. 37, Nov.18- Dec.26 , Pp.2037-2044.

❖ Katherine Mckee, (1999), in her paper "Micro Level Strategies for Supporting Livelihoods", Journal of the Society for International Development

❖ Talwar Sabanna (2001): "The Service Sector for Growth and Employment" The Indian Journal of Labour Economics; Vol. 38 , No. 4, Oct- Dec, Pp. 673-680.

❖ Nevil, D. and Demico, S. (1974). Role conflict in women as a function of marital status. Human Relations, 28 (5) :487 -497.

❖ Koran Prasad (2002) Indian Women: Their Health and Productivity; World Bank Discussion Paper 109; Washington DC

❖ Raka Sharan (2005), Labour Reform and Social Safety Net, Indian Journal of Labour Economics, Vol.40, No.3. pp 74-89.

❖ Horton, Susan (1995): "Women and Industrialization in Asia"; Routledge, London Human Development Report 2001.

❖ Artecona & Cunningham (2001) The status of women in the States - Women's economic status in the States: Wide Disparities by Race, Ethnicity, and Region. Washington, Dc: Institute for Women's Policy Research.

❖ Giri, A.K. (2002): " A Post –Modernist Enquiry Into Women's Workforce Participation"; "; The Indian Journal of Labour Economics, Vol. 42 , No. 4,Jan – March, Pp. 557-564

❖ Rani, Uma. (2005)Income, risks and vulnerabilities among women informal workers case study of Surat City. Ahmedabad : Gujarat Institute of Development Research. 45 p.

❖ Ramya Vijaya (2003)): "Female Labour Participation in Productive Work"; Man and Development; Vol XXVI, No. 1, March. Pp. 167-173

❖ Berik, Rodgers & Zveglich (2003) "Globalization Vs Skill based Technological Change: Implications for Unemployment and Wage Inequality";The Economic Journal; Vol. 115, No. 503. April, Pp. 391-393.

❖ Oostendorp (2004): "Trade liberalization: Challenges and Opportunities for women in Southeast Asia, UNIFEM and ENGENDER, New York and Singapore.

❖ Reilly & Dutta (2005): "The Pattern of Globalization and Some Implications for the Pursuit of Social Goals"; The Indian Journal of Labour Economics; Vol. 48,No. 1, Jan-March, Pp. 47-61.

❖ Sinha, Aseema (2007): " Globalization, Rising Inequality, and New Insecurities in India"muse.jhu.edu/journals/journal_of_democracy/.../18.2sinha.html

❖ Menon & Rodgers (2006) "The Challenge of Gender Disparities in India's Economic Development"; The Indian Journal of Labour Economics; LXXXIV (332):123-146.

❖ Yamamoto (2007)   The international trade and gender gap : A survey, Tokyo: Asian Productivity Organization.

❖ Hari Priya (2000)Quality of women's employment: A focus on the South. International Institute for Labour Studies: Decent Work Research

❖ Vankar (2005). The Economic Status of Women: An Analytical Framework,-in The Role of Women in Contributing to Family Income

❖ Export of Leather and Leather products (Facts and Figures 2009-10), Council for Leather Exports – India

❖ Indian Leather Industry – Perspective Planning and Intervention Strategies to Reach US $ 7 billion exports by 2010-2011, CLE New Delhi

❖ NSS 66th Round: Report No. 515(61/10/1), Part II, (July2009-June2010):"Employment and Unemployment Situation in India".

❖ Agrawal, Sarita (1993): "Gender Discrimination in the Labour Market: A Review of Literature"; The Indian Journal of Labour Economics; Vol. 36, No. 2.

❖ Agarwal, Bina. (1985): "Work Participation of Rural Women in Third World -- Some Data and Conceptual Biases"; Economic and Political Weekly; December 21-28, Pp. A-155 to A-164.

❖ Morgan and Olsen (2009) "The Strategic Silence: Gender and Economic Policy"; London: Zed Book with the North-South Institute.

❖ Mehrotra and Biggeri 2005.: "Status of Indian Women"; Kanishka Publisher,New Delhi.

❖ Busse, M. & Spielmann, C. (2003) Gender discrimination and the international division of labour. HWWA Discussion Paper 245 ISSN 1616-4814 Retrieved on April 20, 2009 from *http://www.hwwa.de/Publikationen/Discussion_Paper/2003/245.pdf*

❖ Mathur, A. (1994): "Work Participation, Gender and Economic Development: A Quantitative Anatomy of the Indian Scenario"; The Journal of Development Studies; 30(2): Pp. 466-504.

❖ Mehta,Arati and Menon,Latika (1998): "Status of Indian Women"; Kanishka Publisher,New Delhi.

❖ Mahapatra, Suhasini. (2002): "Women Participation in Labour Force", New Delhi: Rajat Publications, Pp. 46-54.

❖ Labour practices in the Footwear, leather, textiles and clothing industries, International Labour Office, Geneva, 2000

CPSIA information can be obtained
at www.ICGtesting.com
Printed in the USA
BVHW031239091222
653840BV00008B/690